Paint Shop™ Pro 5

fast&easy®

Diane Koers

Premier
Press™

Publisher: Stacy L. Hiquet

Senior Marketing Manager: Sarah O'Donnell

Marketing Manager: Heather Hurley

Associate Marketing Manager: Kristin Eisenzopf

Manager of Editorial Services: Heather Talbot

Project Editor: Sandy Doell

Technical Reviewer: Sonja Shea

Retail Market Coordinator: Sarah Dubois

Copy Editor: Karen Gill

Interior Layout: Shawn Morningstar

Cover Designer: Mike Tanamachi

Indexer: Sharon Shock

Proofreader: Margaret Bauer

Paint Shop™ Pro® 8 is a registered trademark of Jasc Software™. All other trademarks are the property of their respective owners.

Important: Premier Press cannot provide software support. Please contact the appropriate software manufacturer's technical support line or Web site for assistance. Premier Press and the author have attempted throughout this book to distinguish proprietary trademarks from descriptive terms by following the capitalization style used by the manufacturer.

ISBN: 1-59200-097-5

Library of Congress Catalog Card Number: 2003104023

Printed in the United States of America

04 05 06 07 BH 10 9 8 7 6 5 4 3 2

Premier Press, a division of Course Technology
25 Thomson Place
Boston, MA 02210

To my "sister," Penny, who, since we were little girls, has enriched me with her friendship.

Acknowledgments

I am deeply appreciative to the many people who assisted with this book. Thank you for all the time you gave and for your assistance.

To Stacy Hiquet for the opportunity to write this book and for her confidence in me. A very special thanks goes to Sandy Doell for her unending assistance in the book development; to Sonja Shea for (again) checking all the technical angles and keeping me straight; to Karen Gill for her help in making this book grammatically correct; to Shawn Morningstar for laying it all out so nice and easy; and to all those at Premier working behind the scenes whose names I don't know. I really appreciate your fine work.

A special recognition goes to all those on the various Paint Shop Pro newsgroups, especially "Bonesy" Sonja Shea (PSPToybox), Patti Wavinak (Moon's Designs) and Porter, and to all the regulars. Thanks for letting me bug you with my questions and for all the special assistance you provided. I learned and laughed with all of you! To Nancy, Kris, Joe, and everyone at Jasc Software: You are still the nicest group of people I've ever worked with.

To my husband, Vern: Thank you again for all your support and never-ending faith in me. Your help at deadline time is immeasurable.

Finally, and most importantly, I give praise and thanks to God above for all the blessings He's bestowed on me. Without Him, I can do nothing.

About the Author

Diane Koers owns and operates All Business Service, a software training and consulting business formed in 1988 that services the central Indiana area. Her area of expertise has long been in the word-processing, spreadsheet, and graphics areas of computing as well as providing training and support for Peachtree Accounting Software. Diane's authoring experience includes more than 20 books on topics such as PC Security, Microsoft Windows, Microsoft Office, Microsoft Works, WordPerfect, Paint Shop Pro, Lotus SmartSuite, Quicken, Microsoft Money, and Peachtree Accounting, many of which have been translated into other languages such as Dutch, Bulgarian, Spanish, and Greek. She has also developed and written numerous training manuals for her clients.

Active in her church and civic activities, Diane enjoys spending her free time traveling and playing with her grandsons and her Yorkshire terriers.

Contents

Introduction

Welcome to the world of Paint Shop Pro 8.

First, let me say that I'm not a graphics or digital artist. In fact, I'm not any type of artist. I'm a teacher, and I've written this book with the thought in mind that most of us are not graphics artists. We're simply computer users who want to use our computer to create amazing graphics images. Paint Shop Pro 8 can help you create such graphics.

However, creating terrific graphics is not just a matter of drawing something on your screen. It's many steps put together. Most images are created out of several different objects—each with its own special effect—and then assembled to create the final image. Sound complicated? I thought so at first, but it's really not; in fact, the Paint Shop Pro application makes it simple. This book, *Paint Shop™ Pro® 8 Fast & Easy*, takes you through each process one step at a time.

Fast & Easy guides use a step-by-step approach and are written in an easy-to-understand common lingo. Each step is accompanied by a visual representation of your screen so that you can follow along and make sure you are on the right track.

This book is divided into four parts including three appendixes. In Part I, "Getting Started with the Basics," I show you how to control the tools that are used to create the basic objects. Although it's not the most exciting part of the book, it's certainly the most practical. Look out then! Things start to be lots of fun! In Parts II, "Working with Raster Graphics," and III, "Using Vector Graphics & Text," you learn how to assemble the objects and add special effects as well as the basics of creating graphics elements for publication to the Web. Part IV, "Special Photo Projects," includes steps for a couple of particular photographic projects such as removing red eye from photos. Finally, the appendixes show you how to save time with Paint Shop Pro keystroke shortcuts, list Web sites you can go to for cool Paint Shop Pro accessories, and present examples of just a few of the wonderful special effects.

Through this book, you learn *how* to create images, but *what* you create is up to you! Your imagination is the only limit to what you can do with the images after that. This book cannot begin to teach you everything you can do with Paint Shop Pro 8, nor will it give you all the different ways to accomplish a task. What I *have* tried to do is give you the fastest and easiest way to get started with this fun and exciting graphics program.

Who Should Read This Book?

You can use this book as a learning tool or as a step-by-step task reference. The easy-to-follow, highly visual nature of this book makes it the perfect learning tool for a beginning computer user as well as those seasoned computer users who are new to graphics applications. No prerequisites are required from you, the reader, except that you know how to turn your computer on and know how to use your mouse.

By using this *Paint Shop Pro 8 Fast & Easy* guide, any level of user can quickly look up steps for a task without having to plow through pages of descriptions.

Added Advice to Make You a Pro

You'll notice that this book focuses on the steps that are necessary for a task and keeps explanations to a minimum. Included in this book are elements that provide some additional information to help you master the program, without encumbering your progress through the steps:

- **Tips** offer shortcuts when you're performing an action, and they describe a feature that can make your work in Paint Shop Pro quicker and easier.

- **Notes** give you a bit of background or additional information about a feature; they also give advice about how to use the feature in your day-to-day activities.

- **Cautions** are used to warn you of possible disastrous results if you perform a task incorrectly.

This book truly is the *fastest and easiest* way to learn Paint Shop Pro 8. Enjoy!

—Diane Koers

PART I

Getting Started with the Basics

1

Exploring the Basics

Welcome to Paint Shop Pro version 8. If this is your first opportunity to use Paint Shop Pro, you might be a little intimidated by the vast array of tools on the opening screen. Just remember that although Paint Shop Pro is a powerful program, it's also easy to use, which is why many people are choosing it. Don't worry! You'll be creating your first image after just a couple of mouse clicks. In this chapter, you'll learn how to

- Start the Paint Shop Pro application
- Identify toolbars and tool palettes
- Manage files
- Change views

Starting Paint Shop Pro

You can start Paint Shop Pro (PSP) from the Start menu or you might have an icon on your desktop to launch PSP.

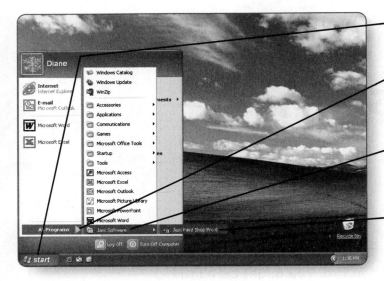

1. Click on **start**. The start menu will appear.

2. Click on **All Programs**. The Programs submenu menu will appear.

3. Click on **Jasc Software**. The Jasc Software submenu menu will appear.

4. Click on **Jasc Paint Shop Pro 8**. The program will begin.

Setting File Associations

The File Format Associations dialog box appears the first time you use Paint Shop Pro. The File Format Associations determine which files your computer opens automatically using the Paint Shop Pro application. Your system now thinks that PSP 8 is your application of choice to open those images.

For example, a friend e-mails you a .tiff photograph that you want to edit. By creating the Paint Shop Pro association, all you need to do is double-click the photograph file. Paint Shop Pro then opens with the image ready to edit. You can associate Paint Shop Pro with up to 60 different file formats.

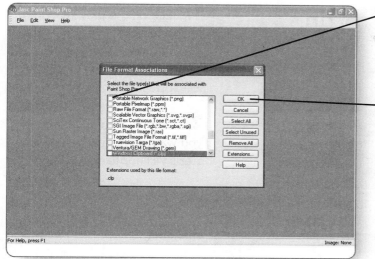

1. **Click** on any **file type** to add or remove the √. Items with a √ will be associated with Paint Shop Pro.

2. **Click** on **OK**. The File Format Associations dialog box will close.

TIP

To later review or change file associations, click on File, select Preferences, and then select File Format Associations.

Understanding the Learning Center

New to Paint Shop Pro version 8 is the Learning Center. The Learning Center is a series of step-by-step short tutorials called Quick Guides that are designed to help you get started with Paint Shop Pro. The Learning Center includes help for simple topics such as opening a file to more advanced topics such as special photo projects.

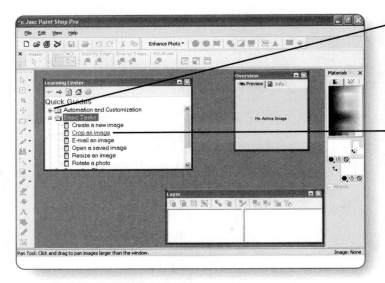

1. Click on the plus sign next to the **topic** you want to review. The plus sign will turn into a minus sign and a series of tasks will appear.

2. Click on the **specific topic** you want to review. A series of steps will appear.

The Learning Center window includes several buttons to assist you:

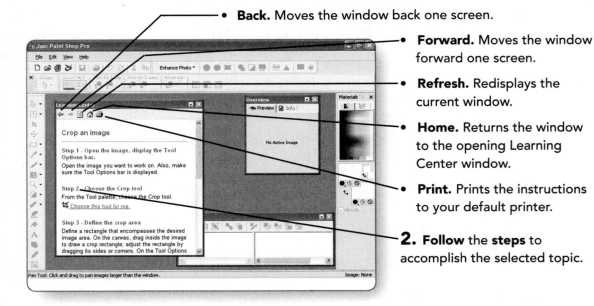

- **Back.** Moves the window back one screen.

- **Forward.** Moves the window forward one screen.

- **Refresh.** Redisplays the current window.

- **Home.** Returns the window to the opening Learning Center window.

- **Print.** Prints the instructions to your default printer.

2. Follow the **steps** to accomplish the selected topic.

The bottom of the Learning Center window might display related topics you want to review.

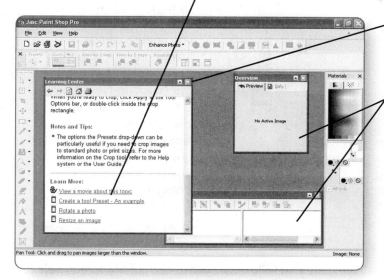

3. **Click** the **Close button**. The Learning Center window will close.

By default, Paint Shop Pro displays two additional palettes, the Layer Palette and the Overview Palette. You'll learn about these items in later chapters. For now, close the Layer and Overview Palettes by clicking on their Close buttons.

TIP

To redisplay the Learning Center window, click Learning Center from the Help menu or press the F10 key.

Examining Screen Objects

The Paint Shop Pro window, called the *workspace*, is full of toolbars and palettes. Each has a specific purpose to assist you in creating or editing images. As you read through this book, you'll use and learn more about each of these objects. Paint Shop Pro groups many objects into two categories: toolbars and palettes. Toolbars display buttons for the most common tasks, and palettes display information and help you select tools, modify options, manage layers, select colors, and perform other editing tasks.

NOTE

To easily work with the remainder of this chapter, you need a canvas or image on your screen. Click on the New icon and then click on New. Click OK to accept all the default choices. You'll learn about the options in the New Image dialog box in Chapter 2, "Working with Paint Shop Pro Files."

The mini table that follows describes each of the screen objects.

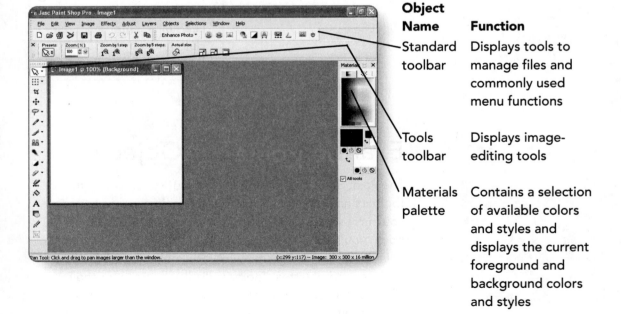

Object Name	Function
Standard toolbar	Displays tools to manage files and commonly used menu functions
Tools toolbar	Displays image-editing tools
Materials palette	Contains a selection of available colors and styles and displays the current foreground and background colors and styles

NOTE

You'll learn lots more about the Materials palette in Chapter 5, "Understanding the Materials Palette."

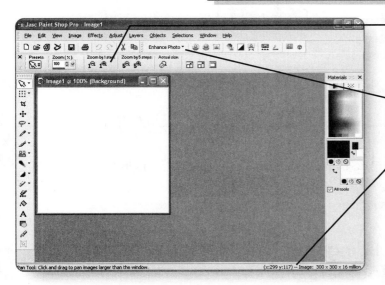

Tool Options palette Displays options for the currently selected tool

Photo toolbar Displays commonly used tools when you're working with photographs

Status toolbar Displays image details such as a description of a tool or cursor coordinates

Additionally, although they are not displayed by default, Paint Shop Pro includes other toolbars and pallets.

Object Name	Function
Browser toolbar	Displays useful tools when you're browsing images
Web toolbar	Displays commonly used tools when you're working with Web graphics
Effects toolbar	Displays commonly used effects
Script toolbar	Displays commands for creating and running scripts
Histogram palette	Displays a graph showing the distribution of color and light in an image
Brush Variance palette	Displays additional options for working with brushes
Layers palette	Lists each layer in the current image

Object Name	Function
Overview palette	Displays entire image when you're zooming in to a small area
Scrip Output palette	Displays script actions you make and the results of running scripts
Learning Center palette	Displays tutorials for common tasks

NOTE

You can learn about working with layers in Chapter 9, "Developing Layers."

Hiding and Displaying Toolbars and Palettes

The toolbar or palette you want might not be visible, or you might not need or want some that are displayed. You can easily hide or display toolbars or palettes.

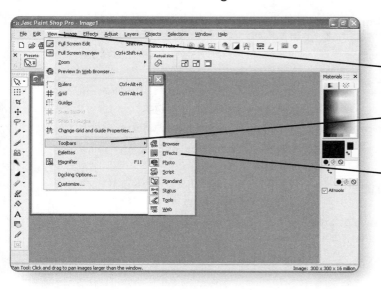

1. Click on **View**. The View menu will appear.

2a. Click on **Toolbars**. The Toolbars submenu will appear.

3a. Click on the **toolbar** you want to display or hide.

OR

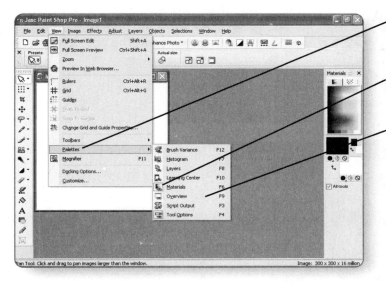

2b. **Click** on **Palettes**. The Palettes submenu will appear.

Currently displayed objects have a box around their icon.

3b. **Click** on the **palette** you want to display or hide.

Docking Toolbars and Palettes

Most toolbars and palettes are docked at an edge of the screen, but if a toolbar is not located in a favorable position for you to access, move it to any position on the screen.

Sometimes, you might move a toolbar accidentally into the middle of the screen, blocking your view of your document. It's easy to move a toolbar or palette into any position.

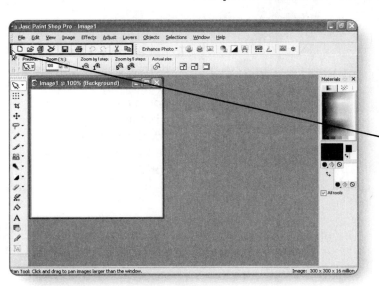

1. **Press and hold** the **mouse pointer** on a toolbar or palette where you see a series of dots. A black border will appear around the object.

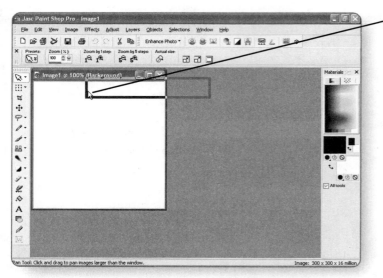

2. Drag the **mouse** into the screen area. The object might change shape.

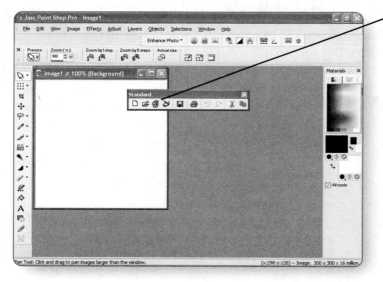

3. Release the **mouse button**. The toolbar or palette will remain in the new position.

TIP

To put an object back in its normal position, press and hold the mouse button over the toolbar title bar and drag it into the desired position, usually at the top of the screen.

Moving Floating Windows

If a floating screen object is in the way of your work, you can easily move it to a new location.

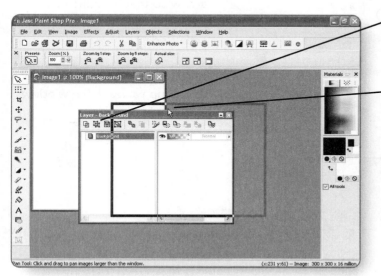

1. **Position** the **mouse** over the title bar of the object you want to move.

2. **Drag** the **window** to a desired location. You will see an outline of the window.

3. **Release** the **mouse button**. The window will move to the new position.

Working with Automatic Rollup

When a palette is not docked, it has a feature called automatic rollup. The objects roll up and close when your mouse is out of their vicinity but open automatically as you hover your mouse in their area. The automatic rollup feature applies only to palettes, not to toolbars.

The automatic rollup arrow points to the left when the feature is active and points upward when the window is locked.

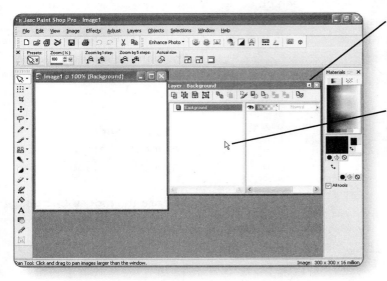

1. If necessary, **click** the **locking arrow** so that it points to the left. The rollup feature will be activated.

As the mouse is displayed over the rollup window, the window will remain open.

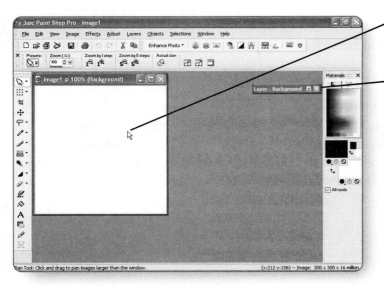

2. Move the **mouse pointer** out of the palette window.

The window will roll up and only the title bar will remain visible.

3. Move the **mouse pointer** back into the palette window area. The window will reopen to its original size.

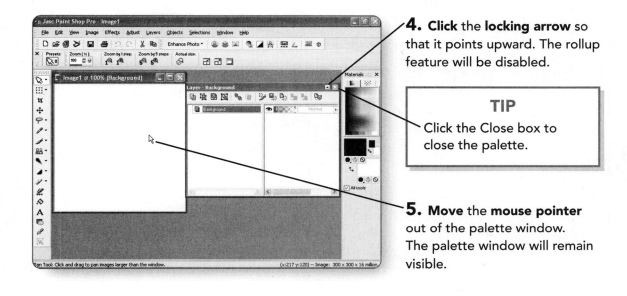

4. Click the **locking arrow** so that it points upward. The rollup feature will be disabled.

TIP

Click the Close box to close the palette.

5. Move the **mouse pointer** out of the palette window. The palette window will remain visible.

Modifying the Screen Appearance

As you work on an image, Paint Shop Pro includes several tools to change screen appearance and assist you when you're working with an image.

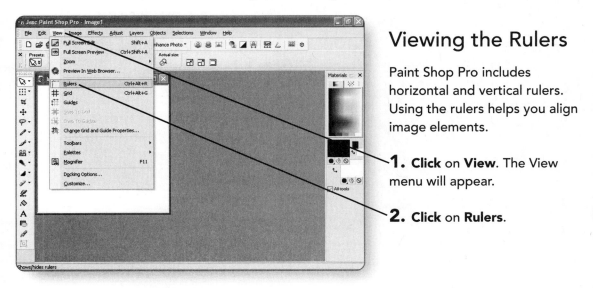

Viewing the Rulers

Paint Shop Pro includes horizontal and vertical rulers. Using the rulers helps you align image elements.

1. Click on **View**. The View menu will appear.

2. Click on **Rulers**.

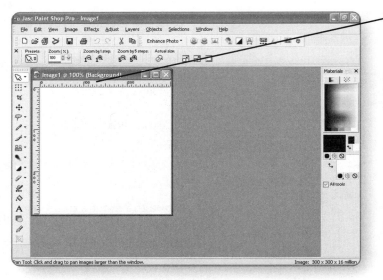

The rulers will display with measurements in pixels.

3. Repeat the preceding **steps** to hide the rulers.

Displaying the Grid

Displaying the grid places nonprinting equally spaced vertical and horizontal lines on the screen. Use the gridlines to help you align image elements.

1. Click on **View**. The View menu will appear.

2. Click on **Grid**.

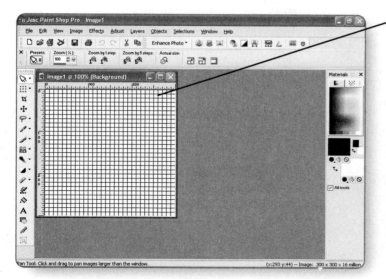

The grid will appear onscreen.

3. Repeat the preceding **steps** to hide the grid.

TIP

Change the spacing between the lines of the grid by selecting Change Grid and Guide Properties from the View menu.

2

Working with Paint Shop Pro Files

Very shortly, you'll be creating a new graphics file or working with one that was created previously. As you arduously work with your graphics image or make changes to it, you will probably need to stop periodically and do something else—take a break, eat dinner, pay the bills, walk the dog, and so forth. You need to save your file so that you can return to it whenever you are ready. Saving your file stores it on your computer, not just in the computer's temporary memory, and files it away for the future. That's what this chapter is about—working with those files. In this chapter, you'll learn how to

- Create a new file with preset characteristics
- Save files
- Close files
- Browse and open existing files
- Set Autosave options

Working with Files

If you've worked with other Windows applications, you're probably familiar with file concepts such as opening, naming, saving, and closing. Paint Shop Pro uses the same associations that Windows mandates.

Creating a New File

Unlike some programs you might use, Paint Shop Pro doesn't automatically open with a blank document for you. You might want to begin with an existing photograph or image, or you might want to create a document from scratch. If you want to create a new document, Paint Shop Pro first requires several pieces of information.

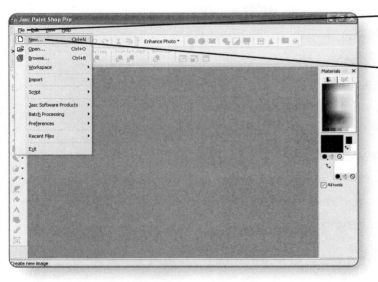

1. Click on **File**. The File menu will appear.

2. Click on **New**. The New Image dialog box will open.

TIP

You can also create a new file by pressing Ctrl+N or by clicking on the New button.

Determining Image Size

Paint Shop Pro requires you to predetermine the size of the new image. You can determine the size in inches, centimeters, or the default *pixels*. Pixel, which stands for picture element, is the individual square (or dots of light) that are used to make up an image—in particular, a raster image. You'll learn about raster images in later chapters. In terms of measurement, a pixel is the smallest element that can be assigned a color. Most graphics artists prefer to work in pixels.

TIP

If you are going to use your image for the Web, you should not create images larger than 600 pixels wide or 440 pixels tall. This ensures that everyone who sees the Web image will be able to see it in its entirety. As an example, if you're designing a Web page headline, you might want to make it a maximum size of 600 wide × 175 tall so that it doesn't take up the entire screen height.

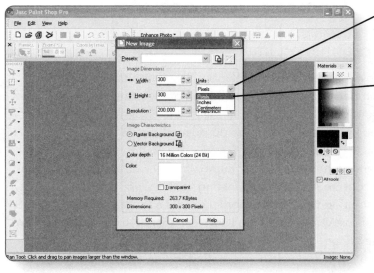

1. Click on the **down arrow** ( ) in the **Units** section. A selection list will appear.

2. Click on your preferred **unit of measurement**. The selection will display in the list box.

In most Paint Shop Pro dialog boxes, you will see three ways to enter numeric measurements:

- Highlight the existing number and then type a number in the text box.

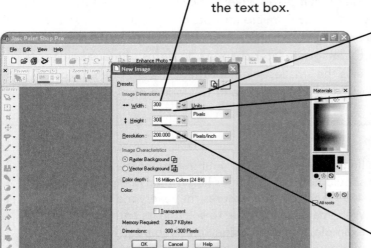

- Click the up/down arrows until the number you want appears.

- Drag the slider bar until the number you want appears.

3. Change the current **width** to the desired width. The new measurement will replace the existing measurement.

4. Change the current **height** to the desired height. The new measurement will replace the existing measurement.

Determining Image Resolution

Now let's talk about resolution. Resolution measures the number of pixels in a specific unit of measurement. The higher the resolution, the more detail that is displayed. The resolution you need depends on the purpose of the image.

Here's a general rule of thumb: If you're designing a graphic for onscreen use or for posting to the Web, set your resolution to 72 pixels per inch. That's the resolution of most Web browsers and e-mail applications. If you're going to print the image, go with a higher resolution, such as 600 pixels per inch or 1200 pixels per inch, depending on your printer.

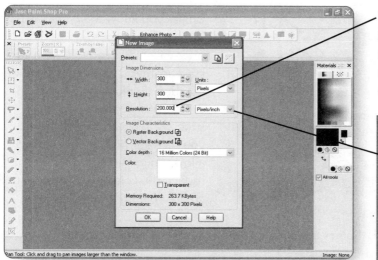

1. Change the current **resolution** to the desired resolution. The new measurement will replace the existing measurement.

Determining Image Characteristics

The lower section in the New Image dialog box deals with the background color of your new image and the number of available colors, called the *color depth*.

You also must decide the type of background you need for your image: raster or vector. Basically, raster graphics use pixels to store information about the image, whereas vector graphics store graphics information in a mathematical format. You'll learn about working with each type of graphic as you progress through this book, beginning with raster graphics.

1. **Select** a **background type**. The option will be selected.

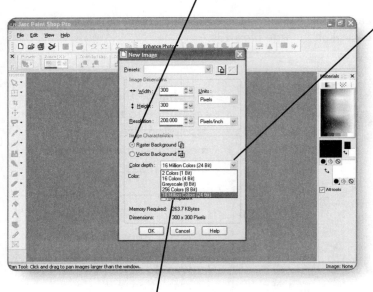

2. **Click** on the **down arrow** (⌄) next to Color depth. A list of options will appear.

Unless you know that your image is to be in black and white or grayscale, you probably want to start an image with the maximum number of colors, which is 16.7 million. Many Paint Shop Pro special effects aren't available if you set your maximum colors to a lower number. You can always reduce the color depth after you create your image.

3. **Select** a **color depth**. The option will be selected.

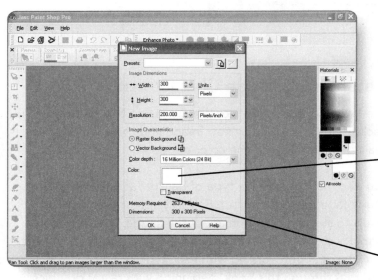

Typically, the background color, which is like the color of a canvas, is black or white. However, other selections are available. New to Paint Shop Pro 8 is the ability to easily add a texture to your background.

4. **Click** on the background **color box**. The Material dialog box will open.

TIP

If you don't want color for the background of your image, click the Transparent button.

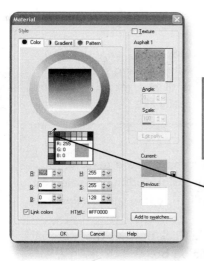

You can select your color from the predefined color box or click anywhere in the color circle to select a more precise color.

TIP

You will learn lots more about the Material dialog box in Chapter 5, "Understanding the Materials Palette."

5. **Click** on the **background color** you want. A sample will appear in the Current box.

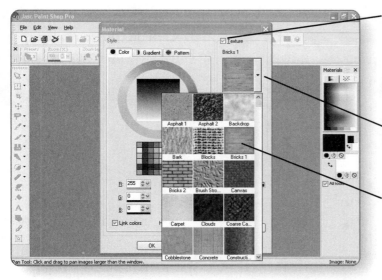

6. **Click** the **Texture check box** if you want a textured effect on your background. A √ will appear, and the textured options will become available.

7. **Click** on the **arrow** next to the textured effects. A palette of textures will appear.

8. **Click** on the **texture** you want to use. The texture name will display.

TIP

Optionally, experiment with rotating the texture until you get an effect you really like.

A sample of the texture, plus the color option you selected, will appear in the Preview box.

9. Click on **OK**. The Material dialog box will close.

10. Click on **OK**. You're ready to begin creating an image.

Saving a File

Saving a file in Paint Shop Pro is identical to saving a file in most Windows applications. Don't make the mistake of waiting until you've finished working on a project to save it. Save your file early in its creation. Saving your work early and often can save you lots of grief if your computer locks up or a power failure occurs.

Saving a File the First Time

When you first create a file, it has no name. If you want to view, edit, or publish that file to the Web, it must have a name. Paint Shop Pro asks for a name the first time you save the file, and after that, the name you give it appears in the title bar at the top of the screen.

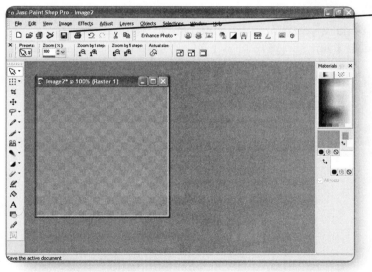

1. **Click** on the **Save button**. The Save As dialog box will appear.

TIP

You can also save a new file by pressing Ctrl+S or by choosing Save from the File menu.

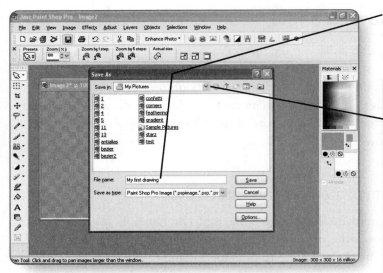

2. Type a **name** for your file in the **File name text box**. The file name will display.

Optionally, you can select a file type in which to save your image. Paint Shop Pro allows you to save your image in many different file types, including Web type formats such as GIF, JPEG, or PNG. However, it's usually best to save the file as the default Paint Shop Pro (.psp) format until you are finished with it. Then, if you need a different file format, you can resave it with the new format. See Chapter 17, "Designing Web Page Components," for more information on saving a .psp file into a Web format.

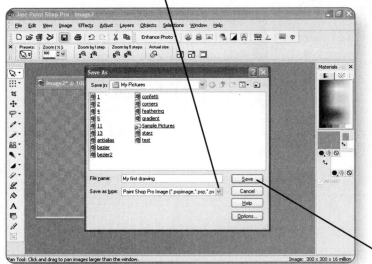

3. Click on **Save**. Paint Shop Pro will save your file.

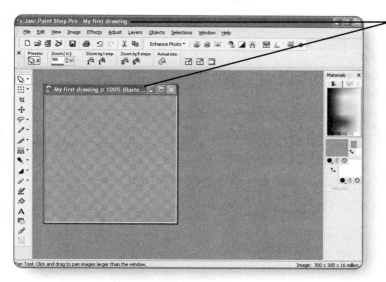

The name you specified will appear in the window title bars.

Resaving a File

As you continue to work on your file, you should resave it every 10 minutes or so to help ensure that you do not lose your changes.

If you have made changes to a file but not yet saved those changes, Paint Shop Pro displays an asterisk (*) next to the filename in the title bar.

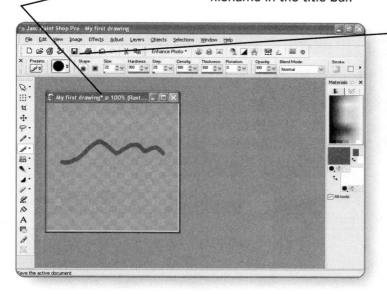

1. Click on the **Save button**. The file will be resaved with any changes. No dialog box will open because the file is resaved with the same name and in the same folder as previously specified.

TIP

If you want to save the file with a different name, in a different folder, or as a different file type, click on File and then choose Save As. The Save As dialog box will prompt you for the new name or folder. The original file will remain as well as the new one.

Opening Files

Opening an image file puts a copy of that image into the computer's memory and onto your screen so that you can work on it. If you make changes, be sure to save the file again. You can open files you've created and saved, files you've downloaded from the Internet, files you've downloaded from your digital camera, or files you've scanned from a scanner.

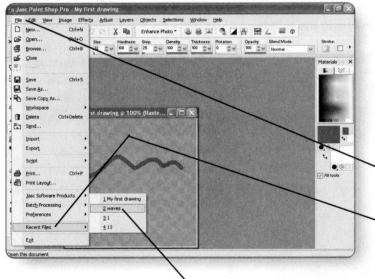

Opening a Recently Opened File

Paint Shop Pro tracks the previous four files you've worked with, making it easy to select one of them through the File menu.

1. Click on **File**. The File menu will appear.

2. Click on **Recent Files**. A submenu of your recent files will appear.

3. Click on the **filename** you want to open. The image file will open on your screen, ready for you to edit.

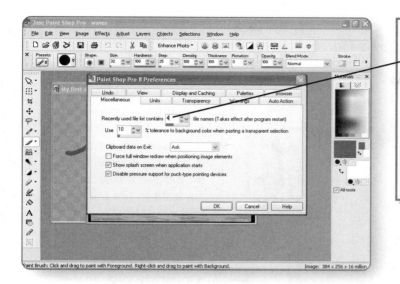

NOTE

To change the number of recently used files, click General Program Preferences from the File, Preferences menu. The Miscellaneous tab specifies the number of recently used files.

Opening an Existing File

To work on a previously created file—whether it's a file you created from scratch, a photograph, or a piece of clip art from another program—you can use the Open dialog box to locate your file. You can also open multiple files and easily switch between them.

1. Click on the **Open button**. The Open dialog box will appear.

TIP

You can also open an existing file by pressing Ctrl+O or by choosing Open from the File menu.

2. Click on the **image** you want to open. The filename is highlighted.

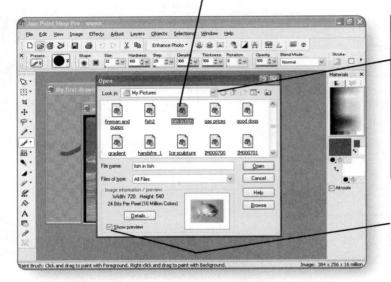

3. Optionally, **click** on the **Show Preview check box**.

A thumbnail (small illustration) of the image will appear.

4. Click on **Open**. The image is placed on your screen, ready to edit.

Duplicating a File

If you have a file you would like to practice with, but you don't want to risk damaging the original file, you can use the Paint Shop Pro Duplicate command. The Duplicate command opens another window with an exact duplicate of the currently open window. You can then close the original and practice on the duplicate.

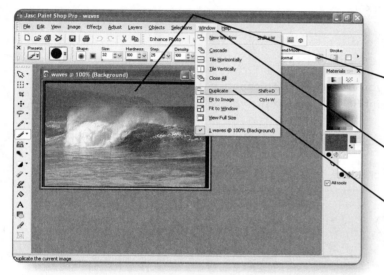

1. Open a **file**. The file will appear in the Paint Shop Pro windows.

2. Click on **Window**. The Window menu will appear.

3. Click on **Duplicate**. A second window, an exact copy of the first, will appear.

The original file is still open. If you don't want to work on it, you must close it.

The duplicate file has no name. If you want to keep it, you must save it.

Closing Files

When you are finished working on an image, you should close it. Closing is the equivalent of putting it away for later use. When you close a file, you are only putting the file away—not closing the program. Paint Shop Pro is still active and ready to work for you.

Closing a File

If you close a file with changes that have not been saved, Paint Shop Pro prompts you with a message box.

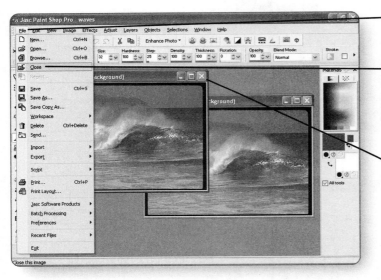

1a. **Click** on **File**. The File menu will appear.

2a. **Click** on **Close**. The file is put away.

OR

1b. **Click** on the **Close button**. The file is closed. By choosing this method, you combine steps 1 and 2.

NOTE

If you have not saved your file, choose Yes to save the changes or No to close the file without saving the changes.

Closing All Windows

If you are working with multiple graphics image windows, you can close them all at a single time. Instead of following a prompt to save each file individually, Paint Shop Pro provides a window where you can check which of the open files you want to save.

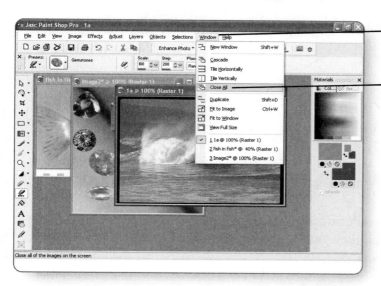

1. Click on **Window**. The Window menu will appear.

2. Click on **Close All**. The Close All Files dialog box will open.

> **TIP**
> Optionally, click the Paint Shop Pro Close button.

Any files that have not already been saved are listed in the top left. By default, each unsaved filename has a √ indicating that you want to save the file.

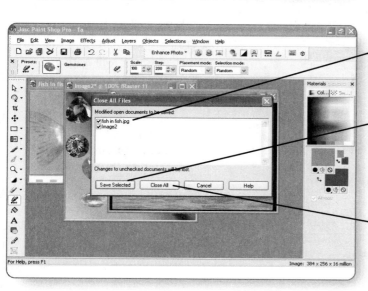

3. Remove the √ from any file you don't want to save the changes for.

4. Click on **Save**. Paint Shop Pro will save the remaining checked files.

> **TIP**
> Optionally, click on Close All to close all open files without saving any open files.

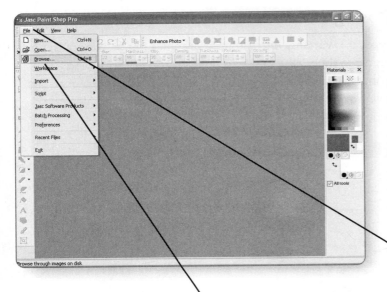

Browsing Images

A useful feature provided with Paint Shop Pro is the Browse feature. Browsing lets you view thumbnails of your images. Browsing the thumbnails allows you to look at many images at the same time to quickly select the image you're looking for.

1. Click on **File**. The File menu will appear.

2. Click on **Browse**. The Browse window will open.

The left side of the Browse window is similar to the Windows Explorer window, which displays a tree structure of your disk drives.

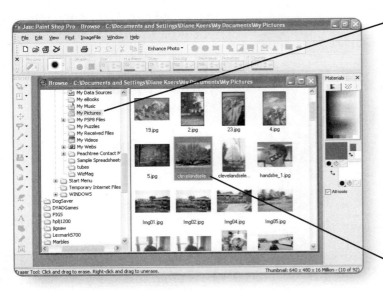

3. Click on the **folder** you want to browse. Thumbnails of graphics files located in the selected folder will appear.

NOTE

See Chapter 7, "Printing Images," for information on printing thumbnails of your images.

4. Double-click on the **image** you want to open. The image will appear onscreen.

TIP

To open multiple files at the same time, hold down the Ctrl key and click on each additional file you want to open. Press the Enter key when the files are selected.

The Browse window will stay open in the background. Click on the Close button to close it.

Working with Multiple Windows

Paint Shop Pro includes the ability to work on a number of different image files at the same time.

1. Click on **Window**. The Window menu will appear with a list of all open Paint Shop Pro files.

2. Click on the **image file** you want to display. The selected image will become the active file.

The currently active window will display a √ next to the name.

Occasionally, you might want to view two or more documents next to each other so that you can compare them.

3. **Click** on **Window**. The Window menu will appear.

4. **Click** on **Tile Vertically**. The entire work area will be divided among the open image files.

TIP

To edit an image, click anywhere on the window for that file.

Setting Autosave

Paint Shop Pro has a feature called Autosave that periodically saves your document for you. After a crash, when you boot up and reopen Paint Shop Pro, the program opens a recovered saved version of the files you were working on at the time of the crash.

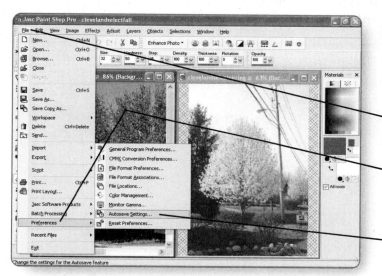

1. Click on **File**. The File menu will appear.

2. Click on **Preferences**. The Preferences submenu menu will appear.

3. Click on **Autosave Settings**. The Autosave Settings dialog box will open.

4. Click on **Enable Autosave**. The option will appear with a √.

Paint Shop Pro allows you to specify the time intervals for the Autosave to save your work.

5. Optionally, **click** on the **up/down arrows** ( ) to increase or decrease the amount of time between each Autosave.

6. Click on **OK**. The Autosave Settings dialog box will close.

CAUTION

Use caution with the Autosave feature. If you are just practicing and want to start over and you have Autosave activated, you might have changes to your image you don't want.

3

Discovering Drawing Tools

In Chapter 1, "Exploring the Basics," you discovered many of the different screen objects that Paint Shop Pro provides. The two objects you'll probably use the most are the Tools toolbar and the Tool Options palette. The Tools toolbar contains tools that you'll need to create and edit images, whether you create the images from scratch or edit a photograph or other artwork. Although it is beyond the scope of this book to use every available tool, we'll take a look as some of the more commonly used tools. In this chapter, you'll learn how to

- Identify commonly used tools
- Draw with the Paint Brush and Airbrush tools
- Set Paint Brush options
- Draw lines and preset shapes
- Use Undo

Identifying the Tools

The Tools toolbar displays icons representing the drawing tools that are available in Paint Shop Pro. Some tools have an arrow next to them, which indicates that there are several similar type tools grouped together. Click on a tool to select it or click on any tool arrow to see the additional tools.

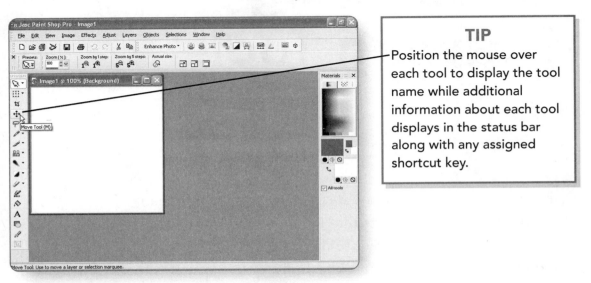

TIP

Position the mouse over each tool to display the tool name while additional information about each tool displays in the status bar along with any assigned shortcut key.

The table that follows lists the tools on the Tools toolbar and a general description of their functions. The tools are listed top to bottom.

Tool	Function
Pan tools	Increase or decrease the magnification and view area of the displayed image
Deform tools	Rotate, resize, skew, or distort the image
Crop tool	Eliminates areas of an image
Move tool	Moves a selection to a different area of an image
Selection tools	Make selections for editing, copying, or removing
Dropper tools	Select a foreground and background color or replace one color with another
Paint Brush tools	Paint an image by using a paintbrush, air brush, or warp brush shape
Clone brushes	Create brush strokes that duplicate part of an image, such as for removing blemishes from photos
Smudge brushes	Create several different effects that are similar to smearing paint
Lighten/Darken brushes	Increase or decrease lightness
Eraser tools	Replace colors in an image with the background color or transparency
Picture Tube tool	Paints images and shapes
Flood Fill tool	Fills an area with a color, pattern, or gradient
Text tool	Creates text areas and objects
Preset Shapes tool	Draws rectangles, squares, ellipses, circles, stars, and callout clouds
Pen tool	Draws lines, polylines, and freehand lines
Object Selection tool	Lets you move, resize, reshape, and rotate vector objects

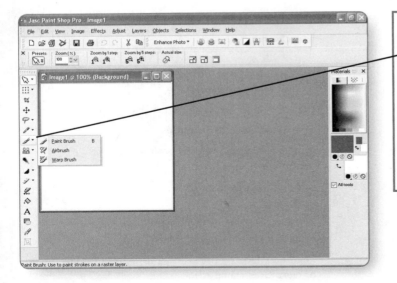

Many tools have an arrow beside them indicating that additional tools are available that are similar to the displayed tool. Click on the arrow and then click on the tool you want to use.

Changing Tool Options

Each tool has its own set of options. After you select the tool you want to use but before you actually use the tool, select from the available options on the Tools Options palette.

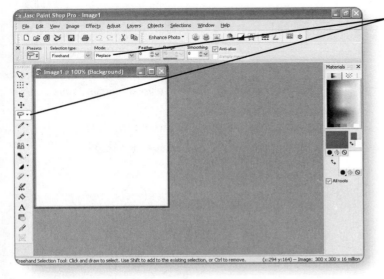

1. **Click** on a **Selection tool**. The Tool Options palette will display selection options.

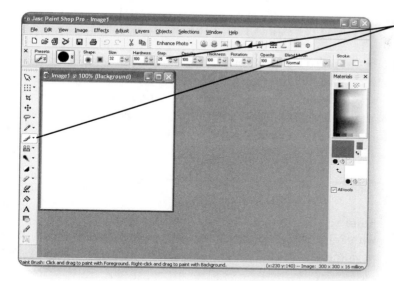

2. Click on a **Paint Brush tool**. The Tool Options palette will show paintbrush options.

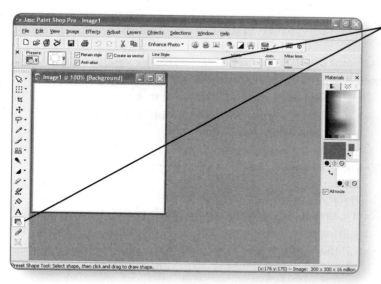

3. Click on the **Preset Shapes tool**. The Tool Options palette will display preset shape options.

Drawing with the Tools

Paint Shop Pro is a wonderful program for working with pre-existing graphics images, but it is even better when you need to draw or paint your own images. For the samples in this chapter, start with a new image 300 pixels wide by 300 pixels high and with a white background. Select the highest available color depth.

TIP

Refer to "Creating a New File" in Chapter 2, "Working with Paint Shop Pro Files," for instructions on creating a new image.

Painting with the Paint Brush

The Paint Brush is the tool you'll probably use most often to draw basic shapes. Most images are simple combinations of basic shapes. You can draw and paint freehand style using the Paint Brush by using the mouse pointer as the brush tip.

Drawing with the Paint Brush

Begin by using the Paint Brush tool to draw on your canvas. Don't worry if it doesn't look like much to begin with. With just a little practice, you'll learn how to control your mouse to control the brush.

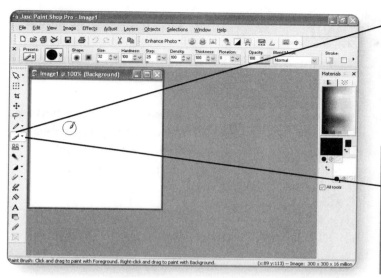

1. Click on the **Paint Brush tool**. The mouse pointer will appear as a paintbrush tip. The circle surrounding the paintbrush illustrates the stroke size.

TIP

If you don't see the Paint Brush tool, click the arrow next to the brush tools to display a submenu of brush tools.

2. Select a **brush size**. A higher value will result in a larger, wider brush stroke, whereas a lower value will produce a thinner line. Sizes range from a 1 for the thinnest line to 500 for the widest line.

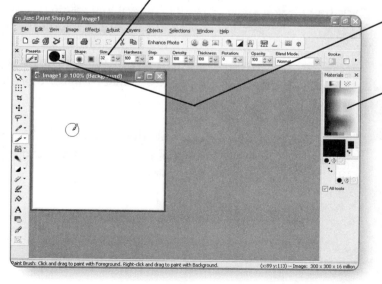

A sample of your brush with the selected settings will appear in the Preview button.

3. Click on a **color** from the Materials palette. A sample will appear in a color swatch box.

NOTE

You'll learn lots more about the Materials palette in Chapter 5, "Understanding the Materials Palette."

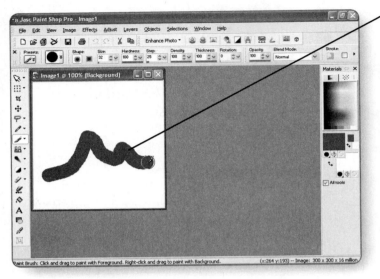

4. Click and drag the **mouse** across a section of your image window. A brush line will appear.

5. Release the **mouse button**. That's it! You've just painted with the Paint Brush tool.

Selecting Brush Options

Combining different brush options can provide a variety of different effects. Try changing other paintbrush options and redrawing a line to see what happens.

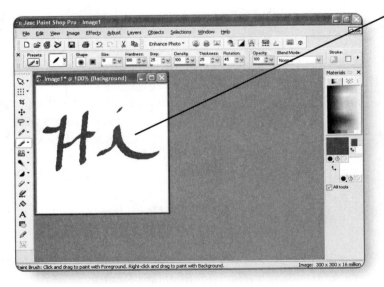

For example, if you take a round shape brush, set the thickness to 25, the rotation to 45, and the hardness to 100, you get a brush stroke that is similar to a ribbon or calligraphic stroke.

The table that follows describes some of the brush options and their uses.

#	Tool	Use
❶	Shape	Identifies whether the brush tip is rounded or squared. Rounded tip brushes create a smoother edge, whereas squared tips create a firmer edge.
❷	Hardness	Defines how the painted item edges blend into the background or other items. A higher value or "harder" brush stroke produces a crisper edge, whereas a lower value produces a softer edge. Hardness ranges are from 0 to 100.
❸	Step	Labels the distance between brush strokes. A higher value decreases the frequency of the drops of paint as the brush tip touches the image, whereas a lower value produces a smoother and denser effect. Step ranges are from 1 to 200.
❹	Density	Designates the number of pixels that the brush paints. A higher value paints a more solid line, whereas a lower value produces a speckled stroke effect. Density values are from 1 to 100.

#	Tool	Use
❺	Thickness	Selects the thickness of the brush stroke. A lower value draws a thinner stroke, whereas a higher value creates a heavier, thicker stroke. Thickness values range from 1 to 100.
❻	Rotation	Turns the angle of the brush stroke. Rotation is measured in degrees from 0 to 359.
❼	Opacity	Displays the density of a brush stroke. A higher value applies a more solid color effect, whereas a lower value results in softer, more transparent color. Opacity is measured from 1 to 100.

Selecting Preset Options

If you don't want to select all those options each time you want to use the brush tools, you can select from a variety of preset brushes and options included with Paint Shop Pro. You can also select from presets that simulate other drawing utensils, such as crayon, chalk, or charcoal.

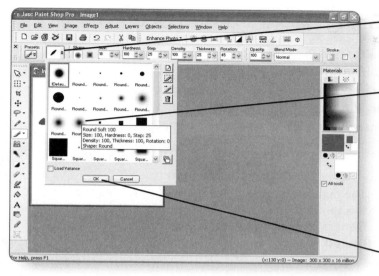

1. Click on the **Presets Preview box arrows**. A list of preset brushes will appear.

2. Pause the **mouse** over any of the brush tips. A ToolTip will appear showing the brush settings.

3. Click the **preset brush** you want to use. A border will surround the selection.

4. Click on **OK**. The preset brush list will close.

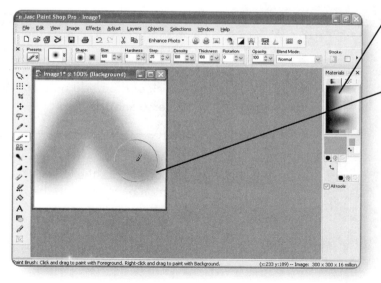

5. Click on a **color** from the Materials palette. A sample will appear in a color swatch box.

6. Paint the **image** as desired.

Going Backward with Undo

Paint Shop Pro includes an Undo command that reverses the command made to the current image. It can remove painting or drawing operations, color alterations, filter effects, and so on. It cannot undo a modification that has been closed or changes to the filename or file format.

> **NOTE**
>
> The number of operations you can undo depends on the settings in the Undo tab in the File, Preferences, General Program Preferences menu. The maximum is limited only by that setting and the disk space in your computer.

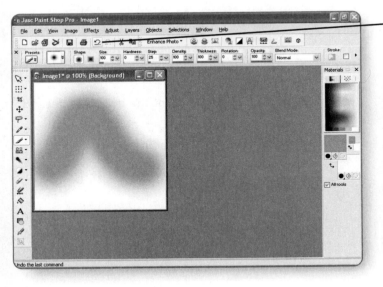

1. Click on the **Undo button.** Paint Shop Pro will reverse the previous step.

Each click of the Undo button will reverse another step.

> **TIP**
>
> Optionally, use the Undo function by clicking on the Edit menu and choosing Undo or pressing Ctrl+Z.

Another method to correct errors or make changes is by using the Eraser tools. You'll learn about using those tools to edit your drawings in Chapter 6, "Editing Images and Drawings."

Operating the Airbrush Tool

Although using the Airbrush tool is similar to using the Paint Brush tool, you'll also find that using the Airbrush tool is similar to painting with a spray can. When you're spray painting, if you stay in one place for a moment, the paint builds up. The same reaction occurs when you use the Airbrush tool. You'll notice this behavior even more if you set the Opacity fairly low in the Tool Options palette. Using the Airbrush tool is different from spray painting in one big way: The Airbrush tool doesn't drip!

The Airbrush tool is really a variation of the Paint Brush tool, so Paint Shop Pro lists the Airbrush tool under the Paint Brush selections.

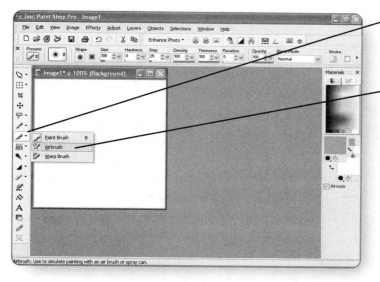

1. **Click** the **arrow** next to the Paint Brush tool. A submenu of paint tools will appear.

2. **Click** on the **Airbrush tool**. The mouse pointer will turn into an airbrush tip.

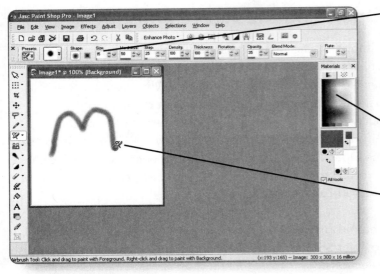

3. Set any desired **options** from the Tool Options palette. You'll find the same options for the Airbrush tool that you have with the Paint Brush tool.

4. Click on a **color** from the Materials palette. A sample will appear in a color swatch box.

5. Click and drag the **mouse** across a section of your image window, pausing every few seconds. A line will appear.

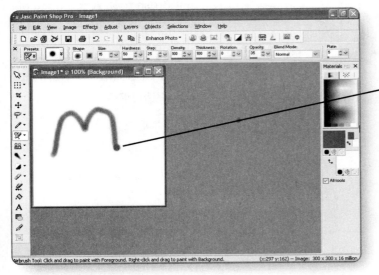

6. Release the **mouse button**. That's it! You've just painted with the Airbrush!

In the example you see here, the Paint Brush opacity is set at 35. You can see that the paint thickened when the mouse movement stopped.

Drawing a Preset Shape

You don't have to be a superlative artist to draw shapes and other items with Paint Shop Pro because it includes many common preset shapes, including rectangles, triangles, stars, and ellipses and fun shapes such as flowers, happy faces, telephones, and musical notes.

Drawing a Rectangle

When you're drawing a shape such as a rectangle, you can select the thickness and style of the outer lines, as well as the corner shapes or miters.

Keep the following facts in mind when you're drawing shapes:

- If you click and drag from the top of the canvas toward the bottom, the image shape will be drawn from corner to corner.

- If you click and drag from the bottom of the canvas toward the top, the image shape will be drawn upside down.

- If you click and drag using the right mouse button instead of the left button, the image will be drawn from the midpoint to the outer edges.

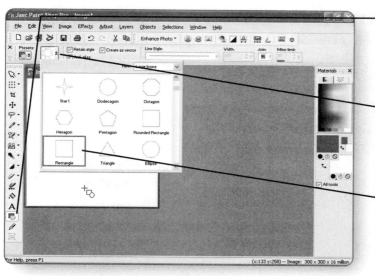

1. Click on the **Preset Shape tool**. The mouse pointer will appear as a black cross with a square and circle on it.

2. From the Tool Options palette, **click** on the **Shape list arrows**. A list of shapes will appear.

3. Click on **Rectangle** or another desired shape. The option will appear in the shape box.

The Retain style check box will maintain the shape and appearance as you see it in the drop-down box. Uncheck this option to use your own line style, corners, or colors.

4. **Remove** the **Retain style** √. The √ is removed.

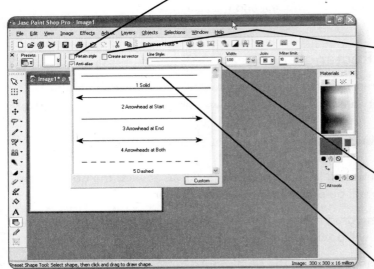

5. **Click** on the **Line Style arrows.** A list of line styles will appear, including solid, dotted, dashed, and other lines.

6. **Click** on a **line style**. The selected style will display in the Line Style box.

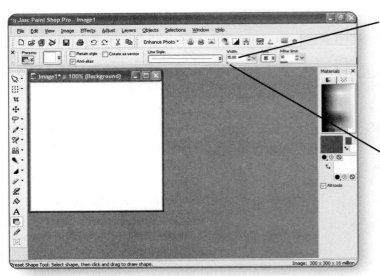

7. **Click** the **line width up or down arrows** (‡) to select a border line width. The number you select is indicated in pixels.

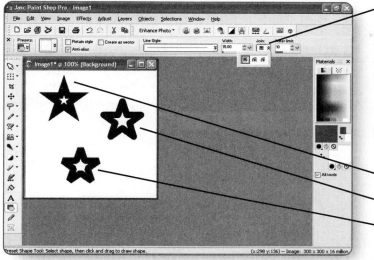

If you are using one of the thicker line widths and a shape other than an ellipse, you can choose the types of corners you want your shape to take. The corners are called the *join*, indicating how you want the corners joined together. Join choices include these:

- Mitered corners
- Round corners
- Beveled corners

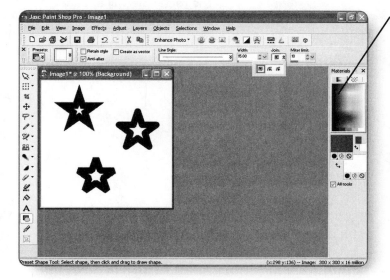

8. Click on a **color** from the Materials palette. A sample will appear in a color swatch box.

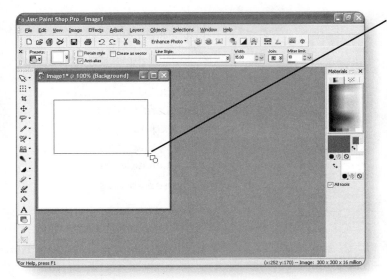

9. Click and drag in the image window. An outline of a rectangle will appear.

10. Release the **mouse button**.

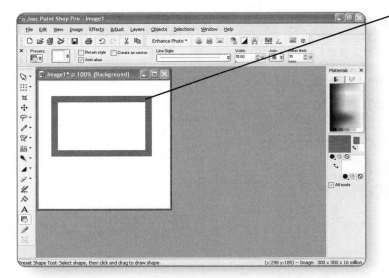

The rectangle will appear on the screen.

Creating the Perfect Shape

Who says you can't draw a perfect circle? With Paint Shop Pro's Ellipse tool, you can. You can draw perfect squares, perfect circles, perfect stars, and so forth. The Shift key is the secret to constraining your drawing shapes. Holding down the Shift key when you're drawing any shape restricts the shape to a ratio so that all sides remain equal.

1. Click on the **Preset Shape tool**. The mouse pointer will appear as black cross with a square and circle on it.

2. From the Tool Options palette, **click** on the **Shape List arrows**. A list of shapes will appear.

3. Click on **Ellipse** or another shape. The option will appear in the shape box.

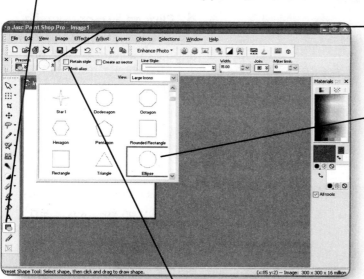

4. Remove any √s from Retain style. The check box will be blank.

5. Remove any √s from Create as vector. The check box will be blank.

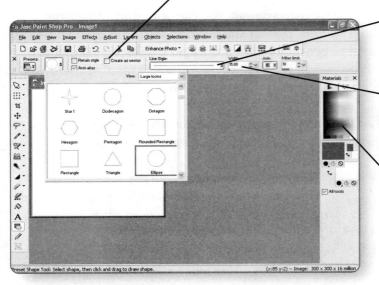

6. Click on a **line style**. The selected style will display in the line style box.

7. Select a **line width (thickness)**. The number you select is indicated in pixels.

8. Click on a **color** from the Materials palette. A sample will appear in a color swatch box.

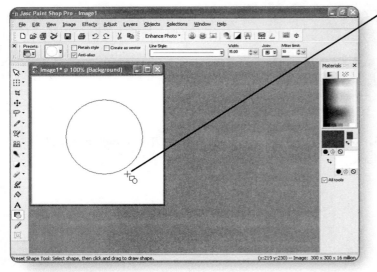

9. Press and hold down the **Shift key** on your keyboard while you **click and drag** in the image window. The shape will appear on your document.

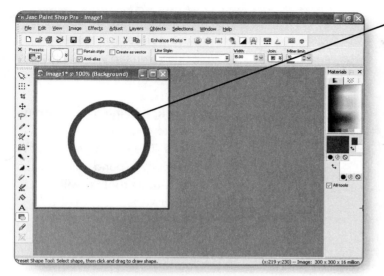

10. Release the **mouse button** and then **release** the **Shift key.** The symmetrical shape will appear on the screen.

Using the Pen Tool

Although the Paint Brush tool you used earlier allowed you freedom in drawing by emulating a real paintbrush, the Pen tool is more like a drafting tool, drawing straighter, more distinctive lines. You can use the Pen tool to draw polygons and other similar objects as well as draw freehand.

When you're working with the Pen tool (along with a few other tools), the Tool Options toolbar is broken into two separate bars. Most computer screens and resolutions aren't large enough to display all the tools, so Paint Shop Pro hides a portion of the available options.

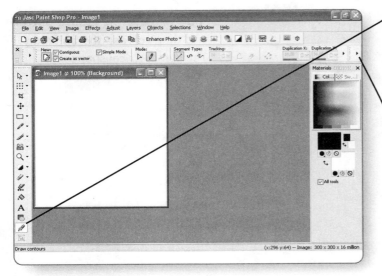

1. Click on the **Pen tool**. The mouse pointer will appear as a black arrowhead with a plus below it.

2. Click the **Line Style options arrow** to display more tool options. The Line Style options toolbar will expand, and the Tool Options toolbar will contract.

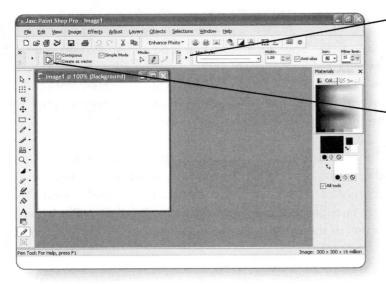

3. Click the **Tool Options arrow**. The Tool Options toolbar will expand and the Line Style Options toolbar will contract.

The Pen tool, like some features in Paint Shop Pro, requires you to let it know when you've completed drawing a particular shape. The term used is *final apply*. When you want to change attributes while you're drawing with the Pen tool, you need to click the New Shape button, indicating that you want to start a new type of line.

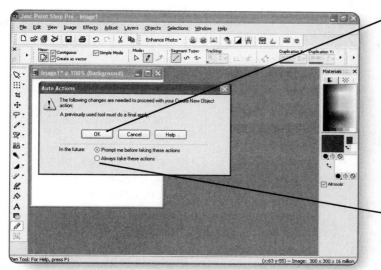

When you begin to draw the new line, Paint Shop Pro might display an Auto Actions dialog box asking you to do a final apply for the previous line. At this point, you can click on OK to apply the previous lines and begin the next line.

> ### TIP
> To avoid future dialog boxes asking about final apply, you can click the Always take these actions option before you click on OK.

Drawing Lines

You can easily create straight lines, thick lines, thin lines, and even lines with arrows by using the Pen tool and the Line Segments option.

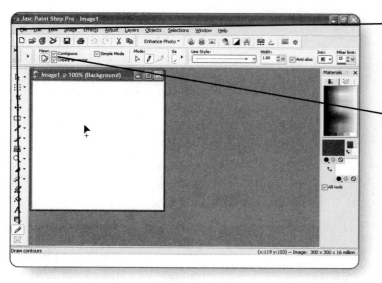

1. Click on the **Pen tool**. The mouse pointer will appear as a black arrowhead with a plus below it.

2. From the Tool Options palette, **remove** the √ from Contiguous. You'll work with contiguous lines in the next section.

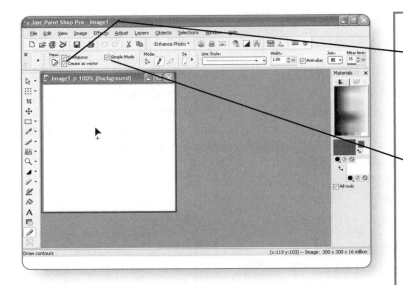

NOTE

For now, remove any √ from Create as vector. You'll work with vector images in Chapter 13, "Constructing Vector Objects."

Keep the Simple tool mode selected if you want to draw a line and change options for the next line. For example, if you draw a blue line and then you want a red line, being in Simple mode means you don't have to select the New Shape button each time you want to make a change.

3. **Click** on the **Drawing Mode tool**. The option will become selected.

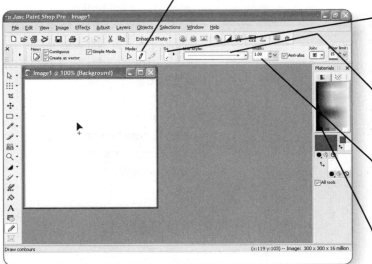

4. **Click** the **Line Segments tool** in the **Segment Type section**. The option will become selected.

5. **Click** on a **line style**. The selected style will display in the Line Style box.

6. **Select** a **line width**. The number you select will be indicated in pixels.

7. **Click** on a **color** from the Materials palette. A sample will appear in a color swatch box.

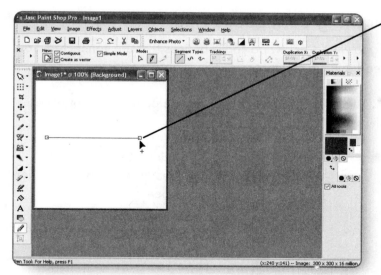

8. Click and drag on the **canvas** to draw your line. A thin black line with boxes on the end will indicate your starting and ending line points.

TIP

To constrain your lines and make them perfectly straight or at 45-degree angles, hold down the Shift key while you're drawing the line.

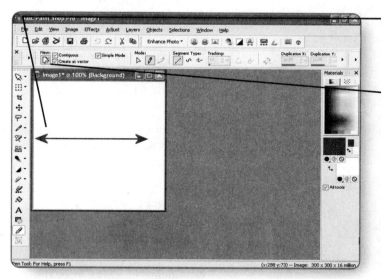

9. Release the **mouse button**. A line will appear on your canvas.

10. Click the **New Shape button** if you are not using Simple mode. Paint Shop Pro will accept the line you drew.

Drawing Contiguous Lines

If you want to draw polygons or lines that are connected, you need to have the contiguous lines option selected.

1. Click on the **Pen tool**. The mouse pointer will appear as a black arrowhead with a plus below it.

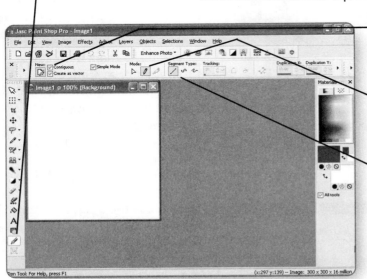

2. Click on **Contiguous** if it's not already selected. The option will appear with a √.

3. Click on the **Drawing Mode tool**. The option will become selected.

4. Click the **Line Segments tool** in the **Segment Type section**. The option will become selected.

5. Click on the **line style option button**. The line style options toolbar will become visible.

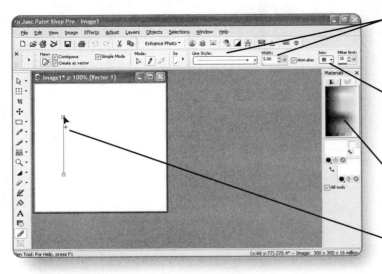

6. Click on a **line style** and **width**. The selected options will display.

7. Select a **corner Join preference**. Select from mitered, rounded, or beveled corners.

8. Click on a **color** from the Materials palette. A sample will appear in a color swatch box.

9. Click and drag to draw a **line**. A line will appear on your screen.

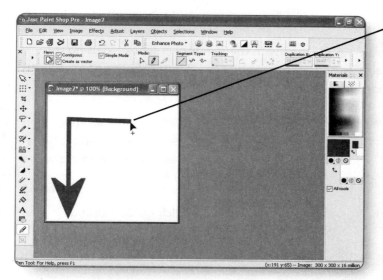

10. **Click** your **mouse** in another location on the canvas. A second line will appear, connected to the first line.

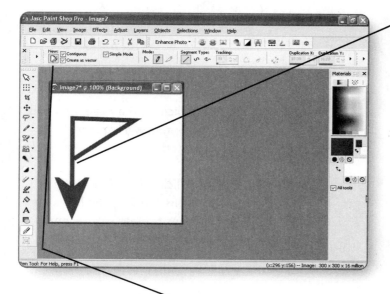

11. **Continue clicking** for each point of your line or polygon. Each line will connect to the previous line.

12. **Click** the **New Shape button**. Paint Shop Pro will accept the lines you drew.

Drawing Freehand

Drawing freehand with the Pen tool is similar to using the Paint Brush tool except that the Pen tool lines appear slightly more crisp and sharp than with the Paint Brush tool.

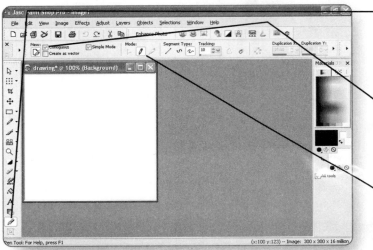

1. Click on the **Pen tool**. The mouse pointer will appear as a black arrowhead with a plus below it.

2. Click on **Contiguous** if you want your drawn lines to be connected. The option will appear with a √.

3. Click on the **Drawing Mode tool**. The option will become selected.

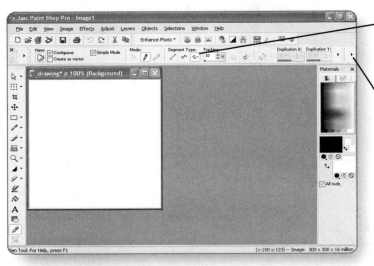

4. Click on the **Freehand tool**. The option will become selected.

5. Click on the **line style options button**. The line style options toolbar will become visible.

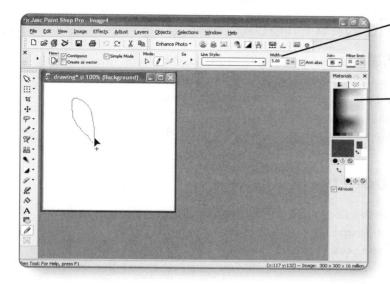

6. Select a **line width**. The number you select will be indicated in pixels.

7. Click on a **color** from the Materials palette. A sample will appear in a color swatch box.

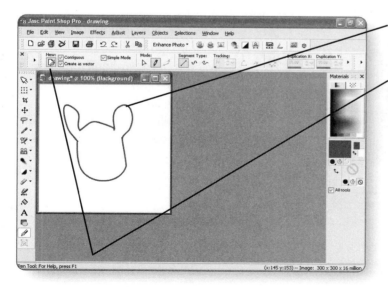

8. Click and drag freely on the **canvas** to draw your lines.

9. Click the **New Shape button** each time you want to start a new draw line.

Viewing Your Work

It's all in the way you look at things. When you're working creatively, sometimes you need to see the finest detail and other times you need to stand back and look at the overall image perspective. Paint Shop Pro includes several tools to help you get a better look at your work.

Zooming In and Out

Use the Zoom feature to zoom in and magnify portions of your image for close-up detail work. You can also zoom out to see your entire image. The Zoom feature is available under the View menu, but you'll find it easiest to use the Zoom tool on the Tools toolbar.

1. Click on the **Zoom tool**. The Zoom tool is located in the Pan Tools submenu.

As you move your mouse over your image, the mouse pointer will turn into a magnifying glass.

2. Click on the **image**. The image will zoom in. Each click of the mouse will zoom the image closer.

The window title bar displays the current zoom percentage.

3. Click the **right mouse button**. The image will zoom out. Each click of the mouse will zoom the image out.

TIP

Optionally, if your mouse has a scroll wheel, you can use the scroll wheel to quickly zoom in and out of your image

The Zoom Tool Options palette also contains buttons to help you review your image.

• Zoom to a specific percentage.

• Zoom in or out by small steps.

• Zoom in or out by large steps.

• Zoom to actual size (100%).

Seeing the Overview Palette

Paint Shop Pro version 8 is the Overview palette. When you have zoomed in on a small area for a detailed operation, you might find it useful to see the entire image while you work. That's the purpose of the Overview palette.

> **NOTE**
>
> Paint Shop Pro might operate more slowly when the Overview palette is open.

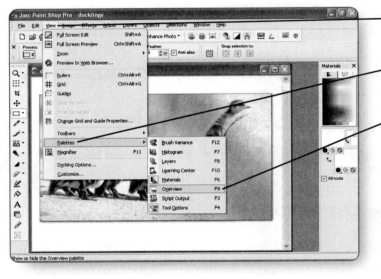

1. Click on **View**. The View menu will appear.

2. Click on **Palettes**. The Palettes submenu will appear.

3. Click on **Overview**. The Overview palette will appear.

> **TIP**
>
> A quick way to display or hide the Overview palette is to press the F9 key.

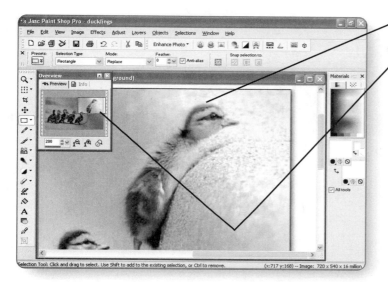

4. Zoom in on an **image**.

The Overview window will still display the entire image, but it will place a rectangle around the currently viewed area.

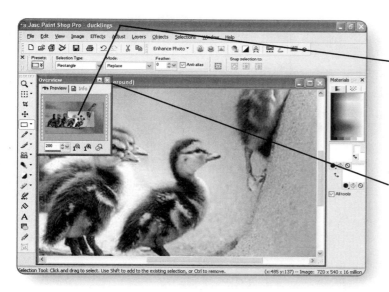

TIP

To quickly move from one area of the image to another, drag the Overview rectangle to the new area you want to view.

When you're finished with the Overview palette, click the Close button to put it away.

4

Working with Selections

To make changes to a portion of an image—whether the image is one you've created, a photograph, or another type of artwork—you need to tell Paint Shop Pro what you want to change before you can specify how you want to change it. This is called making a selection. You can then make your change to the isolated selected area without affecting the rest of the image. You also need to select an area if you want to copy or cut it to the Windows Clipboard for use in other programs or images. Paint Shop Pro includes several different selection tools. In this chapter, you'll learn how to

- Use the selection tools
- Understand feathering
- Discover the Magic Wand
- Add, subtract, and remove selections

Selecting with the Shape Selection Tool

The *Selection tool* is what Paint Shop Pro calls the easiest to use of the three tools used to make selections. For the sake of distinguishing between the terms *Selection tool* and *selection tools*, we'll call the Selection tool the Shape Selection tool. (The other two are the Freehand and Magic Wand tools—more about them later in this chapter.) All three tools are displayed from the Selection tool on the toolbar:

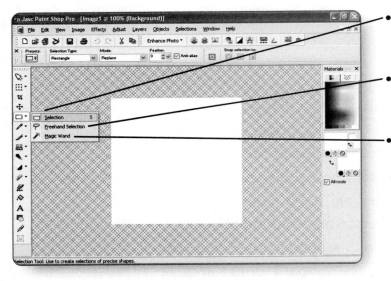

- **Shape Selection tool.** Use this tool to define a common geometric shape option.

- **Freehand Selection tool.** Use this tool to define an irregular shape selection.

- **Magic Wand.** Use this tool to define a selection based on color options.

TIP

You can practice making selections by opening an existing file or creating a new blank image window. Even though the image is blank, you can still see the selections.

Choosing a Selection Shape

The Shape Selection tool allows you to select a portion of your image in any one of 15 different shapes, including circles, rectangles, triangles, stars, and arrows.

TIP

At any time, you can press Ctrl+A to select the entire image.

---

1. Click on the **Shape Selection tool**. The mouse pointer will turn into a cross with a dotted box beside it.

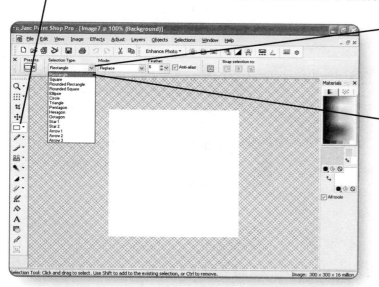

2. Click on the **down arrow** (⌄) next to Selection Type on the Tool Options palette. A list of selection shapes will appear.

3. Click on a **shape**. The selection will appear highlighted in the list box.

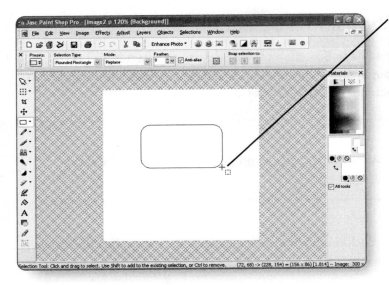

4. Click and drag the **mouse** across a portion of your image window. A solid line will appear around the area you draw.

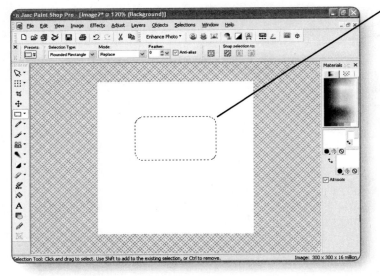

5. Release the **mouse button**. The drawn area will be surrounded with a marquee of "marching ants"—moving dashed lines. The area within the marquee will be your selected area.

Adding Feathering

Feathering is a process that expands your selection and softens the edges of your selection. You won't notice its effect on a blank image, but on an actual image, you can easily see the difference.

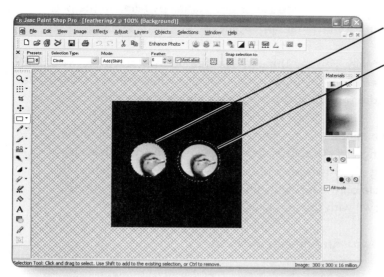

No feathering

Feathered selection

The image on the left was selected without feathering, and the image on the right was selected with feathering set to 10. Notice the softer edges as well as the extension of the selection area.

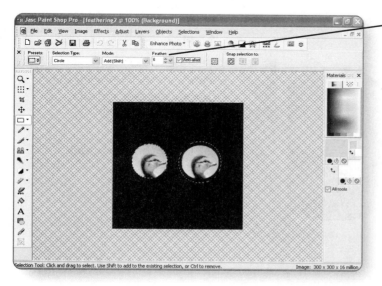

1. Click on the Feather **up or down arrow** (⬍) on the Tool Options palette. The higher the feathering value, the softer the edges.

2. Draw your **selection** as you learned in the previous section.

Understanding Anti-Alias

Anti-alias is certainly a mouthful of a word! It's a graphic term that digital artists use to refer to mathematical calculations and pixels on a screen. When an image is aliased, it has a somewhat jagged edge. Therefore, using anti-alias smoothes the edges of slanted lines and curves by filling in the pixels, giving a smoother appearance.

Actually, you see the anti-alias feature not only when you select portions of an image but also when you are using some of the tools, such as the Preset Shapes tool or the Draw tool.

The image you see here is zoomed in to show the effect of using anti-alias. The circle on the right with the hard jagged edge is drawn without the anti-alias feature, whereas the circle on the left with smoother blending of the edges is drawn with the anti-alias feature.

Drawn with Anti-alias checked

Drawn without Anti-alias checked

1. Place a √ in the **Anti-alias check box** to activate the anti-alias feature. Removing the √ deactivates the anti-alias feature.

2. Draw your **selection**.

Removing All Selections

If you've selected an area in error, or when you've completed whatever you wanted to do to a selection, you need to remove the marquee of selection marks. Removing a selection does nothing to your image—it only removes the selection marks.

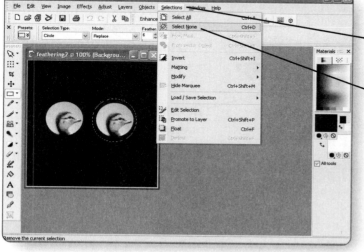
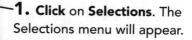

1. Click on **Selections**. The Selections menu will appear.

2. Click on **Select None**. The marquee will disappear and the area will no longer be selected.

TIP

Optionally, press Ctrl+D to remove all selection marks.

Using the Freehand Tool

Selecting with the Freehand Selection tool gives you a great amount of freedom in drawing the area you want to select. Use this tool to select irregularly shaped areas of an image.

Using your mouse with the Freehand Selection tool might feel a little clumsy at first. You'll find out later in this chapter how to add to and subtract from your selection if you didn't get it quite right with the Freehand Selection tool.

TIP

Selecting with the Freehand Selection tool is much easier if you are zoomed in on the area that you want to select.

---

1. Click on the **Freehand Selection tool**. The mouse pointer will turn into a cross with a "lasso" beside it.

TIP

You can choose both the feathering and anti-alias features from the Tool Options palette for use with the Freehand tool.

2. Click and hold the **mouse button** and **draw** around the **area** you want to select. A line will appear as you draw.

3. Release the **mouse button**. The marquee will appear around the selected area.

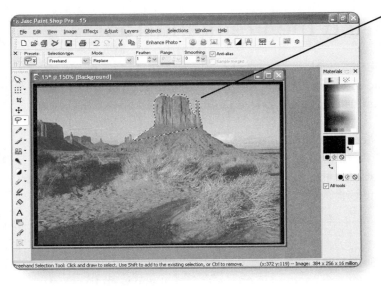

Making Magic Wand Selections

The third selection tool, the Magic Wand, works differently from the other two selection tools. The Shape and Freehand selection tools allow you to select an area of the image, but the Magic Wand works by selecting pixels of equal or similar colors or brightness.

The selections are made based on one of four values. With RGB Value, the Magic Wand selects pixels based on the amount of color they contain. With Hue, it selects pixels based on the position in the color wheel. With Brightness, the Magic Wand selects pixels based on the amount of white they contain. And with All Pixels, it selects only areas that contain pixels; no transparent areas are selected. You'll learn about the color wheel and RGB in Chapter 5, "Understanding the Materials Palette."

1. **Click** on the **Magic Wand tool**. The mouse pointer will turn into a black cross with a magic wand beside it.

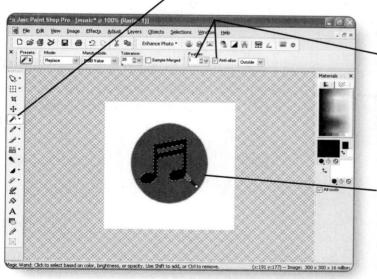

TIP

You can choose both the feathering and anti-alias features from the Tool Options palette for use with the Magic Wand tool.

2. **Click** the **mouse** on an edge of the image you want to select. The marquee will appear around the selected area. In this example, the musical note is selected.

Modifying Selections

For whatever reason—whether you have multiple objects to select, your hand wasn't quite steady enough when you made the initial selection, or you've just changed your mind—you might need to modify a selection. You don't need to deselect and start over. You can add to or subtract from your initial selection.

Reversing the Selection

Sometimes it's easier to select all the areas *except* the area you want to edit. If that's the case, Paint Shop Pro includes a method that allows you to reverse your selection area.

1. Select the **areas** you don't want. The marquee will appear around the selected area. In this example, we want to change the area surrounding the musical note, not the actual musical note, but it's easier to use the Magic Wand tool and select the note.

2. Click on **Selections**. The Selections menu will appear.

3. Click on **Invert**. The selected area will reverse to the non-selected area.

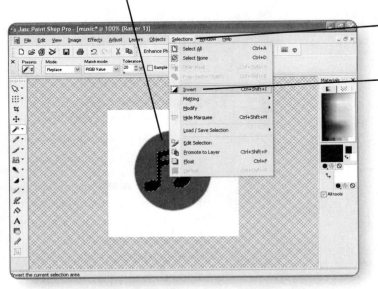

The entire image *except* the musical note is now selected.

Expanding a Selection Area

Did you make a complex selection only to find you made it too tight or forgot to feather it? You can expand your selection with the Selections menu.

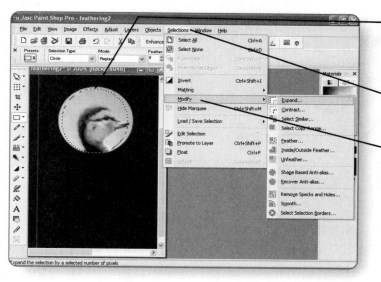

1. **Make** a **selection**. The marquee will appear around the selected area.

2. **Click** on **Selections**. The Selections menu will appear.

3. **Click** on **Modify**. The Modify submenu menu will appear.

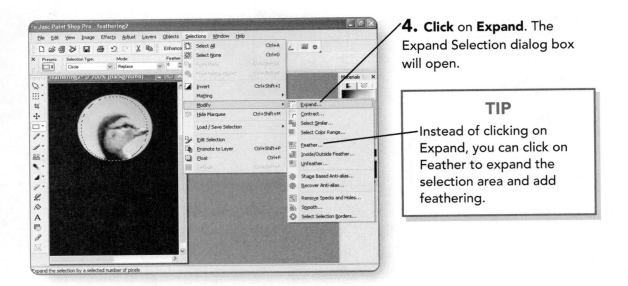

4. Click on **Expand**. The Expand Selection dialog box will open.

TIP

Instead of clicking on Expand, you can click on Feather to expand the selection area and add feathering.

5. Enter the **number of pixels** you want to expand the selection. The expanded area will be indicated by a black border.

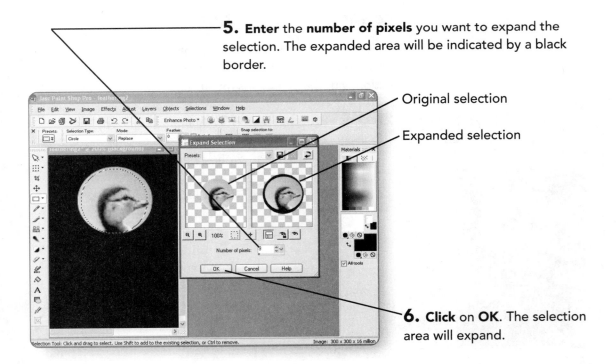

Original selection

Expanded selection

6. Click on **OK**. The selection area will expand.

Adding to a Selection

After you make an initial selection, you can add to it. You can mix and match between the Freehand Selection tool and the Shape Selection tool when you're adding to a selection.

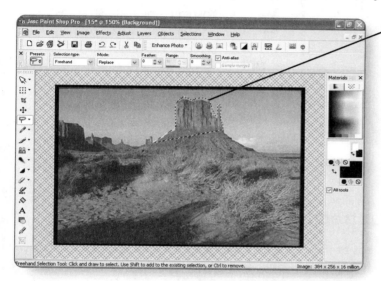

1. **Select** an **area**. You can add to a selection made with any of the selection tools.

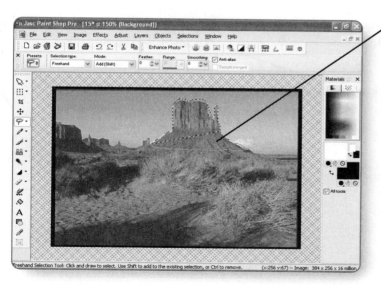

2. **Hold** down the **Shift key** and **select** a **second area**. The mouse pointer will display a plus sign.

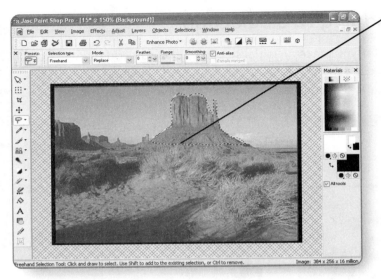

3. Release the **Shift key**. Both the original selection and the newly selected area will appear with a marquee.

You can repeat these steps to add as many areas from a selection as needed.

Subtracting from a Selection

Just as easily as you can add to a selection, you can subtract areas from a selection. This function works with selections you made using either the Shape Selection tool or the Freehand Selection tool.

1. Make a **selection**. The marquee will appear around the selected area. In the example seen here, there is too much selection on the left side of the mountain.

2. Hold down the **Ctrl key** and **select** a **second area**. The mouse pointer will display a minus sign.

3. Release the **Ctrl key**. The original selection will appear without the newly selected area.

You can repeat these steps to subtract as many areas from a selection as needed.

5

Understanding the Materials Palette

Color and style are probably the most important elements when you're creating and working with graphics. Even minor changes to color settings can dramatically alter your image. Style takes into account special combinations such as gradients, patterns, and textures, including the appearance of brick, wood, leather, or sand. Paint Shop Pro provides all these options on the Materials palette. In this chapter, you'll learn how to

- Understand color models
- Make background and foreground color selections
- Change patterns and gradients
- Create color special effects
- Work with grey scale
- Control transparency

Defining Color Models

Before you select colors, you should have a basic understanding of how Paint Shop Pro determines colors. Although there are several methods or models, Paint Shop Pro uses two main ways to define color: RGB and HSL.

Understanding RGB

RGB stands for Red, Green, and Blue, the colors used by most monitors and video output devices. If you're old enough, you might remember when you had to adjust your TV color because the people's faces were too red or too green. You were working with RGB settings. All colors on the screen, whether on your television or computer screen, are a combination of red, blue, and green.

Appreciating HSL

The second color model, HSL, illustrates Hue, Saturation, and Lightness. HSL uses RGB values but allows you, the user, to modify the RGB values even further.

- **Hue.** The shade or tint of an RGB color.
- **Saturation.** The amount of grey in a hue. The higher saturation produces more vivid color, whereas a lower saturation produces more gray.
- **Lightness.** The quantity of light in a color. The higher the lightness value, the whiter the image becomes. At a low value, the image becomes darker or black.

Making Color Selections

Within every tool are two defined areas: foreground and background. For example, if you are just creating a box with a perimeter around it, Paint Shop Pro uses just the foreground color. If the box has a filled-in center, Paint Shop Pro uses the background color.

The color swatches at the bottom of the Materials palette represent the current foreground and background colors. The smaller boxes, called the color boxes, indicate only the color, whereas the larger swatches, called the materials boxes, indicate the color along with a pattern or texture. The first box (the one to the left) is the foreground color, whereas the box on the right is the background color.

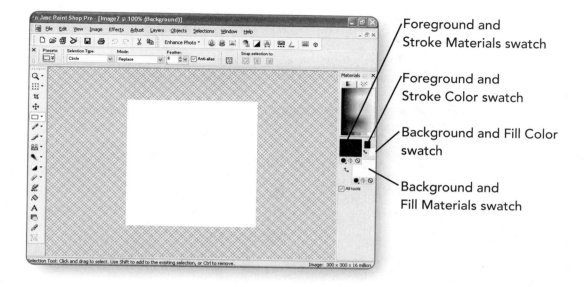

Foreground and
Stroke Materials swatch

Foreground and
Stroke Color swatch

Background and Fill Color
swatch

Background and
Fill Materials swatch

Choosing from the Color Panel

The fastest way to choose a color is by using the Available Color panel that is provided on the Materials palette.

1. Position the **mouse pointer** over the color you want to select. The mouse pointer will appear as an eyedropper.

The color and its RGB values will appear in the preview box.

2a. Click the **left mouse button**. The color you select will become the new foreground color.

OR

2b. Click the **right mouse button**. The color you select will become the new background color.

Selecting from the Color Dialog Box

To finely tune the color, hue, saturation, and lightness of your selection, use the Color dialog box.

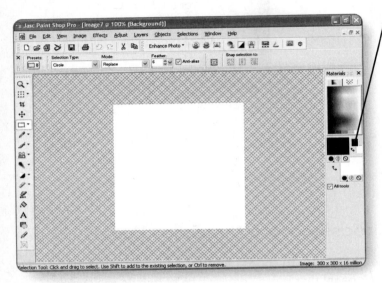

1. Click on the **foreground and stroke color box**. The Color dialog box will open.

TIP

To select a background color, click on the background color box (the second box).

The Color dialog box consists of several elements:

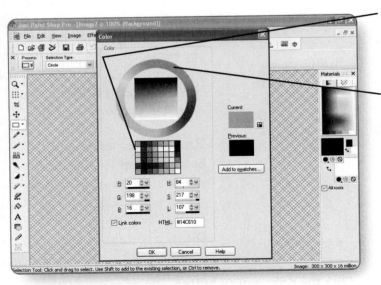

- **Basic Colors palette.** This palette represents 48 of the more common colors in a Materials palette.

- **The color wheel.** The color wheel represents various hue values. Click on a color or drag the little circle to select a color. Then you must select a saturation/lightness.

Saturation/Lightness box. After you've selected a color, adjust the saturation and lightness by clicking the mouse or dragging the little circle until the sample box represents the color you want.

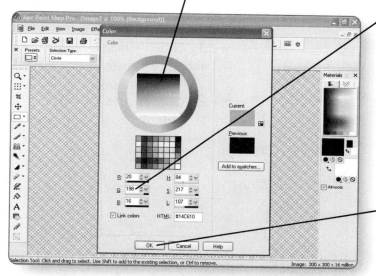

RGB and HSL values. Here you can see the RGB and HSL values of your selected color or enter and adjust the values of the color you want to be displayed.

3. **Click** on a **color**. The Current box displays the newly selected color.

4. **Click** on **OK**. The Color dialog box will close and the newly selected color will appear in the foreground (or background) color box.

Reversing Color Selections

Paint Shop Pro provides an easy way to reverse your foreground and background colors without your having to select them both again.

1. **Click** on the **color swatch double arrow.** The two color boxes will reverse.

Adding a Border

Give your image a colored border. Paint Shop Pro uses the background color to create a straight-edged border around the perimeter of the entire canvas.

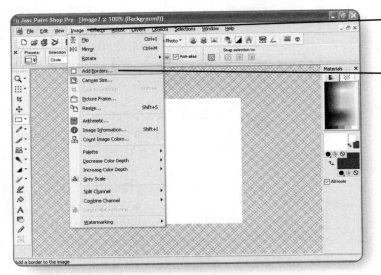

1. Click on **Image**. The Image menu will appear.

2. Click on **Add Borders**. The Add Borders dialog box will open.

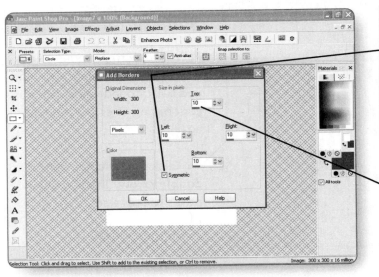

TIP

If you want all four edges to have the same size borders, be sure there's a √ in the Symmetric check box.

3. Select a **size** (in pixels) for each border. The higher the value, the thicker the border will appear.

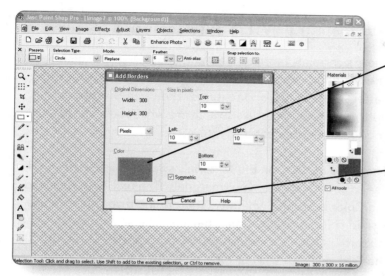

TIP

If you want a border color different from the sample, click the Color box and select a different color.

4. Click on **OK**. The Add Borders dialog box will close.

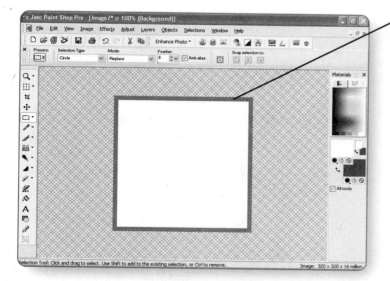

The border will appear around the canvas.

Working with Materials

There's certainly more to life—and images—than color. The Materials swatches on the Materials palette work with patterns, gradients, and textures. The three buttons at the bottom of each Materials swatch are what you'll use to set your pattern, gradient, or texture.

The three buttons on the Materials swatches are what you'll use to set the style of your materials. The first button, called the Color button, is where you determine if you want to use a solid color, a gradient, or a pattern. The second button, the Texture button, is an on/off toggle button where you turn the Texture feature on or off. The third button, called the Transparency button, is where you designate that you want nothing for the foreground or the background. The Transparency button is also an on/off toggle button.

- The solid circle represents solid colors.

- The small dots represent textures.

- The circle with the line represents the international "No" symbol and means "transparent" or none of the other choices.

- The vertical stripes represent gradients.

- The horizontal stripes represent patterns.

Generating Gradients

Gradients are created from the gradual blending of colors. Paint Shop Pro includes multiple pre-designed gradients. Many more gradient designs are available free from the Web—and if you're really creative, you can even design your own.

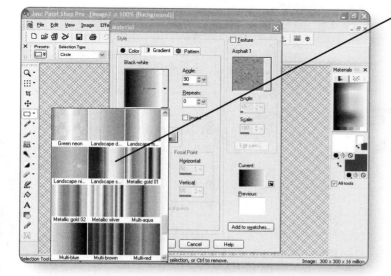

1. Click on a **swatch**. The Materials window will open.

2. Click on the **Gradient tab**. The Gradient tab will appear on top.

3. Click on the **Gradient preview box**. A selection of gradients will appear.

4. Click on the **gradient** you want to use. A sample will appear in the Materials swatch.

5. Optionally, **adjust** the **angle** of the texture. You can rotate the pattern up to 359 degrees.

6. Click on a **gradient style**. You can have the gradient originate from the sides, from the inside, from the outside, or from a corner.

Experiment a little. You'll find many different variations of the selected gradient.

TIP

To reverse the gradient pattern, click the Invert check box.

7. Click on **OK**. The Materials dialog box will close.

TIP

Click on the color switcher to reverse the foreground and background styles.

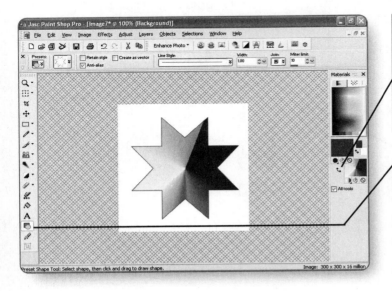

8. Select a **tool** and **draw** the **line or shape** you want to use. The line or the fill pattern will include the gradient you selected.

This figure illustrates a star drawn by using a gradient fill style.

Picking Patterns

In addition to gradients, Paint Shop Pro includes many different patterns to use in the foreground or background of images. You can also use any existing image, such as a drawing or a photograph, as a pattern.

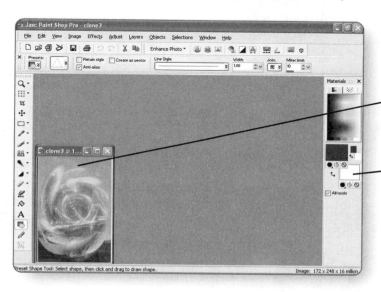

If you want to use an existing image as the pattern, you must open the image first.

1. Open an **image**, whether it's a photo or drawing. The image will appear on the screen.

2. Click on a **swatch**. The Materials window will open.

TIP

If you want the line to have a pattern, use the Foreground and Stroke swatch; however, if you want the interior of a shape to have the pattern, click the Background and Fill swatch.

3. Click on the **Pattern tab**. The Pattern tab will appear on top.

4. Click on the **Current Pattern arrow**. A selection of patterns will appear.

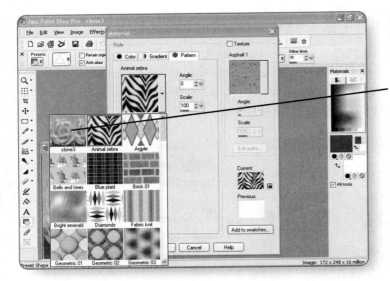

Notice that the currently open image also appears as a pattern choice.

5. **Click** on the **pattern** you would like to use. A sample will appear in the preview box.

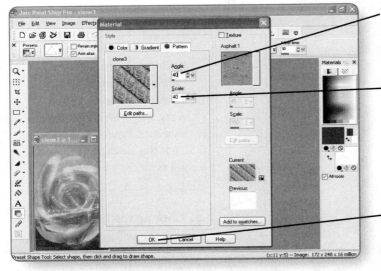

6. Optionally, **adjust** the **angle** of the pattern. You can rotate the pattern up to 359 degrees.

7. Optionally, **adjust** the **scale** of the pattern. If you are going to fill a small image with the pattern, you might want to make the pattern smaller and tighter.

8. **Click** on **OK**. The Materials dialog box will close and the pattern will appear in the Background and Fill Properties swatch.

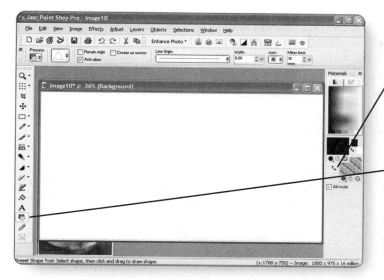

TIP
Click on the color switcher to reverse the foreground and background styles.

9. Select a **tool** and **draw** the line or shape you want to use. The line or the fill pattern will include the pattern you selected.

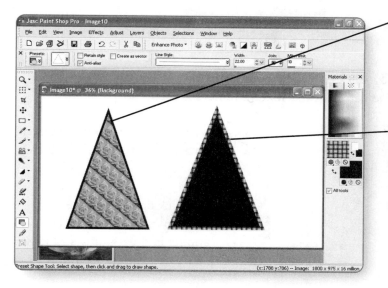

This image represents a triangle drawn by using the preset shape tool with the open image pattern as the background (fill) pattern.

This image represents a triangle drawn by using the preset shape tool with the green weave pattern as the foreground (stroke) pattern.

Tinkering with Textures

Using texture effects gives an image a three-dimensional appearance as though the image were created on a textured surface. Similar to using patterns, the top swatch is the foreground or stroke texture whereas the lower swatch is the background or fill texture.

1. **Click** on a **Materials swatch**. The Material window will open.

2. **Click** on the **Color tab**. The Color tab will appear on top.

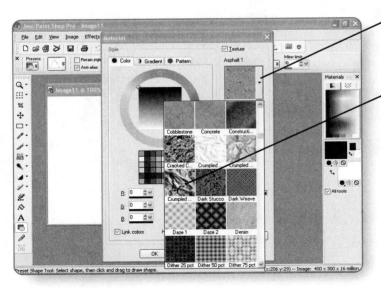

> **NOTE**
>
> You can use textures with Colors, Patterns, or Gradients.

3. **Click** on the **Texture check box**. A √ in the box will indicate that the Texture feature is activated.

4. **Click** on the **texture swatch arrow**. A selection of textures will appear.

5. **Click** on the **texture** you want to use. A sample will appear in the Materials window, combined with the current color.

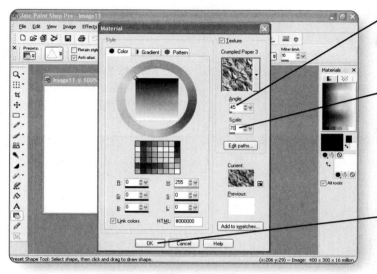

6. Optionally, **adjust** the **angle** of the texture. You can rotate the pattern up to 359 degrees.

7. Optionally, **adjust** the **scale** of the texture. If you are going to fill a small image with the texture, you might want to make the texture smaller and tighter.

8. **Click** on **OK**. The Materials dialog box will close and the texture will appear in the Materials swatch.

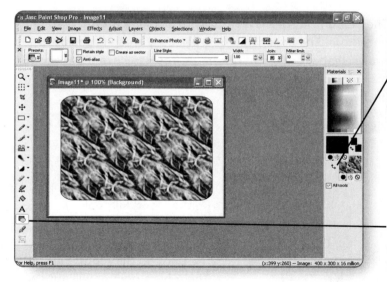

TIP

Click on the color switcher to reverse the foreground and background styles.

9. **Select** a **tool** and **draw** the **line or shape** you want to use. The line or the fill pattern will include the texture you selected.

A rounded corner rectangle with the crumpled paper texture and a solid color grey style.

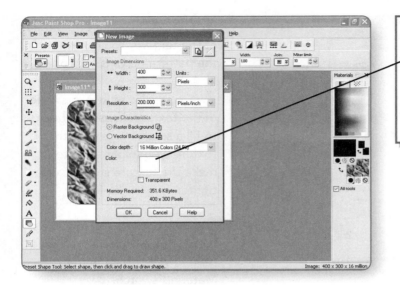

TIP

When you're creating a new image, you can select a solid color, gradient, pattern, or texture for the background.

Using the Flood Fill Tool

The Flood Fill tool fills an area with a color, pattern, gradient, or texture. The area could be a selected area, an enclosed drawn shape, or the entire canvas. You can have the Flood Fill tool replace a selected area, the entire canvas, or a drawn enclosed image.

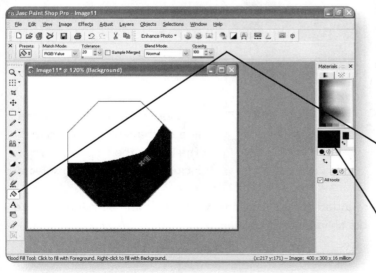

TIP

To confine the fill to a specific area, make a selection before using the Flood Fill tool.

1. **Click** on the **Flood Fill tool**. The mouse pointer will appear with a cross and a paint bucket.

2. **Select** a **color**, **pattern**, **gradient**, **or texture**. A sample will appear in the Materials swatch.

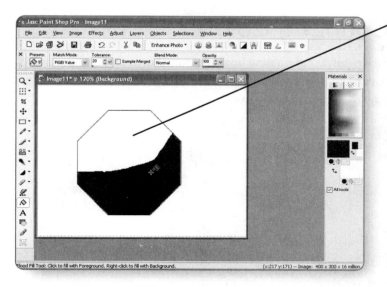

3. Click inside the **area** you want to fill. If you click with the left mouse button, the object will fill with the style of the foreground swatch. If you click with the right mouse button, the object will fill with the style of the background swatch.

Locking Color Choices

Toward the bottom of the Materials palette is an All Tools check box. When the Lock check box is unchecked, the colors and styles are unlocked. This means that each tool you use can have its own combinations of colors, patterns, gradients, and textures. When unlocked, if you switch tools (such as from the

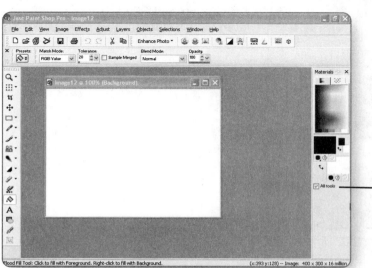

Paintbrush to the Flood Fill tool), the color and style selections change from the Paintbrush colors and styles to the same colors or styles in effect the last time you used the Flood Fill tool.

If you lock the colors, the current settings are used for all tools.

1. Click the **All tools check box**. A √ indicates that all tools will use the current settings, and no √ means that each tool will use its own settings.

Counting Colors

When you create a new image, you have to select the maximum number of colors to be in that image. Want to know how many are actually in a particular image?

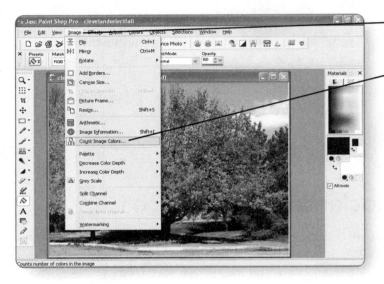

1. Click on **Image**. The Image menu will appear.

2. Click on **Count Image Colors**. An information dialog box will open stating the total number of colors in the current image.

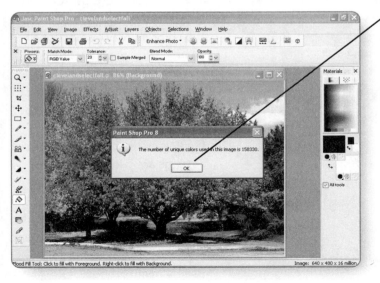

3. Click on **OK**. The dialog box will close.

Creating a Negative Image

Just like a negative you get when you take your photos to the drugstore for processing, you can create a negative of any image. Creating a negative reverses all the color values in an image to their exact opposite.

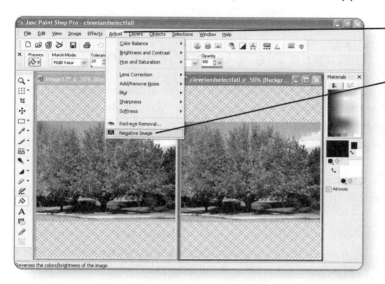

1. Click on **Adjust**. The Adjust menu will appear.

2. Click on **Negative Image**. Paint Shop Pro will reverse all color values in the current image.

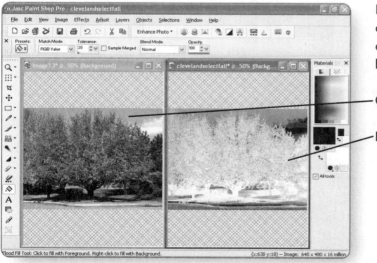

In this example, two exact copies of a photograph are displayed. The second one has been applied as a negative.

—Original image

—Negative image

Introducing Grey Scale

Another color model used by Paint Shop Pro is grey scale, which is what you use with black-and-white images. The images are not purely black and white, however; they are made up of 256 shades of grey. Any image you create can be in grey scale, and any existing image can be converted to grey scale.

Creating a New Grey Scale Image

When you create a new image, you're required to specify the number of colors. Instead of the 16 million colors you've been working with so far, for a new grey scale image, you'll specify grey scale as the image type.

1. **Click** on the **New button** (or click New from the File menu). The New Image dialog box will appear.

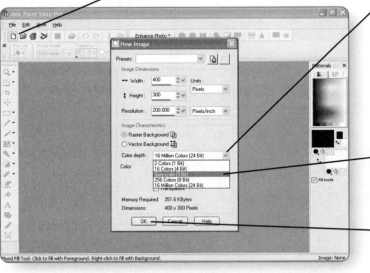

2. **Click** on the **Color depth arrow**. A list of available options will appear.

3. **Click** on **Greyscale**. The option will display in the New Image dialog box.

4. **Click** on **OK**. A new image window will appear.

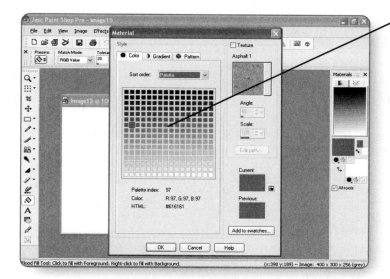

Only shades of grey will appear in the color selections.

Converting an Image to Grey Scale

If you have an existing color image, whether a photograph or drawing, you can easily convert it to grey scale.

1. Open an existing **image**. The image will appear on the screen.

2. Click on **Image**. The Image menu will appear.

3. Click on **Grey Scale**. The image will convert to grey scale.

6

Editing Images and Drawings

After working with your image, you will probably want to make a few changes. Perhaps you've changed your mind about some of the colors or you don't want part of an image. Changes and corrections are easy to make using the Paint Shop Pro tools. In this chapter, you'll learn how to

- Use the eraser tools
- Crop and resize an image
- Distort an image with the warp brush
- Replace colors
- Work with the clone brush

Clearing the Screen

When you are practicing your drawing techniques, you might decide that it would be easier to start over. You can close the current file without saving it and set up a new file, but there is an easier way. Paint Shop Pro includes a Clear feature that clears the current screen. Actually, it clears the current layer, but you'll learn more about layers in Chapter 9, "Developing Layers."

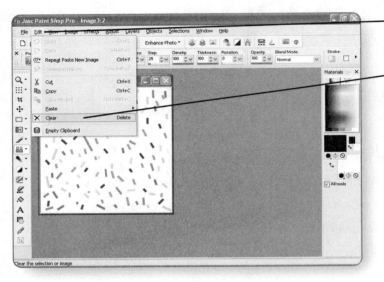

1. Click on **Edit**. The Edit menu will appear.

2. Click on **Clear**. The current image layer will be replaced with the current background color.

> ### NOTE
> If there is any part of the image you want to save, you should save it before you choose Edit, Clear. No warning is displayed prior to clearing the image.

Working with the Erasers

Paint Shop Pro includes two eraser tools—an Eraser and a Background Eraser—that work similarly to a pencil eraser except that you have several options from which you can select. Erase options are the same options available to a paintbrush in that you can select the eraser size, opacity, hardness, and step.

Using the Eraser

Use the regular Eraser tool to replace colors in an image with the background color or with a transparency. If you are working on a background layer, the Eraser tool replaces the erased area with the current background/fill style. If you are working on a Raster layer, Paint Shop Pro replaces the erased area with a transparent area. You'll learn more about Raster layers in Part II, "Working with Raster Graphics."

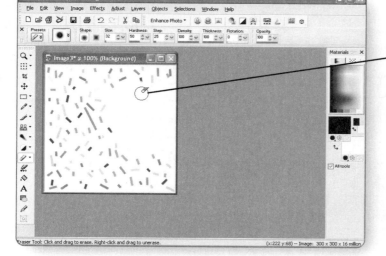

1. Select the **Eraser tool**. The mouse pointer will look like a pencil with an eraser.

2. Select a **color** for your background. Paint Shop Pro will replace whatever you erase with the current background color.

> **TIP**
> To confine the erasing to a specific area, select the area before you use the Eraser tool.

3. Click and drag the **mouse pointer** over the area you want to erase. The erased area will be replaced with the background color.

> **TIP**
> Click and drag with the right mouse button to replace the erased area with the foreground color.

Erasing with the Background Eraser

The Background Eraser tool is new to Paint Shop Pro 8. Although it's similar to the regular Eraser tool, the Background Eraser tool works more from the center of the brush and works to erase around a specific area, which can give you softer erased edges. For example, if you have a photograph of a bird and you want just the bird—without the trees and other items in the background—the Background Eraser tool is what you want to use.

The Background Eraser tool works only on raster layers and does not work on the background layer. If your image is not on a raster layer, Paint Shop Pro displays a dialog box prompting you to promote it to a full layer. Click on OK and then proceed with the Background Eraser tool.

The center of the Background Eraser tool is the key to using this feature, so it works best if you can easily see the center. To make the center easier to spot, turn on the Precise Cursor option.

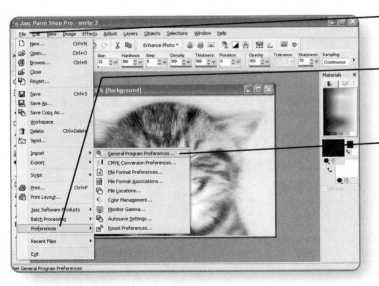

1. Click on **File**. The File menu will appear.

2. Click on **Preferences**. The Preferences submenu will appear.

3. Click on **General Program Preferences**. The Paint Shop Pro 8 Preferences dialog box will open.

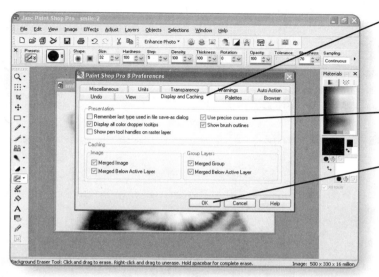

4. Click on the **Display and Caching tab**. The Display and Caching tab will come to the front.

5. Click on **Use precise cursors**. The option will have a √.

6. Click on **OK**. The Paint Shop Pro 8 Preferences dialog box will close.

7. Click on the **Background Eraser tool**. The mouse pointer will appear as a circle with centering sights.

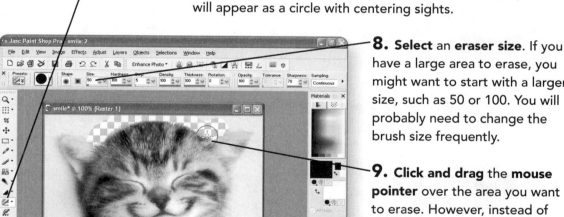

8. Select an **eraser size**. If you have a large area to erase, you might want to start with a larger size, such as 50 or 100. You will probably need to change the brush size frequently.

9. Click and drag the **mouse pointer** over the area you want to erase. However, instead of using the brush edge, as you would with the regular Eraser tool, don't worry about anything but the center of the brush where the crosshairs are located. The erased area is replaced with a transparency.

TIP

To restore an area completely and quickly, hold down the spacebar and then drag the right mouse button over the erased area.

The image with the background intact

The image with the background erased

Cropping an Image

Cropping an image allows you to eliminate extra pieces of an image you don't want. When you use the Crop tool, you select a rectangular area of the image you want to keep. Paint Shop Pro then deletes the area outside the rectangle.

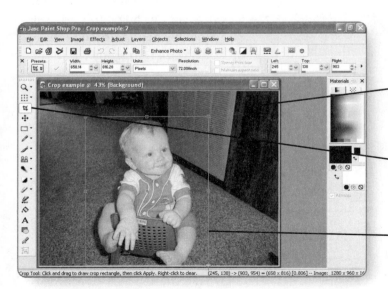

1. Open the **image** you want to crop. The image will appear on the screen.

2. Click on the **Crop tool**. The mouse pointer will change to a plus with a crop symbol behind it.

3. Draw a **rectangular area** around the area of the image you want to keep. A line with small handles will appear around the selected area.

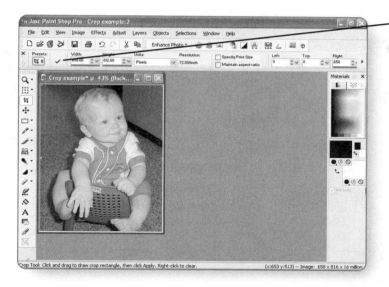

4. Click on the **Apply tool**. The excess image will be deleted.

> **NOTE**
> Cropping an image can reduce the file size.

Resizing the Canvas

Although resizing an image canvas seems similar to cropping an image, when you resize the image, you are not removing a portion of the image; you're only making the entire image smaller or larger.

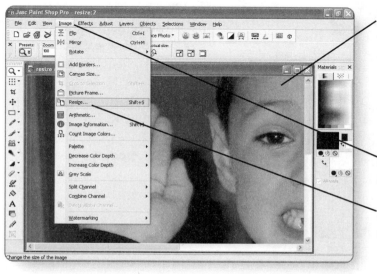

1. Open the **image** you want to resize. The image will appear on the screen.

2. Click on **Image**. The Image menu will appear.

3. Click on **Resize**. The Resize dialog box will open.

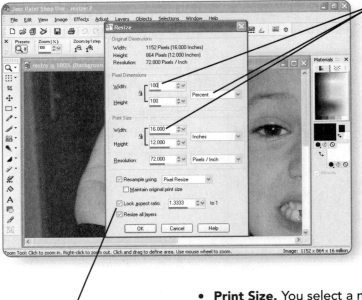

The current image size is displayed.

4. Click a **resize method**.

Paint Shop Pro provides three different methods to resize an image:

- **Pixel Size.** You select a new size by choosing a new measurement in pixels.

- **Percentage of Original.** You select a new size based on a percentage to increase or decrease from the original.

- **Print Size.** You select a new size by changing the physical dimensions.

When the Lock aspect ratio option is checked, the image size is changed proportionately. If you change the width, the height will change automatically.

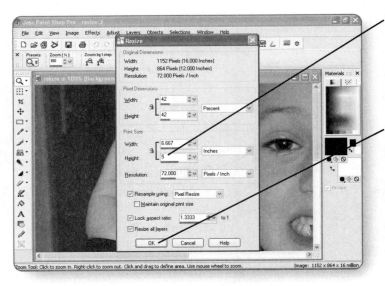

5. Click the new image **size** in pixels, percentage, or actual size. The other measurement boxes will reflect the change as well.

6. Click on **OK**. The Resize dialog box will close, and the image will appear in the new size.

Distorting with the Warp Brush

New to Paint Shop Pro 8 is the Warp Brush, which allows you to distort an image almost as if it were made of rubber. You can push, twist, stretch, or shrink a portion of your image.

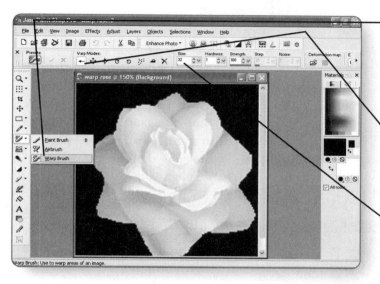

1. **Click** the **Warp Brush**. It is one of the three tools on the Brush tool list. The mouse pointer will become a circle with an x and a paintbrush.

2. **Select** a **warp mode**. You can push a portion of the image or twirl it clockwise or counterclockwise.

3. **Make** any brush **option selections**. Similar to other brush tools, you can select options such as size, hardness, or step.

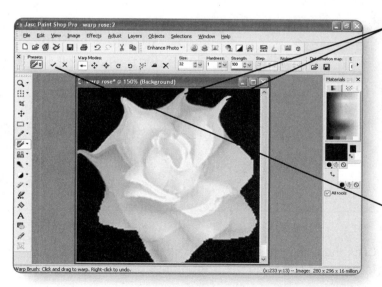

4. **Click and drag** in the **image** the area that you want to distort. In this image, the Warp Brush tool made some of the top rose petals smoother and pointed.

5. **Click** the **Apply button**. Paint Shop Pro will accept your changes.

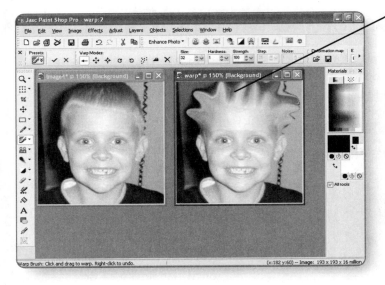

Another image with lots of warping to the hairdo

Picking Up Colors

Searching through 16 million plus colors can be an overwhelming task. If you need a specific color for your image, and that color is used elsewhere in your image or in another image, you can use the color dropper to pick up an existing color.

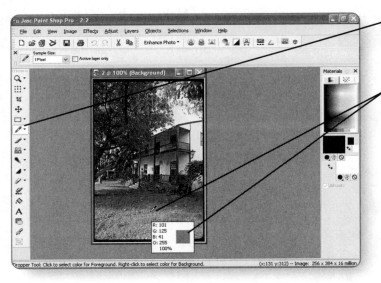

1. **Click** on the **Dropper tool**. The mouse pointer will look like an eyedropper.

2. **Pause** the **mouse** over any portion of your image. The color dropper will display the RGB colors at the point of your mouse pointer.

3. **Click** the **mouse button**. The dropper will pick up the current color and load it into the color swatch.

TIP

Click the left mouse button to pick up the color as the foreground color and the right mouse button to pick up the color as a background color.

Replacing Colors

Paint Shop Pro includes a Color Replacer tool that uses the color swatches to replace one color in an image with a new color. You can use either the foreground/stroke color or background/fill color. You can paint with the brush strokes to replace only those areas the brush touches, or you can double-click the image to replace the color throughout.

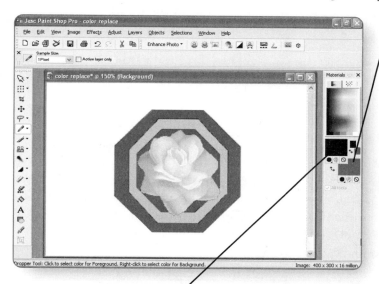

1. Select on the Background Materials swatch the **color** you want to replace. In this example, the purple area on the outer ring and inner ring of the octagon need to be replaced.

TIP

Use the Dropper tool to select the color you don't want.

---

2. Select on the Foreground Materials swatch the **color** you want to use instead of the original color. Again, in this example, the purple area will be replaced with a solid black area.

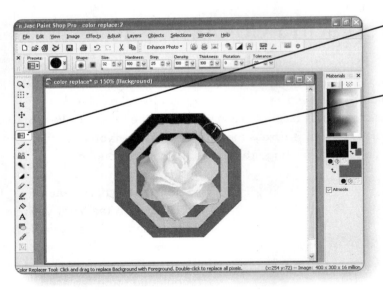

3. **Click** on the **Color Replacer tool**. The mouse pointer will appear as a paintbrush.

4a. **Click and drag** the **mouse pointer** across the area you want to replace. The background color will be replaced with the foreground colors.

NOTE

It's okay if the mouse pointer goes over another color. It will only replace pixels with the background color.

OR

4b. **Double-click** anywhere on the **image** to replace all pixels in the image with the background color with the foreground color. All background color pixels will be replaced instantly with the foreground color.

TIP

To restrict the color replacing to a specific area, make a selection before you use the Color Replacer.

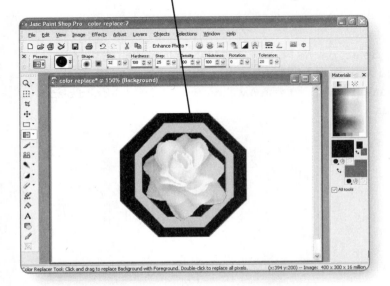

Working with the Clone Brush

The Clone Brush is a wonderful tool for superimposing one image or part of an image onto another. You can also use it to duplicate portions of an image.

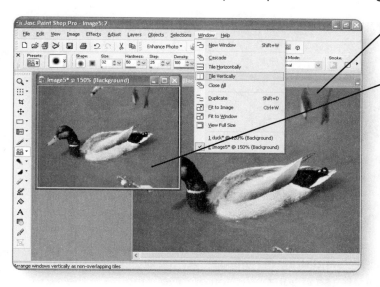

1. **Open** the **image** you want to duplicate.

2. **Open or create** the **image** you want to duplicate to. It can be a duplicate of the first image or a completely different image.

In the example seen here, the original image is duplicated and made smaller.

Display the two images side by side.

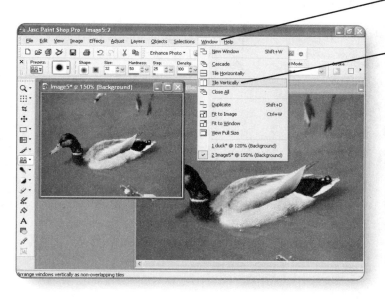

3. **Click** on **Window**. The Window menu will appear.

4a. **Click** on **Tile Vertically**. The two images will appear next to each other.

OR

4b. Manually **move and resize** the **windows** so that they are displayed side by side.

5. **Click** on the **Clone brush**. The mouse pointer looks like a rubber stamp.

6. **Right-click** the **mouse** on the area of the image that you want to duplicate. It won't look like anything happens, but Paint Shop Pro is remembering the image where you clicked.

7. **Click and drag** the **mouse** over the area you want to replicate the image to. As you drag your mouse in the second image, you begin to see the first image.

The original image displays a moving cursor, which indicates the current position.

TIP

Each time you want to replicate the original area, you need to right-click the mouse on the original area again.

This once lonely duck now has many companions.

7

Printing Images

Many projects that are created in Paint Shop Pro are for electronic production. Sometimes, however, you'll want to print your image to paper. You'll find that printing in Paint Shop Pro is similar to other Windows programs, but Paint Shop Pro includes several handy options from which you can benefit. In this chapter, you'll learn how to

- Change page settings
- Print your work
- Work with Print Layout
- Print multiple images on a page
- Print thumbnails

Printing a Single Image

Printing an open image in Paint Shop Pro is identical to printing in other Windows applications. As you prepare to print your image, you can determine several typical printing options, including margins, orientation, and some image placement options. Use the Print dialog box to set all these options.

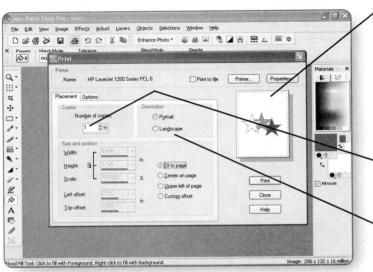

1. Click the **Print** button on the Standard toolbar. The Print dialog box will open.

TIP

Optionally, click on the File menu and select Print to open the Print dialog box.

The preview window displays the image with the currently selected print options. As you change any option, the preview box displays the image with the changes. From the Placement tab, you can select the following settings.

- **Number of copies.** Use this to specify the number of copies you want to print.

- **Orientation.** You can print the image in portrait or landscape (lengthwise).

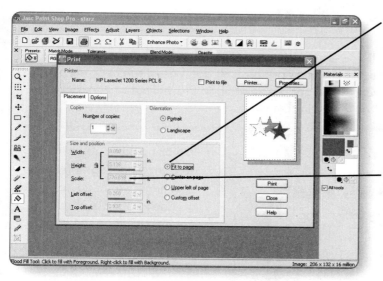

- **Position.** By default, the image prints in the center of the page. If you select Fit to page, the image will, without losing proportions, resize so that the entire image fits to the smaller of either the page height or page width.

- **Scale.** You can change the size of the image (without losing proportions) by changing the scale. You must first select the Custom offset option under Size and position.

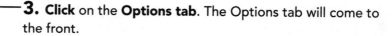

3. Click on the **Options tab**. The Options tab will come to the front.

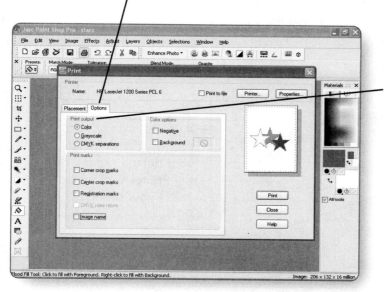

The Options tab deals with color and print marking options, such as these:

- **Print output.** If you are working on a color image and printing to a color printer, but you want to print the image in black and white, click the Greyscale option. Paint Shop Pro replaces the colors in the image with greys of equal lightness, giving the effect of a black-and-white image.

NOTE

If you are printing a color image to a noncolor printer such as a laser printer, you don't need to check the Greyscale option. Paint Shop Pro will automatically print the image in that way.

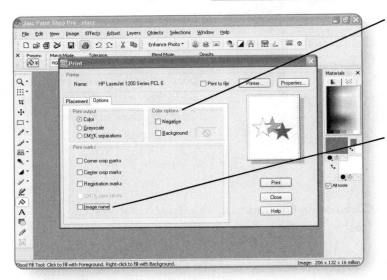

- **Color options.** You can opt to print a photograph image as a negative, or you can click on Background and select a color to print on the page around the image.

- **Print marks.** From this section, you can opt to print various crop marks and other symbols indicative of the actual image size. You can select a single option or multiple options. Checking the Image name option prints the filename on the page along with the image.

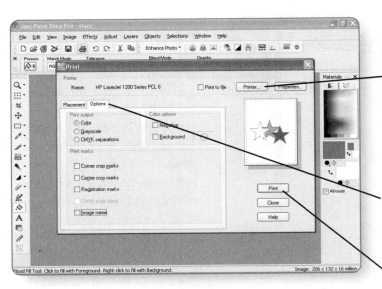

TIP

If you want to print to a printer different from your default printer, click the Printer button and select your printer.

3. Select any desired **settings**. The preview window will reflect your selected options.

4. Click on **Print**. The image will print with your specifications.

Printing Multiple Images

Printing multiple images on a single sheet of paper can save you money, especially if you're printing photographs on photo paper. Printing multiple images allows you to select which images to print as well as their size and placement on the page.

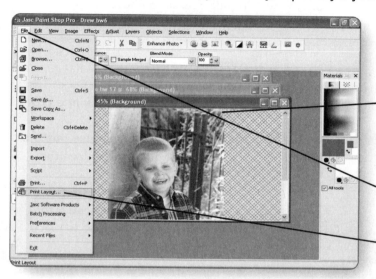

1. Open any **images** you want to print. The open images will appear in cascading windows in the Jasc Paint Shop Pro window.

2. Click on **File**. The File menu will appear.

3. Click on **Print Layout**. Paint Shop Pro will switch the view to Print Layout mode.

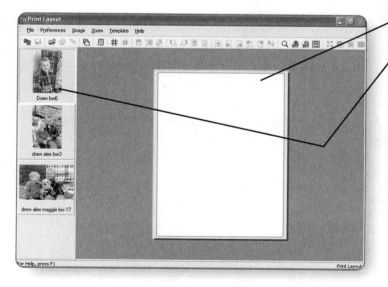

A blank layout page will appear.

The open images will appear as thumbnails on the left side of your screen.

Next, you need to lay out the images on the page. You can determine where you want the images and resize them if you want to.

NOTE

Print Layout also includes templates to assist you with arranging your images. You'll learn lots more about Print Layout in the "Printing Standard Photo Sizes" section later in this chapter.

4. **Drag** the first **image** you want to place on the page. The mouse pointer will turn into an arrow with a small white box.

5. **Release** the **mouse button**. Paint Shop Pro will place the image on the page.

6. **Repeat steps 4** and **5** for each image you want to place on the page.

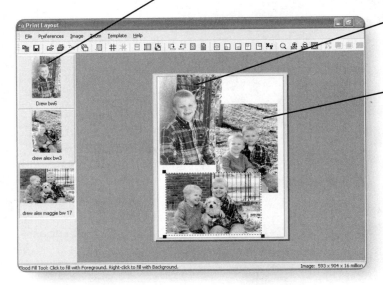

TIP

To delete an image you don't want, click on the unwanted image and press the Delete key.

If the images are not the size you want, you can resize the images to better fit on your page.

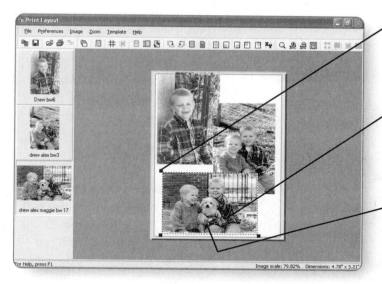

7. Click on a **placed image**. Four sizing handles will appear around the selected image corners.

8. Position the **mouse pointer** over any of the handles. The mouse pointer will turn into a white double-headed arrow.

9. Click and drag the **handle** to resize the image. A set of dashed outlines will indicate the new size as well as the original size.

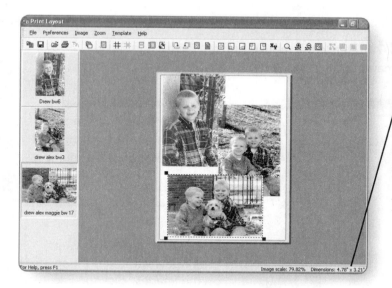

TIP
Look in the lower-right corner of the status bar for exact size dimensions.

10. Release the **mouse button**. The image will adjust to the new size.

If you placed the images into position but decide they might look better in a different position, you can use your mouse to easily move the images to any position on the page.

11. **Click** on the **image** you want to move. The image will be surrounded with selection handles.

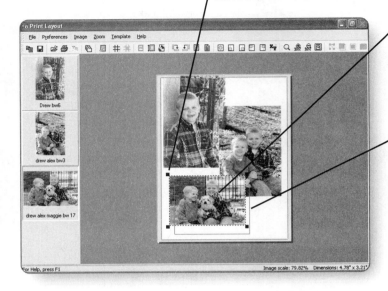

12. **Place** the **mouse pointer** anywhere in the body of the image. The mouse pointer will appear as a cross with four arrowheads.

13. **Click and drag** the **mouse** until the image is at the desired position. A set of dashed outlines will indicate both the new position and the original position.

14. **Release** the **mouse button**. Paint Shop Pro will move the image to the new location.

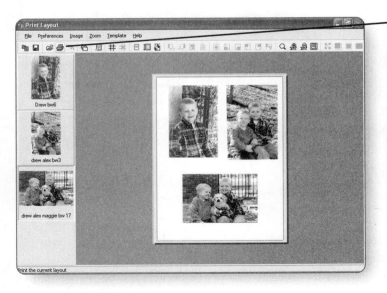

15. When you're finished resizing and moving images, **click** on the **Print button**. Paint Shop Pro will print the multiple images.

TIP

To close the Print Layout window without printing the images, click the File menu and select Close Print Layout.

Using Auto Arrange

Don't want to take the time to do all that moving and resizing? Let Paint Shop Pro's Auto Arrange feature do the work for you.

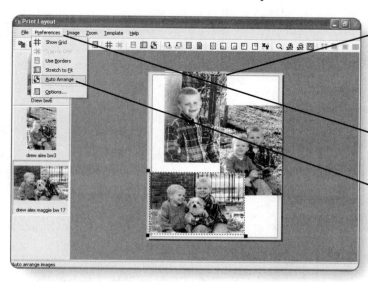

1. Place the **images** on the page as you learned in the previous section, but don't be concerned about size or exact placement.

2. Click on **Preferences**. The Preferences menu will appear.

3. Click on **Auto Arrange**. Paint Shop Pro will rearrange the images to fit the page.

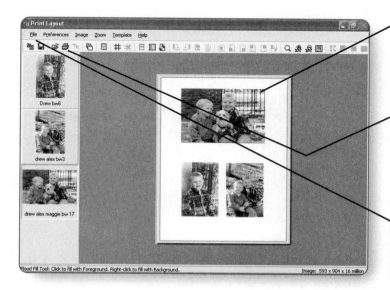

Auto Arrange divides the paper into sections of size comparable to the number of images and places an image in each section.

Click on the Print button when you're ready to print the multiple images.

TIP

To close the Print Layout window without printing the images, click the File menu and select Close Print Layout.

Printing Standard Photo Sizes

In an earlier section, "Printing Multiple Images," you used the Print Layout box to print multiple images on a single sheet. The Print Layout can also assist you when you need to print standard photo sizes of an image. For example, you have a great photograph of your new grandchild and you want to share copies with others. You can select from layouts that include a single 8 × 10 size, choose one with eight wallet sizes to a page, or even select combinations of a single 5 × 7 plus four wallet sizes to a single page. The Print Layout even includes sizes that fit standard Avery forms.

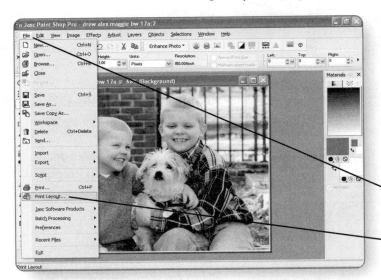

1. Click on **File**. The File menu will appear.

2. Click on **Print Layout**. Paint Shop Pro will switch the view to Print Layout mode.

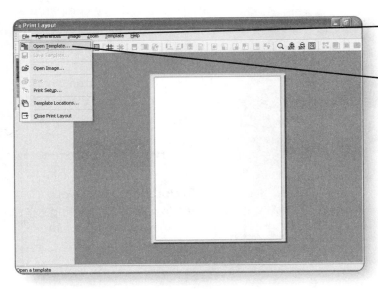

3. Click on **File**. The File menu will appear.

4. Click on **Open Template**. The Templates dialog box will open.

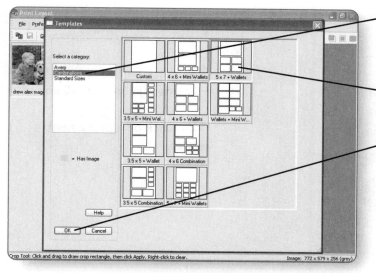

5. Click on a **category**. A list of available template sizes will appear.

6. Click on the **template** you want to use.

7. Click on **OK**. The Templates dialog box will close.

8. Click on the **image** you want to use if you have more than one image open. The image will be selected.

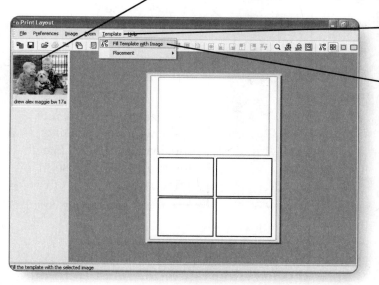

9. Click on **Template**. The Template menu will appear.

10. Click on **Fill Template with Image**. The template will fill with the selected image.

If your images do not fill the template cells completely, you might want to line them up differently.

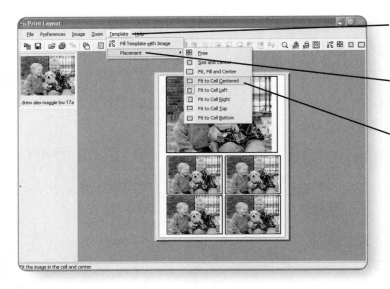

11. **Click** on **Template**. The Template menu will appear.

12. **Click** on **Placement**. The Placement submenu will appear.

13. **Click** on a **placement option**.

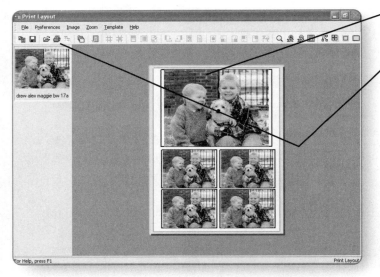

In this figure, the image is centered to each frame.

14. **Click** on the **Print button**. The page with the images will print.

TIP

To close the Print Layout window without printing the images, click the File menu and select Close Print Layout.

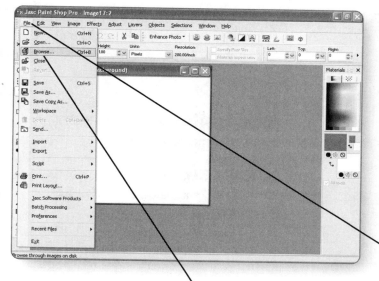

Producing Thumbnails

In Chapter 2, "Working with Paint Shop Pro Files," you learned about the Paint Shop Pro Browse feature that allows you to view thumbnails and open your images easily. You can also print the thumbnail images you see in the Browse window.

1. Click on **File**. The File menu will appear.

2. Click on **Browse**. The Browse window will open.

3. Locate and click on the **folder** with the images you want to print. The images will appear in the Browse window.

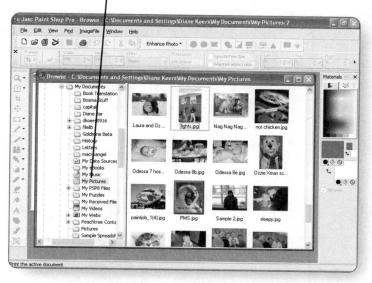

TIP

If you don't want to print thumbnails of all the images in the current folder, hold down the Ctrl key and click on the images you do want to include.

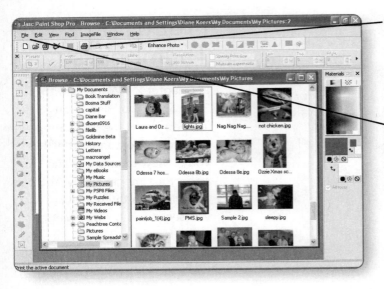

4a. Click on the **Print button**. The Browser Print dialog box will open.

OR

4b. Click on **File**. The File menu will appear.

5b. Click on **Print**. The Browser Print dialog box will open.

With the standard template, Paint Shop Pro will print 25 thumbnail images to a page.

6. Click on **Use the standard template**. The option will be selected.

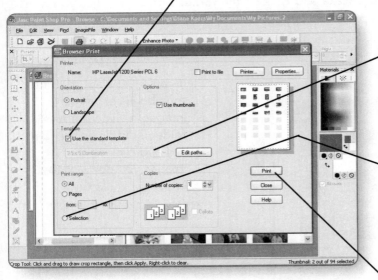

TIP

There are a number of other layouts other than 25 thumbnails to a page. Click the Template arrow to select a different layout.

7. Click the **Selection option** if you have selected specific images to print. If you do not have images selected, the option will be unavailable.

8. Click on **Print**. The thumbnails will print with up to 25 images per page.

As a heading to the pages, Paint Shop Pro will print the path to the images.

8

Using Help and Getting Assistance

Although you'll find many answers to your questions in this book, sometimes you'll need additional assistance. Paint Shop Pro supplies you with several types of support. In this chapter, you'll learn how to

- Use the Help Topics feature
- Obtain context help
- Locate help on the Web
- Contact Jasc Software

Searching the Program for Help

In Chapter 1, you learned how to accomplish specific tasks by using the new Learning Center window. Sometimes, however, you might have a simple issue stumping you and need help with it. If you get stuck and don't know what to do next, you'll find online help just a mouse click away.

Using the Help Topics

The Help Topics feature presents help information in a folder-like format, making it easy for you to browse available topics.

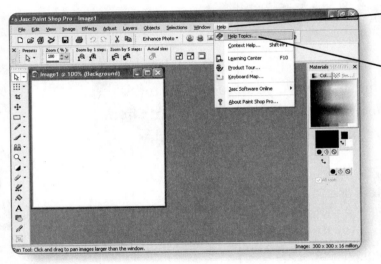

1. Click on **Help**. The Help menu will appear.

2. Click on **Help Topics**. The Paint Shop Pro Help window will open with the Contents tab on top.

TIP

Optionally, press F1 to open the Help window.

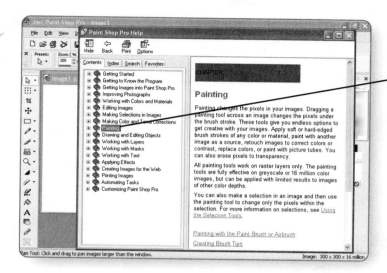

Available topics are listed on the left.

3. Double-click on a **general topic**. The topic's folder will open and a list of other specific topics or other general topics will appear beneath it.

> **NOTE**
>
> A *general topic* contains specific topics and is signified by a book. A specific topic is indicated by a yellow paper with a question mark on it. Some general topics might have other general topics listed under them.

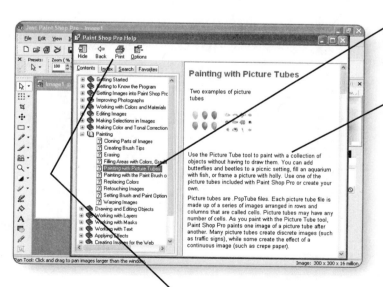

4. Click on the **specific topic** you want to view. The specific topic will be highlighted.

Paint Shop Pro will display the information on that topic in the Help window on the right.

Click on the Printer icon to print the displayed topic.

Using the Help Index

If you don't find what you need in the Help topics, try looking through the extensive alphabetical help index.

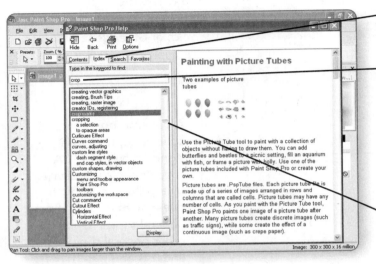

1. Click on the **Index tab**. The Help Index window will appear.

2a. Type the **first characters** or **word** of your keyword. The keywords list will jump alphabetically to the word that you typed.

OR

2b. Scroll through the **list of keywords** until you find your keyword.

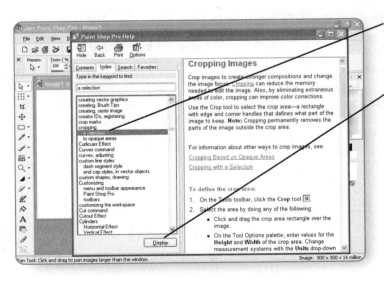

3. Click on the **topic** you're interested in. The topic will be highlighted.

4. Click on **Display**. The information will display in the Paint Shop Pro Help window.

5. Click on the **Close button**. The Help window will close.

Obtaining Context Help

There are so many objects on a Paint Shop Pro screen that it's hard to remember what each item is or does. Use the Context Help feature to identify the various buttons and components.

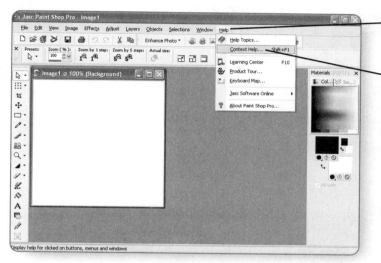

1. **Click** on the **Help menu**. The Help menu will appear.

2. **Click** on **Context Help**. The mouse pointer will change to a pointer with a question mark.

TIP

Optionally, press Shift+F1 to access the Context help feature.

3. **Position** the **pointer** over any button, item, or menu selection on the screen.

4. **Click** the **mouse button**. A detailed help window will open explaining the function of the item you clicked on.

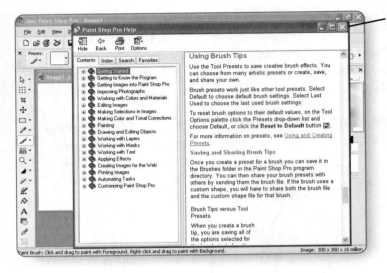

5. Click on the help window **Close button**. The help window will close.

Getting Assistance with a Dialog Box

Paint Shop Pro provides help with the dialog boxes that are used in its application.

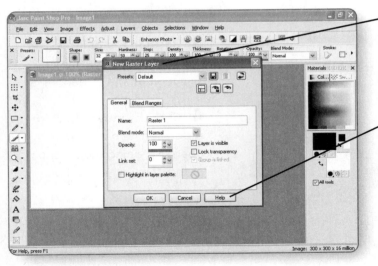

1. Click on a **menu selection** that results in a dialog box. (Hint: Any menu selection that ends with an ellipsis (...) results in a dialog box.)

2. Click on **Help** in the dialog box. A help window will open with information that is specific to the open dialog box.

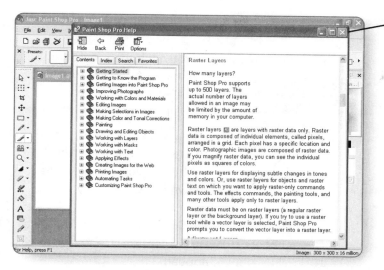

3. Click on the Paint Shop Pro Help window **Close button**. The window will close.

Getting Help on the Web

With Internet access, you'll find lots of help on the Jasc Software Web site. The site provides answers to many Frequently Asked Questions (FAQs), as well as tips, tutorials, updates and patches, a chat room, and a search engine.

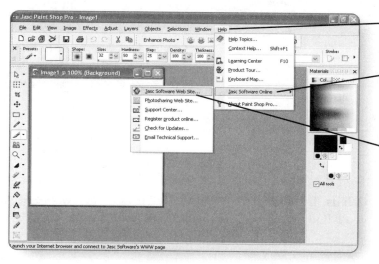

1. Click on **Help**. The Help menu will appear.

2. Click on **Jasc Software Online**. A submenu menu will appear.

3. Click on **Jasc Software Web Site**. Your default Web browser will launch and display the Jasc Software home page.

You'll find the Jasc Software home page at http://www.jasc.com.

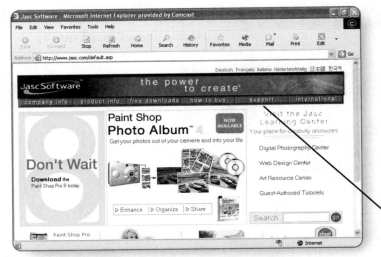

NOTE

You might be prompted to connect to your Internet Service Provider (ISP).

Web pages change frequently, so the ones you see online might not look like the ones shown here.

4. Click on **Support**. The Jasc Customer Care Center page will appear.

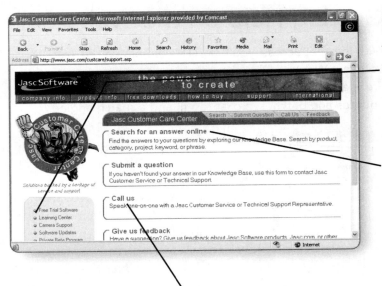

From the Jasc Customer Care Center page you have options to choose:

- **Learning Center.** Takes you to the Paint Shop Pro Tips and Tutorials page, where you'll find other Paint Shop Pro resources.

- **Search for an answer online.** Takes you to the Jasc Customer Care Center search page. From there, you can browse through the FAQs, do an online search, or participate in a Jasc chat room.

- **Call us.** Takes you to the Customer Service page where you'll find phone numbers and other Jasc information.

TIP

You might also want to take a look at Appendix B, "Exploring Useful Web Sites," for a list of helpful Web sites that relate to Paint Shop Pro.

Contacting Jasc Software

If you don't find the answer you need from the Jasc Web site, try e-mailing Jasc your question. I've found the company's tech support people to be some of the most helpful support I've ever used. You can e-mail Jasc tech support at techsup@jasc.com.

If you don't have Internet access or you prefer to talk with a live person, try contacting Jasc Software at the support phone number (952) 930-9171. Support is available Monday through Friday, 8 a.m. – 6 p.m. Central Standard Time.

Part I Review Questions

1. What are file associations? *See "Setting File Associations" in Chapter 1.*

2. What are two main elements in the Paint Shop Pro workspace? *See "Examining Screen Objects" in Chapter 1.*

3. What three types of measurements can you use when you're predetermining the size of a new image? *See "Determining Image Size" in Chapter 2.*

4. Which feature that is provided with Paint Shop Pro lets you view thumbnails of your images? *See "Browsing Images" in Chapter 2.*

5. When you're drawing ellipses or other shapes, what key can you hold down to draw a perfect circle or shape? *See "Creating the Perfect Shape" in Chapter 3.*

6. What does feathering do? *See "Adding Feathering" in Chapter 4.*

7. If you want a shape to have a color-filled center, do you select the color in the background or the foreground? *See "Making Color Selections" in Chapter 5.*

8. Will the Background Eraser tool work on all types of layers? *See "Erasing with the Background Eraser" in Chapter 6.*

9. What Paint Shop Pro feature do you use when you want to print multiple images on a single sheet? *See "Printing Standard Photo Sizes" in Chapter 7.*

10. What key can you press to open the Paint Shop Pro help system? *See "Using the Help Topics" in Chapter 8.*

PART II

Working with Raster Graphics

9

Developing Layers

Up to this point, you've learned how to use the Paint Shop Pro tools to create simple objects. The next level of graphics is called layering. You have the option of creating a layer for each object you create in Paint Shop Pro.

Layering is like putting each portion of your graphics image on a separate transparent sheet of paper. You can then shuffle the order of the layers (sheets). Layering makes it much easier to edit or move a particular portion of the image. As you edit one portion of the image, you won't disturb the other portions. If you are making composite images, you'll find layers particularly helpful. In this chapter, you'll learn how to

- Create, duplicate, and delete layers
- View and hide layers
- Change layer opacity
- Merge layers
- Rename layers

Creating Layers

Every Paint Shop Pro image consists of at least one layer—usually called the background layer—that is similar to the canvas of a painting. Paint Shop Pro 8 now supports up to 500 layers per image if it's not limited by the memory in your computer. Images that are created with a transparent background don't have a background layer.

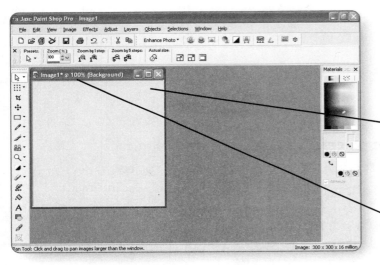

You should use layers when you want to combine several different elements into an image that you might want to control independently of each other.

1. **Create** a **new image canvas** with a nontransparent background.

> **TIP**
>
> Notice that the image title bar displays the current layer, which in the case of a new image is the background layer.

In addition to the background layer that Paint Shop Pro provides, you can create a number of other types of layers in Paint Shop Pro, including raster, vector, masks, and adjustment layers. Raster layers contain pixel-based information, whereas vector layers contain instruction data for drawing vector lines, shapes, and text. The next several chapters in this book deal primarily with raster and mask layers. You'll learn more about vector images in Part III, "Using Vector Graphics & Text." Adjustment layers are beyond the scope of this book and will not be addressed.

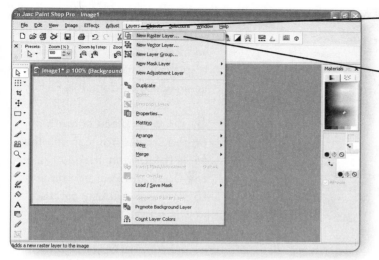

2. Click on **Layers**. The Layers menu will appear.

3. Click on **New Raster Layer**. The New Raster Layer dialog box will open.

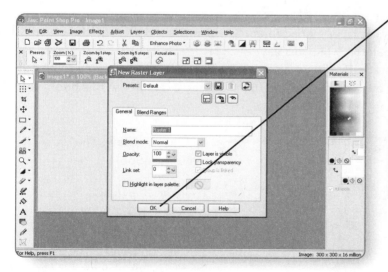

4. Click on **OK**. A new layer will appear on the image.

TIP

You can bypass the New Raster Layer dialog box by holding down the Shift key while you select New Raster Layer.

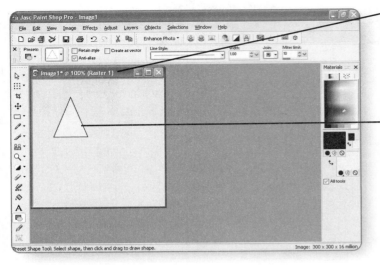

Although nothing will appear to have changed, look at the image window title bar. The title bar displays the name of the new layer, which by default is Raster 1.

5. **Draw or place something** on the screen. You can use the tools to draw an image or use the Copy and Paste commands to place a previously created image on the screen.

Viewing Layers

Most layer management is accomplished through the Layer palette, which displays each layer and its order in the layer stack. By default, Paint Shop Pro will display the Layer palette; however, if you were following the examples in this book, you may have turned it off.

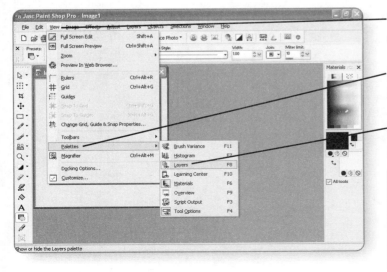

1. **Click** on **View**. The View menu will appear.

2. **Click** on **Palettes**. The Palettes submenu will appear.

3. **Click** on **Layers**. The Layer palette will display on the screen.

TIP

Optionally, you can use the F8 key to toggle the Layer palette on or off.

Paint Shop Pro reveals quite a bit of information in the Layer palette, including the following:

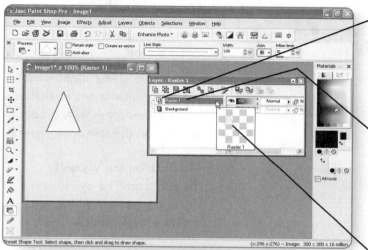

- **Layer type.** Each type of layer represents a different layer type. In our example, you see a clear and a solid box indicating that this is a raster layer.

- **Layer name.** When you start adding lots of layers, you'll want to give each layer a unique name to quickly identify what each layer holds.

TIP

Pause the mouse over the layer name to see a representation of the layer contents.

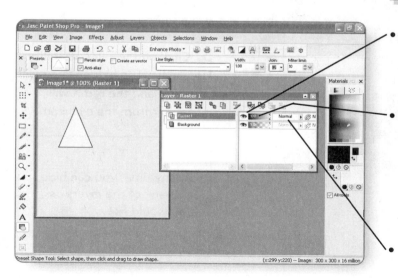

- **Visibility toggle.** The eye icon indicates that the layer is visible. You'll see later in this section how to hide layers.

- **Opacity.** Opacity is the measure of an object to block light transmission—the opposite of transparency. You'll see how to change opacity in the next section, "Changing Layer Opacity."

- **Blend mode.** This feature combines the pixels of the current layer with the pixels of the underlying layers.

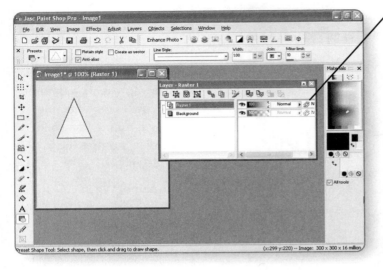

- **Lock transparency.** This option lets you lock transparent pixels in an image so that only the nontransparent pixels can be edited.

On occasion, you might want to hide particular layers so that you can more easily view and edit objects on the remaining layers.

4. Click on the **Visibility Toggle icon.** The eye icon will change to an eye with a red X, and the layer hides.

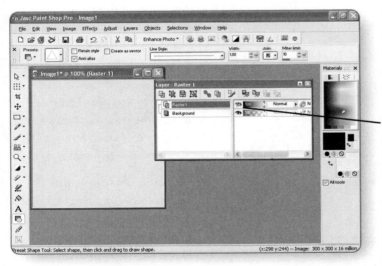

In this example, Raster 1 isn't gone—it's simply hidden. Notice the yellow triangle that was drawn on Raster 1 has disappeared.

5. Click on the same **visibility icon** again. The hidden layer will redisplay and the red X will disappear from the eye icon.

TIP

At any time, you can hide as many of the layers as you would like.

Changing Layer Opacity

When the opacity is lower, the resulting image is more transparent. When the opacity is higher, the image is fully opaque or visible. Background layers do not have opacity control.

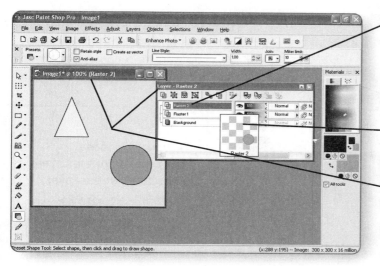

1. On the Layer palette, **click** on the **layer** you want to modify. The layer name will be highlighted, indicating that it is the active layer.

A miniature representation of the layer will display.

The active layer name will appear in both the image title bar and the layer palette.

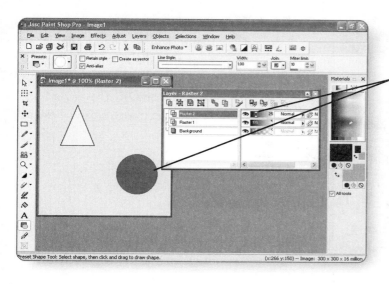

2. Drag the layer **opacity handle** to the left or right. The opacity value will display and the layer image will change as you slide the opacity handle.

In this example, decreasing the opacity makes the red circle more transparent.

Naming Layers

As you add more layers, you might want to more easily identify what each layer represents. Use the Layer Name feature to clearly name each layer. Background layers are already named, so you cannot rename them.

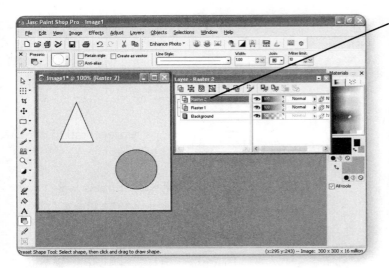

1. From the Layer palette, **double-click** on the **layer name** you want to rename. The Layer Properties dialog box will open.

TIP

Optionally, choose Properties from the Layers menu to open the Layer Properties dialog box.

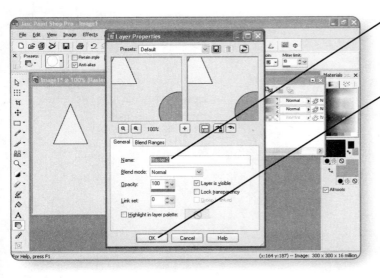

2. Type a new descriptive **name**. The new name will appear in the Name text box.

3. Click on **OK**. The Layer Properties dialog box will close.

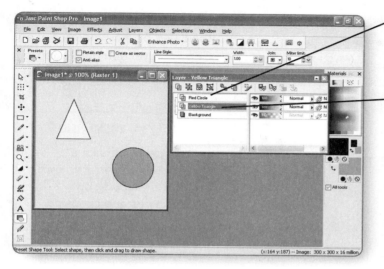

4. Repeat steps 1 through **3** for each layer you want to rename.

The Layer palette will reflect the new layer names.

Duplicating Layers

If you created a layer just the way you want it and you need another similar layer, then you can duplicate the existing layer and modify the new one rather than re-creating the layer.

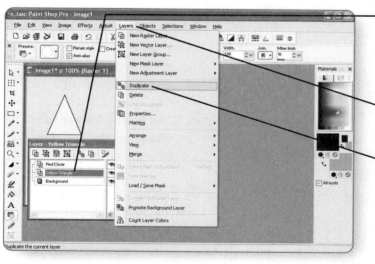

1. From the Layer palette, **click** on the **layer name** you want to duplicate. The layer name will appear in the image title bar.

2. Click on **Layers**. The Layers menu will appear.

3. Click on **Duplicate**. Paint Shop Pro will duplicate the layer.

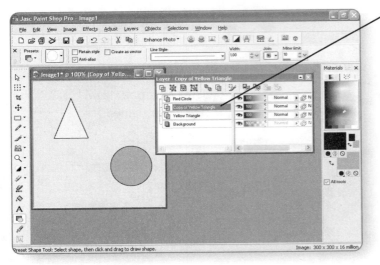

The new layer will appear on the Layer palette and be named Copy of *layer you duplicated*. You might want to rename the layer.

TIP

You can also make a selected area into its own layer by clicking on Selections and choosing Promote Selection to Layer.

Moving a Layered Image

Can't see the new duplicated layer? That's because its image is lying directly on top of the layer it was duplicated from. You'll probably want to move the new layer.

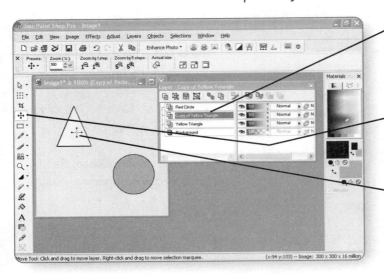

1. From the Layer Palette, **click** on the **layer name** you want to move. The layer name will appear in the image title bar.

2. Click on the **Mover tool**. The mouse pointer will turn into a four-headed arrow.

3. Position the **mouse pointer** over the image.

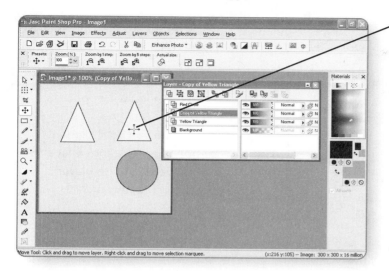

4. Click and drag the **image** to a new position. The image will move onscreen to its new position.

5. Release the **mouse button**. The image will remain in the new position.

Reordering Layers

If your layers are stacked differently than you want, you can change their order. One exception is the background layer, which is always the lowest layer. You can move layers up or down one layer at a time or you can move a layer to the top or bottom of the stack.

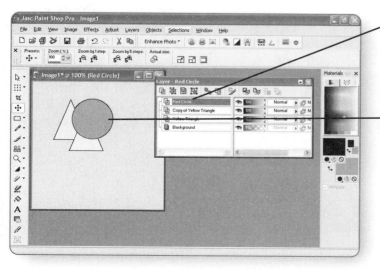

1. On the Layer palette, **click** the **layer** you want to reorder. The selected layer will becomes the active layer.

Notice that in this example, the red circle is on top of the yellow triangles.

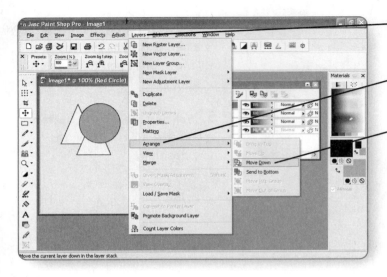

2. Click on **Layers**. The Layers menu will appear.

3. Click on **Arrange**. The Arrange menu will appear.

4. Click on an arrangement **option**. The rearranged layer name appears on the layer palette in the new order.

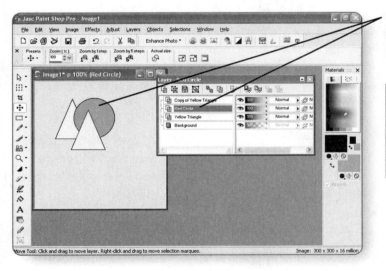

Now the red circle layer is between the yellow triangle layers.

TIP

Optionally, you can move layers by dragging the layers in the Layer palette.

Promoting the Background Layer

As you've seen so far, a raster background layer, created when you open a new image with a nontransparent background, is a little different from the other layers. First, it is always the lowest layer in the stack. Second, it does not have opacity control like the other layers. If you want to control the opacity or transparency of the background layer, you must first promote it to a regular raster layer.

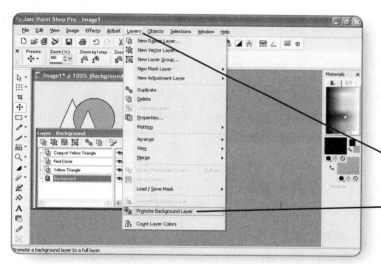

1. Click on **Layers**. The Layers menu will appear.

2. Click on **Promote Background Layer**. The background layer will become a raster layer.

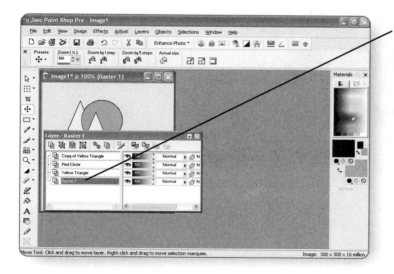

The new raster name will be assigned to the former background layer.

Understanding Layer Groups

After you merge layers, the elements are on a single layer and cannot be manipulated individually. Instead of merging the layers, you might want to group them. You might want to group layers if you want to move items on one layer and want the items on some of the other layers to move along also. Each image can contain multiple layer groups.

Creating Layer Groups

When you create a layer group, Paint Shop Pro assigns a number or name to the group that appears on the Layer palette. Creating groups is a temporary way of merging layers.

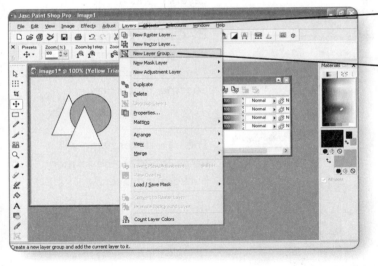

1. Click on **Layers**. The Layers menu will appear.

2. Click on **New Layer Group**. The New Layer Group dialog box will open.

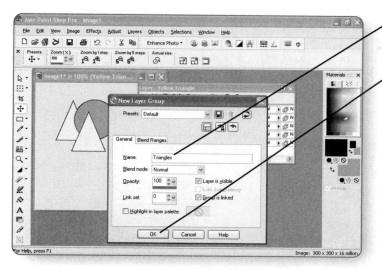

3. Optionally, **type** a **name** for the group.

4. Click on **OK**. The New Layer Group dialog box will close.

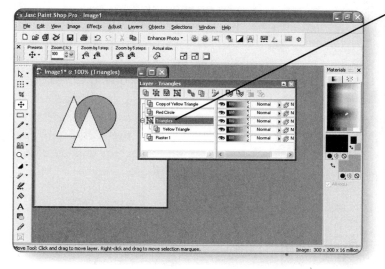

The new group will appear on the Layer palette above the currently selected layer.

Moving Layers to a Group

Paint Shop Pro provides several methods to move a layer into a group. One method involves using the Arrange menu. To move a layer into a group, the layer must first be located directly on top of the group layer.

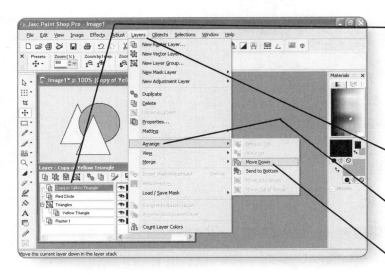

1. Select the **layer** you want to move into a group. The layer will be selected.

If the layer is already directly above the group, skip to step 6.

2. Click on **Layers**. The Layers menu will appear.

3. Click on **Arrange**. The Arrange submenu will appear.

4. Click on **Move Up** or **Move Down** depending on whether the layer needs to be moved up or down from its present location.

5. Repeat steps 1 through **4** as needed to position the layer on top of the group layer.

6. Click on **Layers**. The Layers menu will appear.

7. Click on **Arrange**. The Arrange submenu will appear.

8. Click on **Move Into Group**. The selected layer will appear as part of the group layer.

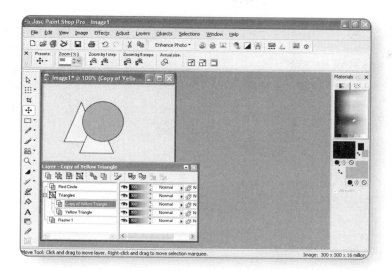

TIP

You can also use your mouse to drag a layer to any position from the Layer palette.

Ungrouping Layer Groups

If you included a layer in a group and no longer want it tied to the group, you can easily move it.

1. Select the **layer** that you want to move out of the group. The layer will be selected.

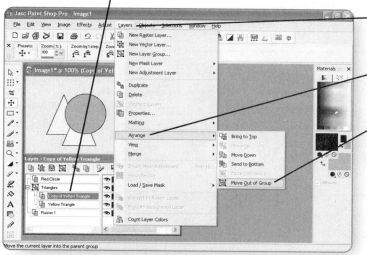

2. Click on **Layers**. The Layers menu will appear.

3. Click on **Arrange**. The Arrange submenu will appear.

4. Click on **Move Out of Group**.

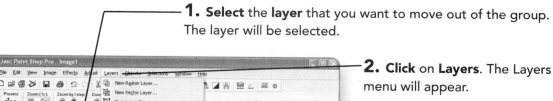

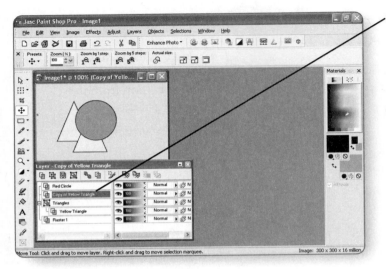

The selected layer will appear directly above the group layer.

Merging Layers

After you get your images in the correct position on their individual layers, you might want to merge the layers. Additionally, many file types, including .jpg, .gif, and .png, allow for only a single layer; as you attempt to save your file as one of these file types, Paint Shop Pro prompts you.

NOTE

After you flatten and merge your layers, other than using the Undo command, you cannot restore the individual layers. You might want to keep a copy of your images with all the layers. Save a copy of the file as a Paint Shop Pro file before you merge the layers.

Merging Down

The Merge Down feature allows you to selectively combine two layers in your image. The two layers must be adjacent to each other.

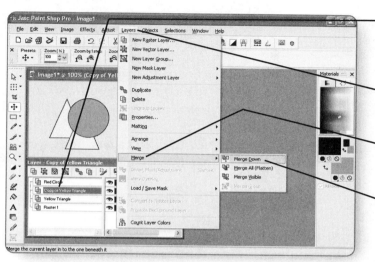

1. From the Layer palette, **click** the **top layer** of the two layers you want to merge.

2. Click on **Layers**. The Layers menu will appear.

3. Click on **Merge**. The Merge submenu will appear.

4. Click on **Merge Down**. The selected layer and the layer below it will merge into one layer.

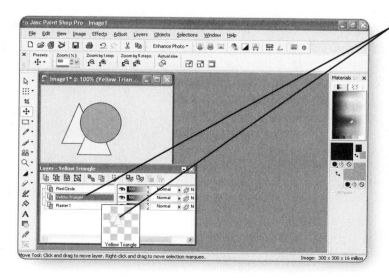

The merged layer retains the name of the lower layer and contains images from both layers.

Merging Groups

When you created a group, the individual group layers were temporarily linked so that if you moved the image on one layer, the other layer images moved proportionately. If you are finished with the group, you can combine the group layers into a single layer by merging the group.

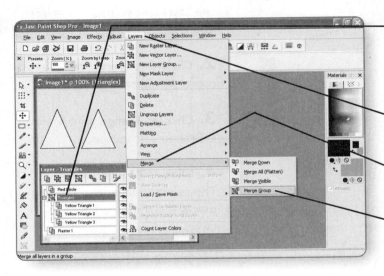

1. From the Layer palette, **click** on the **group** you want to merge. The group layer is selected.

2. Click on **Layers**. The Layers menu will appear.

3. Click on **Merge**. The Merge submenu will appear.

4. Click on **Merge Group**. All the layers in the group will join to become a single layer.

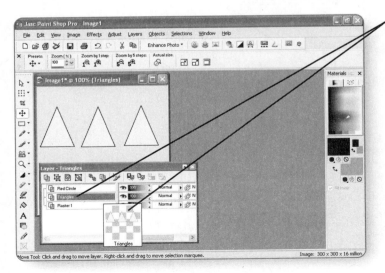

The single layer keeps the group name and contains the images from all the combined layers.

Merging All Layers

When you merge all the layers (called flattening), the image becomes nonlayered. If you have transparent areas in the image, Paint Shop Pro fills them with white.

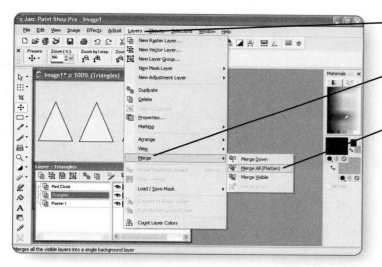

1. Click on **Layers**. The Layers menu will appear.

2. Click on **Merge**. The Merge submenu will appear.

3. Click on **Merge All (Flatten)**. All the layers will combine.

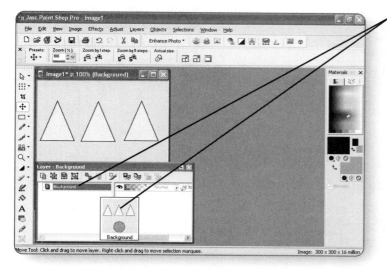

The image now consists of a single background layer with all the components.

Deleting Layers

If you've created a layer you no longer want, you can easily delete it from the Layer palette. If you delete a layer in error, don't forget that you can click on Edit, Undo (or press Ctrl+Z) to reverse your last action.

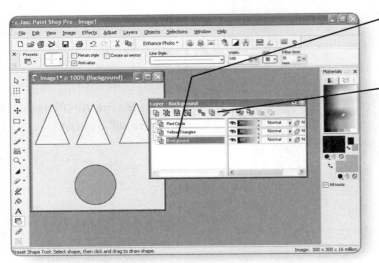

1. **Click** on the **layer name** you want to delete. The layer name will appear in the image title bar.

2. **Click** on the **Delete Layer** icon on the Layer palette. Paint Shop Pro will delete the layer and its contents.

TIP

Optionally, click on the Layers menu and choose Delete.

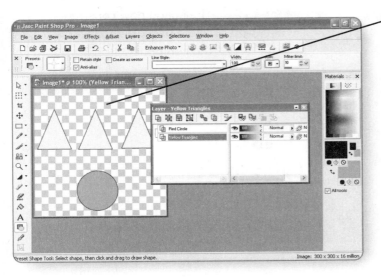

If you delete the background layer, the background of the image will become transparent.

10

Forming Masks

Masking is probably one of the most powerful features of Paint Shop Pro. A mask is a grey scale image that you use to hide and display parts of a layer. Masks are layers that hide portions of other layers without actually deleting them or modifying them. Think of a mask as a stencil that you place over an image to let only part of the image show through. In this chapter, you'll learn how to

- Create and save masks
- Apply and remove a mask
- Edit a mask

Creating a Simple Mask

A mask can cover a layer completely or with varying levels of opacity. Where a mask is black, it completely covers the layer, and where it is white, it leaves the layer uncovered. If you use a grey value between black and white, the mask produces a semi-visible effect.

Although Paint Shop Pro includes a number of masks and hundreds more are available on the Internet, you might want to design your own mask.

For an example, we'll create a mask with a simple oval shape.

> **TIP**
> It's easier to create a mask if you don't have any other images open when you're creating it.

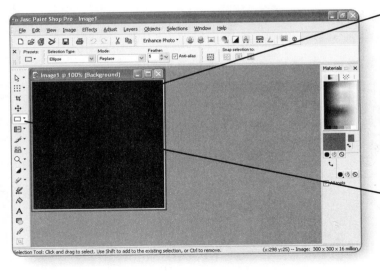

1. Create a **new image** with a black background. When applied, the black portion of a mask will block the image from showing.

Next you need to delete a portion of the black layer so that when the mask is applied, part of the image can show through.

2. Click on the **Selection tool**. The tool will become selected.

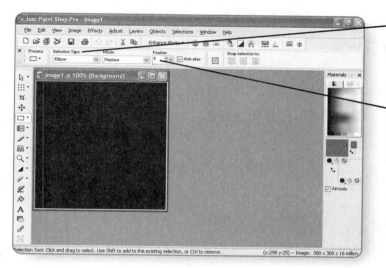

3. Select a **shape**. For this example, an ellipse is needed.

TIP

Set the feathering to 4 or 5 for a nice edge-softening effect.

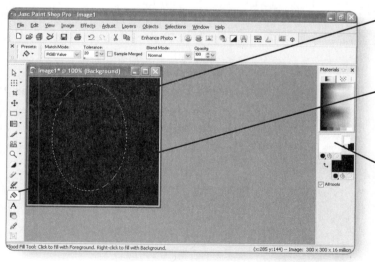

4. Draw an **oval selection** in the black image. A marquee will appear around the selection.

5. Click on the **Flood Fill** tool. The mouse pointer will appear as a paint bucket.

6. Set the **foreground color** to white. Remember that whatever you paint in white will appear through the mask.

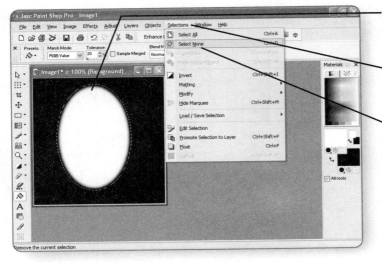

7. Click in the **oval selection**. The oval will fill with white.

8. Click on **Selections**. The Selections menu will appear.

9. Click on **Select None**. The oval will be deselected and the marquee will disappear.

So far, you have an image consisting of an oval. Next, you need to tell Paint Shop Pro that the image is intended for a mask.

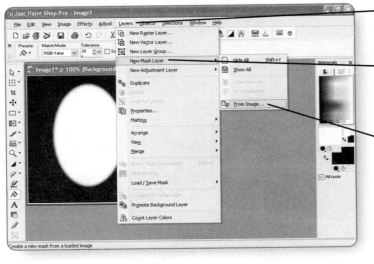

10. Click on **Layers**. The Layers menu will appear.

11. Click on **New Mask Layer**. The New Mask Layer submenu will appear.

12. Click on **From Image**. An Auto Actions dialog box will open.

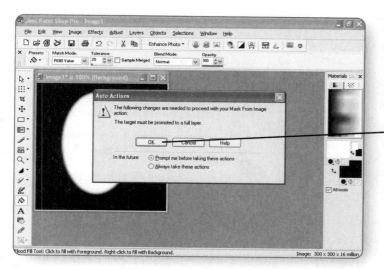

Because the image was originally created as a background layer, the background must first be promoted to a regular layer.

13. Click on **OK**. The Add Mask From Image dialog box will open.

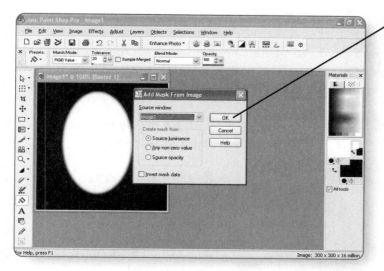

14. Click on **OK**. Paint Shop Pro now knows that the current image is a mask.

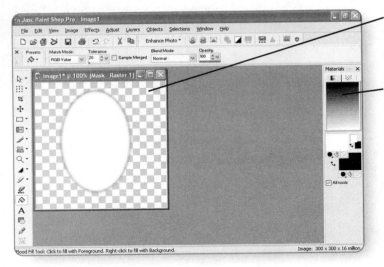

The black portion turns into a transparency (indicated by grey and white checks).

Masks are made up entirely of black, white, or shades of gray.

TIP

Click on File, Preferences, General Program Preferences. Then click on the Transparency tab to determine the way that Paint Shop Pro displays a transparent area on your screen.

Saving Masks

Now that you've created a mask, save it for future use. Paint Shop Pro names mask files with a .pspmask extension to identify it as a mask.

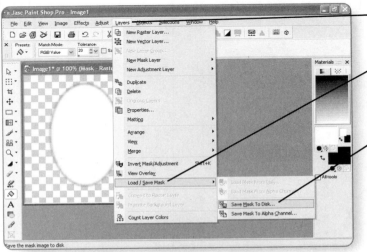

1. Click on **Layers**. The Layers menu will appear.

2. Click on **Load/Save Mask**. The Load/Save Mask submenu will appear.

3. Click on **Save Mask To Disk**. The Save Mask To Disk dialog box will open.

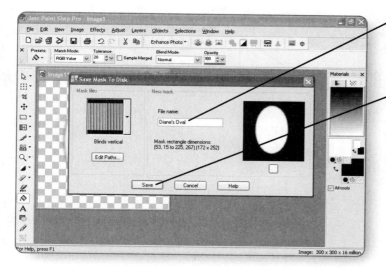

4. Enter a descriptive **name** for the mask. The name will appear in the New mask text box.

5. Click on **Save**. The Save Mask Channel dialog box will close and Paint Shop Pro will store the mask for future use.

You can now close the mask image so that you can apply it to a different image.

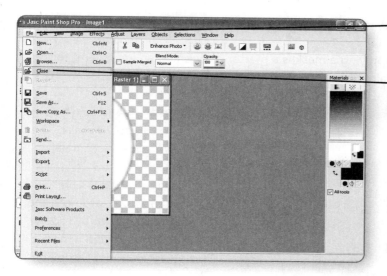

6. Click on **File**. The File menu will appear.

7. Click on **Close**. A message box will open prompting you to save your changes.

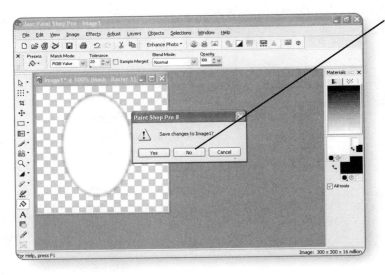

8. Click on **No**. (You've already saved the image as a mask.) The image will close from the screen.

Applying a Mask

Applying a mask is a matter of opening an image and telling Paint Shop Pro which mask you want to apply.

1. Open an **image** to which you want to apply a mask. The image will appear onscreen.

If the image contains only a background layer, promote the background layer to a "regular" layer before applying a mask. This gives you more flexibility when you're editing.

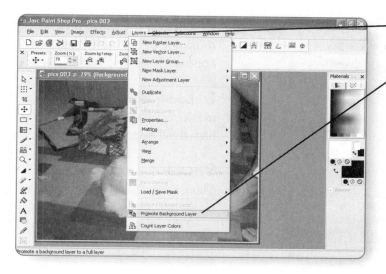

2. Click on **Layers**. The Layers menu will appear.

3. Click on **Promote Background Layer**. The image will no longer be considered a background; it will be a raster layer.

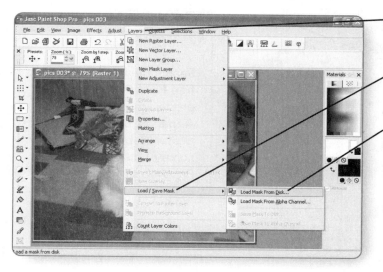

4. Click on **Layers**. The Layers menu will appear.

5. Click on **Load/Save Mask**. A submenu will appear.

6. Click on **Load Mask From Disk**. The Load Mask From Disk dialog box will open.

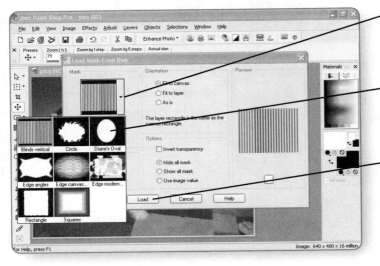

7. Click on the **Mask arrow**. A display of available masks will appear.

8. Locate and click on the **mask** you want to use. The mask name will become highlighted.

9. Click on **Load**. The Load Mask From Disk dialog box will close.

Paint Shop Pro will apply the mask to the image.

TIP

Search the Internet for free Paint Shop Pro predesigned masks. See Appendix B, "Exploring Useful Web Sites," for some popular Paint Shop Pro Web sites.

Masking on Layers

If you foresee the need to further edit the image itself, you might want to apply the mask to a separate layer. Then

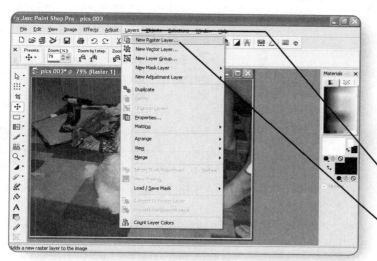

you can edit the image without affecting the mask, applying the two layers together when the editing is complete.

1. Open an **image** to which you want to apply a mask. The image will appear onscreen.

2. Click on **Layers**. The Layers menu will appear.

3. Click on **New Raster Layer**. The New Raster Layer dialog box will open.

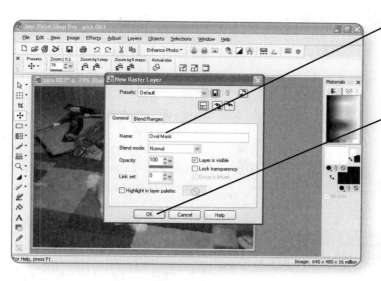

4. Enter a **name** for the new layer, such as **Oval Mask**. The name will appear in the Name text box.

5. Click on **OK**. A new layer will appear in the layer box, although you will see no changes to the image at this point.

Next, you need to give the new blank layer a color, gradient, or pattern.

6. **Click** on the **Flood Fill tool**. The mouse pointer will resemble a paint bucket.

7. **Select** a **color**, **gradient**, or **pattern** from the foreground Materials box. The options will appear in the foreground Materials box.

TIP

Make sure the Mask layer is the active layer.

8. **Click anywhere** on the **blank layer**. The layer "fills" with the new color.

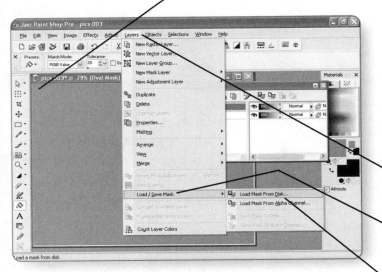

Don't panic! Because you activated the Mask layer, you've just filled up that layer with color. Your original image is as yet untouched.

Now you can apply the mask to the Mask layer.

9. **Click** on **Layers**. The Layers menu will appear.

10. **Click** on **Load/Save Mask**. A submenu will appear.

11. **Click** on **Load Mask From Disk**. The Load Mask From Disk dialog box will open.

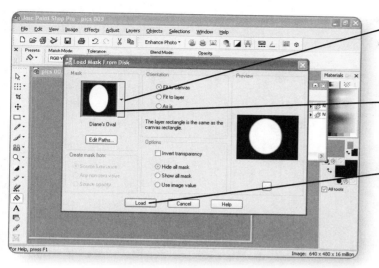

12. Click on the **Mask arrow**. A display of available masks will appear.

13. Locate and click on the **mask** you want to use. The mask name is highlighted.

14. Click on **Load**. The Load Mask From Disk dialog box will close.

Paint Shop Pro will apply the mask to the image layer, but it might be inverted.

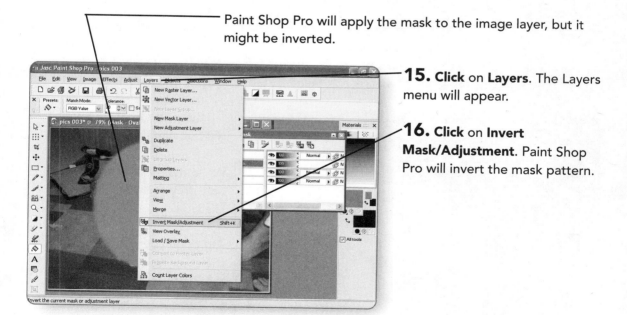

15. Click on **Layers**. The Layers menu will appear.

16. Click on **Invert Mask/Adjustment**. Paint Shop Pro will invert the mask pattern.

The image will now show through the mask.

Editing Masks

When you edit a mask, you aren't changing the actual image. You're changing the masking area or changing the degree of masking. You will select the areas you want to add or delete to the mask and then fill the selected areas with black or white.

1. Click on the **Mask layer**. It will become the active layer.

While the Mask layer is active, only grey scale colors are available.

Although you can use several of the tools, you might find that the Brush tool or the Preset Shape tool is the easiest tool to use to modify the masked area.

2a. Click on a **Paint Brush tool**. The Tool Options palette will display Paint Brush options.

3a. Set any desired Paint Brush **options**. A sample brush will appear in the Preview box.

OR

2b. Click on the **Preset Shapes tool**. The Tool Options palette will display Preset Shape options.

3b. Select a **shape** and **set** any desired **options**.

4. Select black and white as your foreground/background colors. If you want to add to the mask, set black as the background and white as the foreground. If you want to eliminate part of the mask, use black as the foreground and white as the background.

TIP

If you are working on a background layer with a transparency, you don't need to select a color first. As you draw the additions to the mask, additional areas will become transparent.

5. Draw the **additions** to the mask.

For this example, star-shaped cutouts are added to the mask.

Removing a Mask

If you've applied a mask to an image and decide you no longer want it or would like a different mask, you can delete it. Because the mask is a layer by itself, you only need to delete the Mask layer. If you have already flattened the layers, however, you can no longer remove the mask. (This is another good reason to save the image as a .psp file with the layers intact.)

1. Click on the **Mask layer**. The Mask layer will become selected.

2. Click on **Layers**. The Layers menu will appear.

3. Click on **Delete**. A confirmation dialog box will open.

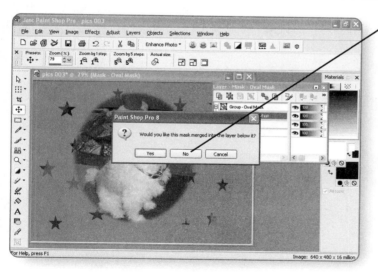

4. Click on **No**. Paint Shop Pro will remove the mask from the image.

NOTE
If you loaded the mask onto its own layer, you might want to delete that layer as well.

11

Designing with Picture Tubes

If you run down to Wal-Mart and look in the school supplies section, you're bound to see lots of ink stamps. You know—the kind that creates an image that you can stamp on the paper over and over again. Well, Paint Shop Pro's picture tubes are similar to those stamps—but even better. You can actually paint images with these tubes. In addition, whereas the stamps you find at the store can each produce only a single image, that's not necessarily the case with tubes. Some tubes might contain only a single image, but many tubes produce several variations of a single image or several different images with a common theme. In this chapter, you'll learn how to

- Use picture tubes
- Modify picture tube size
- Create and install additional picture tubes

Using Picture Tubes

If there were such a prize, picture tubes would win the gold medal as the "most fun feature" of Paint Shop Pro. Picture tubes are amusing little pictures that are created with a click of your mouse button. Use them in combination with other images, and you can create quite a masterpiece.

Creating a Tube Layer

For easier editing, you should place the picture tubes on layers. For ease in editing the image after it is drawn on the screen, place each tube on its own layer. Picture tubes are raster images, so place them on a raster layer.

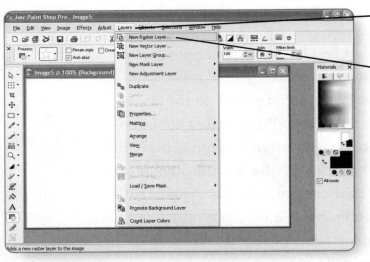

1. Click on **Layers**. The Layers menu will appear.

2. Click on **New Raster Layer**. The New Raster Layer dialog box will open.

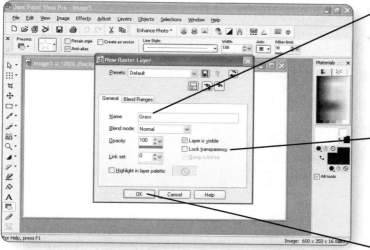

3. Optionally, give the layer a descriptive name by **typing** a new **name** for the layer in the Name text box.

4. **Click** on **OK**. The New Raster Layer dialog box will close.

5. **Click** on the **Picture Tube tool**. The mouse pointer will look like a tube of paint.

6. **Click** on the **preview arrow** in the Tool Options palette. A selection of tubes will display.

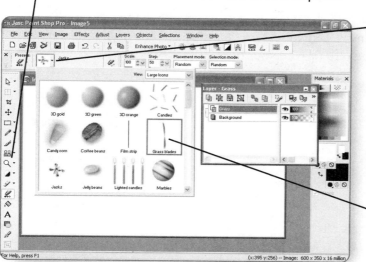

7. **Click** on a **tube**. The selection will appear in the preview box.

You're ready to paint with the picture tube.

Painting with a Picture Tube

Use the Picture Tube tool similarly to the Paint Brush tool. Click or click and drag across the canvas to achieve the look you want.

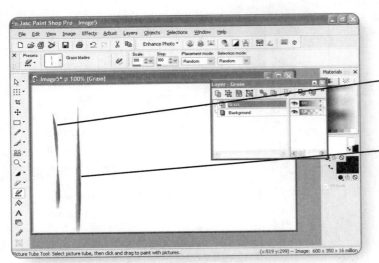

1. Click the **mouse** where you want the image to appear. The image will appear.

2. Click the **mouse** at a different position on the canvas. Depending on the tube you select, another identical or related image will appear.

3. With the mouse button down, **drag** the **mouse** over the canvas. Depending on the selected tube, the screen might begin to fill with your tube images.

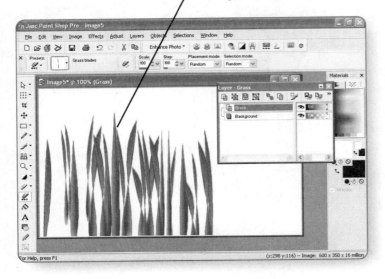

TIP

Draw your picture tubes in a straight line by clicking once at the beginning of the line. Then hold down the Shift key and click a second time at the end of the tube line. Paint Shop Pro draws a straight line using the tube between those two points.

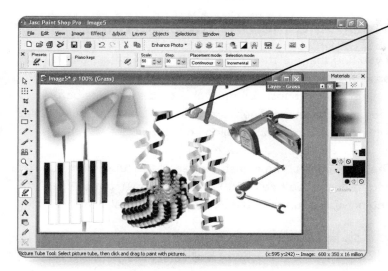

Try drawing with the different tubes. Many of them are more exciting than they appear in the preview box. The Piano Keys, Metal Hose, Metal Springs, and Spiral Garland tubes are perfect examples of the actual tube looking tremendously different from the sample in the preview window.

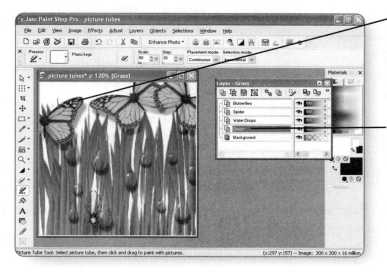

This image was created with just a few mouse clicks by using four different tubes: grass blades, water drops, arachnophobia, and monarch.

Each tube was drawn on a different layer.

Modifying Picture Tube Settings

If you find that a picture tube is painting an image that is too large or too small, too far apart, or too close together, you can edit the settings. You must change the settings before you paint the image. There are two main settings you will use with your picture tubes: scaling and steps.

The Scale control can adjust the size of the tube, from its originally created size of 100, down to 10 percent of its original size or up to 250 percent of its original size.

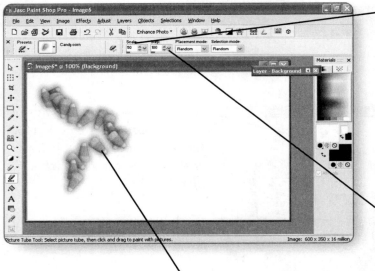

1. Click on the **Scale arrows** and **select** the picture **tube size**. The newly selected number will appear in the Scale box.

The Step control modifies the distance between the intervals in which the tubes appear. The larger the step, the more distance between the tubes.

2. Click on the **Step arrows** and **select** a **step size**. The newly selected number will appear in the Scale box.

3. Paint with the picture tube. Paint Shop Pro will create the images with the new settings.

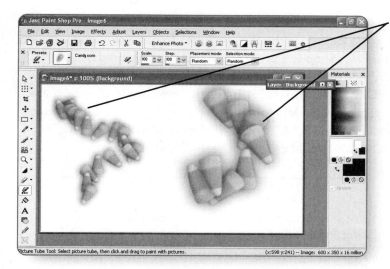

This image reflects the candy corn drawn at 100% on the right and 50% on the left.

Previewing Picture Tubes

A picture tube is really a drawing or series of drawings that is created and saved in a special format. The images are created on a transparent background so that all you see is the image. The easiest way to view picture tubes is with the Paint Shop Pro browser.

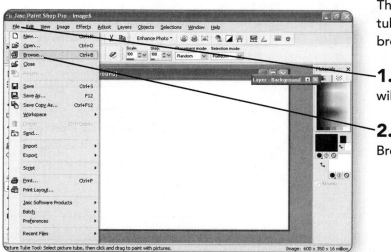

1. Click on **File**. The File menu will appear.

2. Click on **Browse**. The Browse window will open.

By default, the picture tubes that are supplied with Paint Shop Pro are located in the Picture Tubes folder where you installed the Paint Shop Pro program. Typically, this would be C:\PROGRAM FILES\JASC SOFTWARE INC\PAINT SHOP PRO 8\PICTURE TUBES. Tubes that you create or import are typically stored in a folder under your My Documents folder, such as C:\DOCUMENTS AND SETTINGS*YOUR NAME*\MY DOCUMENTS\MY PSP8 FILES\PICTURE TUBES.

TIP

You can specify additional file locations under File, Preferences, File Locations.

---

3. Locate and **click** on the **Picture Tubes folder** or **any folder in which you have tubes**. A thumbnail representation of each tube will appear.

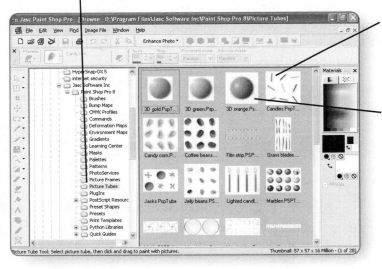

Some picture tubes have multiple items, usually of a different shape, size, color, or angle.

Some picture tubes consist of a single item.

NOTE

Don't double-click on the tube images unless you intend to open them for modification or for exporting.

---

4. Click the **Close button**. The Browse window will close.

Saving New Picture Tubes

Many picture tubes come with the Paint Shop Pro application and even more are available on the CD. You can even find thousands of free picture tubes on the Internet. In most cases, Paint Shop Pro automatically reads the picture tubes, provided that you copy them to one of the locations specified in File, Preferences, File Locations. Sometimes however, you might want to save your own files as picture tubes.

TIP

See Appendix B, "Exploring Useful Web Sites," for some tube sites.

There are a few rules to follow when you're creating picture tubes:

- The image must have a color depth of 24 bit (16 million colors).

- The image must be on a single raster layer.

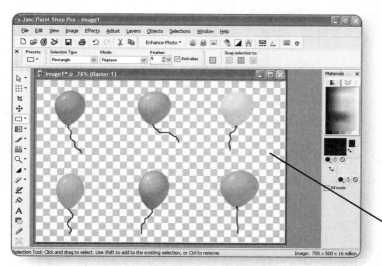

- The background of the image must be transparent.

- If your file has multiple images on it, the items should be symmetrical in position, dividing the canvas space equally between the items. Paint Shop Pro saves picture tube files in a row and column pattern.

1. Create or **open** the **file** that contains the picture tube. The picture tube will appear onscreen.

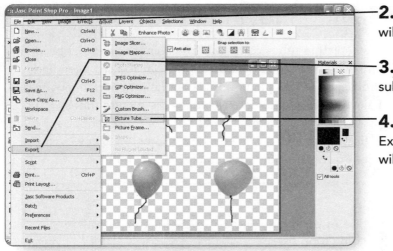

2. Click on **File**. The File menu will open.

3. Click on **Export**. The Export submenu menu will open.

4. Click on **Picture Tube**. The Export Picture Tube dialog box will open.

5. Specify the **number of cells across** in the image. In this example image, the image consists of 3 cells across.

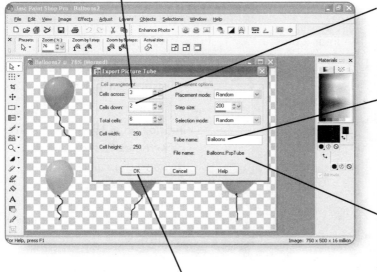

6. Enter the **number of cells down** in the image. In this example image, the image consists of 2 cells down.

7. In the Tube name text box, **type** a **name** for the tube. The name will appear in the text box.

NOTE

Paint Shop Pro 8 saves picture tube files with a file extension of .psptube.

8. Click on **OK**. Paint Shop Pro will add the picture tube to its list.

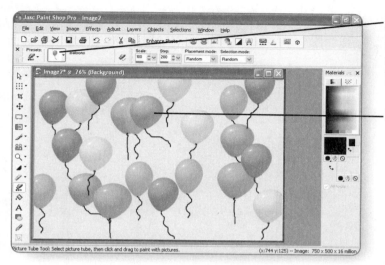

9. Click on the **picture tube preview box** in the Tools Options palette to select the new picture tube.

Happy tubing!

12

Adding Effects, Filters, and Deformations

The terms *effects*, *filters*, and *deformations* are basically synonymous. Some of the earlier versions of Paint Shop Pro separated filters and deformations, and as you access the Internet for tutorials on different projects, you might see them still referred to as filters or deformations. However, Paint Shop Pro now combines them and refers to them as "effects." *Special effects* aren't big enough words to describe what some of these items do for you! In this chapter, you'll learn how to

- Use the Effect browser
- Apply an effect
- Install third-party filters

Discovering Effects

Effects work on the individual layers of an image, so you can apply a different effect for each layer. Effects work only on raster images and only if the image is full-color (16 million) or in certain grey scale settings. Paint Shop Pro includes more than 100 different effects in 11 different categories:

- 3D effects
- Art media effects
- Artistic effects
- Distortion effects
- Edge effects
- Geometric effects
- Illumination effects
- Image effects
- Reflection effects
- Texture effects
- User-defined effects

See Appendix C, "Sample Effects," for a representation of some Paint Shop Pro 8 effects.

Using the Effect Browser

The easiest way to see what an effect applies to your image is with the Effect browser. The Effect browser displays a thumbnail of your open image layer with a sample of each effect with its default settings.

1. Open or **create** the **image** to which you want to apply an effect.

2. From the Layer palette, **click** on the **layer** to which you want to apply an effect. The layer name appears on the image title bar.

TIP

On most filters, selecting an area prior to choosing an effect applies the effect to the selected area only.

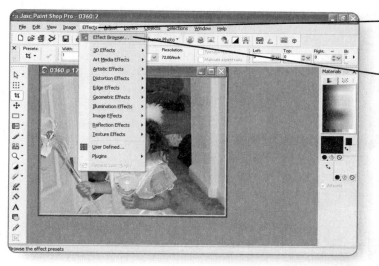

3. Click on **Effects**. The Effects menu will appear.

4. Click on **Effect Browser**. The Effect Browser window will open.

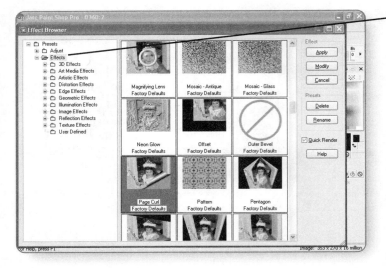

5. Click on the **Effects folder**.

Samples will appear in the preview pane showing the selected layer with each effect at its default settings. As you can see, many effects are dramatic whereas others provide softer and less noticeable change.

NOTE

Some effects require a selection before you can apply an effect.

The category and name of the effect

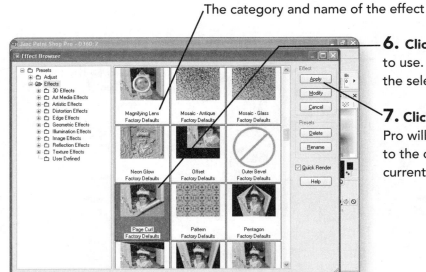

6. Click on an **effect** you want to use. A border will surround the selected effect.

7. Click on **Apply**. Paint Shop Pro will apply the selected effect to the current layer of the current image.

TIP

Remember: If you select an effect you don't like, click the Undo button to reverse your steps. After you have saved and closed a modified image, you cannot undo the previous step.

Selecting from the Effects Menu

If you know the effect you want to apply to an image, you can quickly select it from the Effects menu.

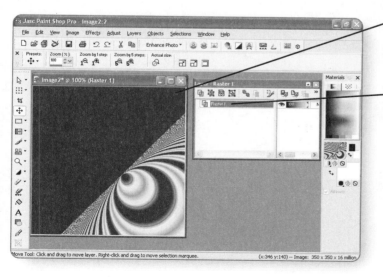

1. Open or **create** the **image** to which you want to apply an effect.

2. Click on the **layer** of the image to which you want to apply an effect. The layer name will appear on the image title bar.

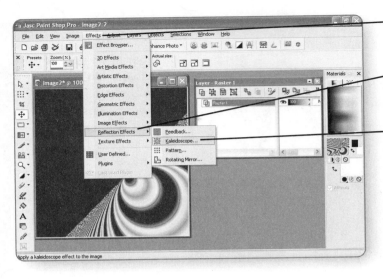

3. **Click** on **Effects**. The Effects menu will appear.

4. **Click** on an **effect category**. A submenu menu will appear.

5. **Click** on an **effect**. Paint Shop Pro will either apply the effect to the current layer of the current image or prompt you with a dialog box for further detail. See the next section, "Working with Effect Dialog Boxes."

NOTE

Effects with an ellipsis … display a dialog box with options. Effects without an ellipsis apply immediately upon selection.

The Kaleidoscope effect applied to the image

Working with Effect Dialog Boxes

Most effects require additional input before the effect can be applied. The options will vary with individual effects.

Standard elements on Effect dialog boxes include the following:

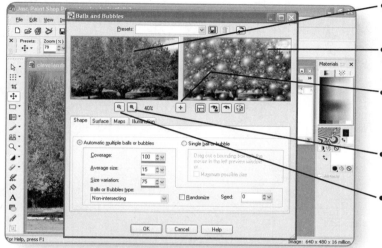

- **Before preview window.** See your image before the effect.

- **After preview window.** See your image after the effect.

- **Move image view.** Select a different area of the image to preview.

- **Zoom In.** See the preview image in a larger perspective.

- **Zoom Out.** See the preview image in a smaller perspective.

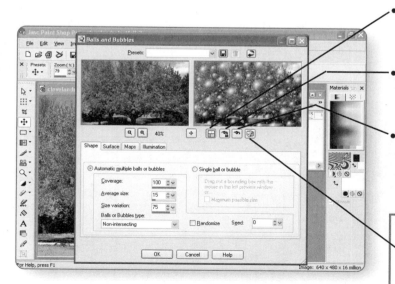

- **Auto Proof.** Click here to see all effect changes on the image window.

- **Proof.** Click here to see the current change on the entire image.

- **Reset.** Click this button to change the effect options to the default values.

NOTE

The Randomize button is discussed in the next section.

The remaining options vary depending on which effect you're working with. In this figure, you see the options for the Balls and Bubbles effect where you can adjust the size, quantity, and spacing of the balls and bubbles.

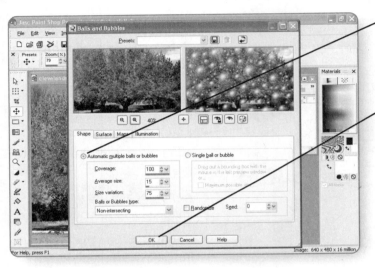

1. **Make** any desired **changes**. The preview window will reflect the effect change to the current layer.

2. **Click** on **OK**. The dialog box will close and Paint Shop Pro will apply the selected effect and settings to the current layer.

TIP

Experiment with the effects and their options. The possibilities are endless!

Discovering the Randomize Button

New to Paint Shop Pro 8 is a Randomize button, which appears in most of the Effects dialog boxes. Because most Effects dialog boxes contain a number of different settings and controls, clicking on the Randomize button selects different combinations of those settings and controls.

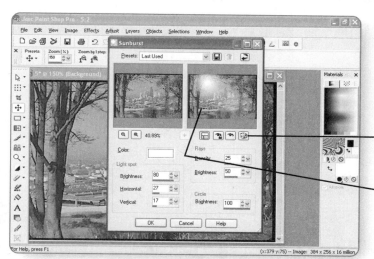

1. Click the **Randomize button** from an Effect dialog box.

The image will preview with a random selection of settings.

2. Click the **Randomize button** again.

The image will preview with a different random selection of settings.

TIP

Each click of the Randomize button selects a completely different combination of effect settings.

3. Click on **OK**. The dialog box will close and Paint Shop Pro will apply the selected effect and settings to the current layer.

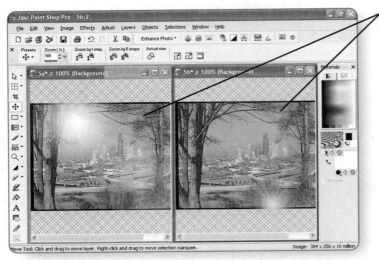

The same image with two different Sunburst effect settings

Working with Third-Party Filters

You've already seen that Paint Shop Pro includes many special effects for you, but additionally, there are hundreds of third-party filters, also called plug-ins, that you can use with Paint Shop Pro. Some are quite pricey whereas others are free. Look around on the Internet, and I think you'll be quite pleased with what you find. Whether you choose Flaming Pear's Blade Pro, Kai's Power Tools, Alien Skin's Eye Candy, or one of the hundreds of others, you'll find unique special effects in each application.

Most third-party filters are compatible with Paint Shop Pro and typically have .8bf as the filename extension, such as swirleypop.8bf or bubblejets.8bf. The .8bf extension is not, however, a requirement in Paint Shop Pro 8.

NOTE

Plug-ins from Adobe Photoshop work if they are from version 5.5 or earlier. Typically, plug-ins from Adobe Photoshop versions 6 or 7 are not compatible with Paint Shop Pro 8.

Installing Third-Party Filters

Each filter manufacturer provides a method and directions to install its filters. When you install the filters, make a note of their file location because you need to tell Paint Shop Pro where, on your computer, you keep those filters. Paint Shop Pro stores instructions to file locations in its Preferences area.

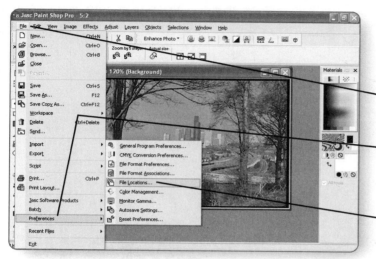

1. Click on **File**. The File menu will appear.

2. Click on **Preferences**. The Preferences submenu menu will appear.

3. Click on **File Locations**. The File Locations dialog box will open.

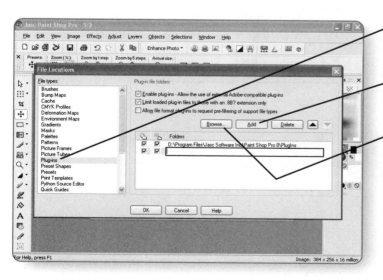

4. Click on **Plug-ins**. A list of plug-in file locations will appear.

5. Click on **Add**. A new blank line will appear.

6. Click on **Browse**. The Browse for Folder dialog box will open.

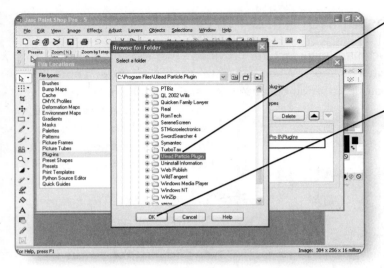

7. Locate and click on the **folder** where the filters are stored. The folder name will be highlighted.

8. Click on **OK**. The file location will display.

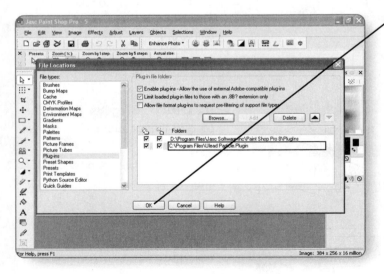

9. Click on **OK**. The File Locations dialog box will close.

Accessing Third-Party Filters

After you've installed the filter and told Paint Shop Pro where to find the filters, new menu choices automatically appear that allow you to access the plug-ins.

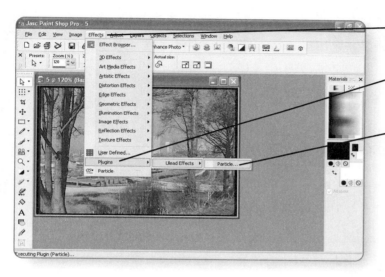

1. **Click** on **Effects**. The Effects menu will appear.

2. **Click** on **Plugins**. The Plugins submenu will appear.

3. **Click** on the **plug-in** you want to use. The filter will apply to your image, or a dialog box might appear prompting you for more options.

TIP

See Appendix B, "Exploring Useful Web Sites," for some third-party filter sites.

Part II Review Questions

1. Do raster layers or vector layers contain pixel-based information? *See "Creating Layers" in Chapter 9.*

2. What is opacity? *See "Viewing Layers" in Chapter 9.*

3. What type of layer is always lowest in a stack of layers? *See "Promoting the Background Layer" in Chapter 9.*

4. Does the black portion of a mask cover or uncover the layer? *See "Creating a Simple Mask" in Chapter 10.*

5. Can you remove a mask from layers that have been flattened? *See "Removing a Mask" in Chapter 10.*

6. Can you adjust the size of a picture tube before you paint with it? *See "Modifying Picture Tube Settings" in Chapter 11.*

7. Name two of the four rules that you must follow when creating Paint Shop Pro tubes. *See "Saving New Picture Tubes" in Chapter 11.*

8. Will effects work on non-raster images? *See "Discovering Effects" in Chapter 12.*

9. What happens when you click the Randomize button in an Effect dialog box? *See "Discovering the Randomize Buttons" in Chapter 12.*

10. What is another name for a third-party effect filter? *See "Working with Third-Party Filters" in Chapter 12.*

PART III

Using Vector Graphics and Text

13

Constructing Vector Objects

Up to this point, you've worked primarily with raster objects, which use pixels to store image information. Vector objects, the other type of Paint Shop Pro object, are stored as separate items with information about each item's position, starting and ending points, width, color, and curve information. Working with vector objects gives you more flexibility in moving and editing the individual objects.

You'll find vector objects especially useful when you're designing logos and making line drawings. In this chapter, you'll learn how to

- Create vector layers
- Draw vector shapes
- Draw vector lines

Creating a Vector Layer

An image can contain both raster objects and vector objects; however, vector objects and raster objects cannot be mixed on a layer. Vector objects must be on a vector layer. If you try to create a vector object on a raster layer, Paint Shop Pro automatically creates a vector layer for you. If the current layer is already a vector layer, Paint Shop Pro adds the new object to the current layer. Paint Shop Pro files can have many vector layers, and each layer can have many objects.

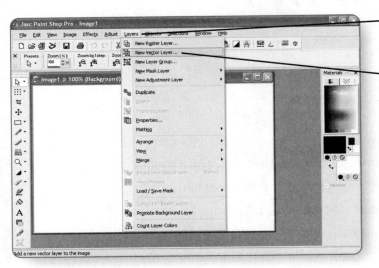

1. **Click** on **Layers**. The Layers menu will appear.

2. **Click** on **New Vector Layer**. The New Vector Layer dialog box will open.

The New Vector Layer dialog box is the same for both vector and raster layers.

TIP

You can bypass the New Vector Layer dialog box by holding down the Shift key while you select New Vector Layer.

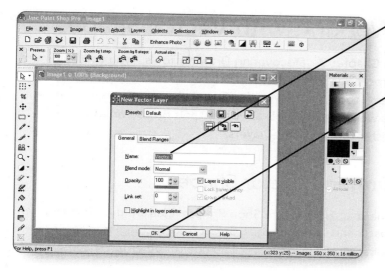

3. **Enter** a **name** for the layer. The layer name will help you identify each vector layer.

4. **Click** on **OK**. The New Vector Layer dialog box will close.

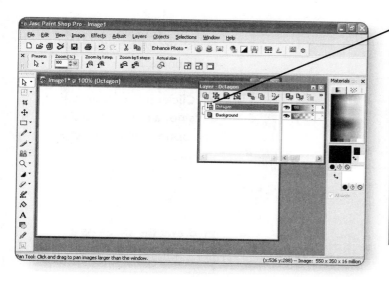

The Layer palette will display the vector icon to the left of a vector layer button.

TIP

Through the Layers menu, you can convert a vector layer to a raster layer, but you cannot convert a raster layer to a vector layer.

Working with Vector Shapes

In Chapter 3, "Discovering Drawing Tools," you used the Preset Shape and Pen tools to create raster objects. These same tools, along with the Text tool, can create vector objects as well. Use the tools as vector tools on vector layers and raster tools on raster layers.

Drawing Vector Shapes

The shapes that Paint Shop Pro provides are the same for both raster and vector images. Select from rectangles, ellipses, stars, curved arrows, and a number of other fun shapes.

1. **Click** on the **Preset Shapes tool**. The Tool Options palette will display preset shape options.

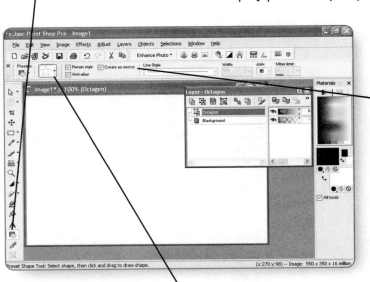

The mouse pointer turns into crosshairs with a square and circle under it.

2. **Click** on **Create as vector** if it's not already checked. The option will be selected.

NOTE

If Create as vector is not checked, Paint Shop Pro draws the shape as a raster object.

---

3. **Click** the **Tool Selection button**. A list of preset shape tools will appear.

The rectangle and other shapes are available to assist you in drawing with accuracy.

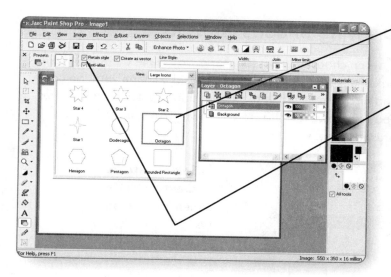

4. Click on a **shape**. The shape will appear in the tool selection button.

For now, leave Retain style checked. We'll look at changing the style later in this chapter.

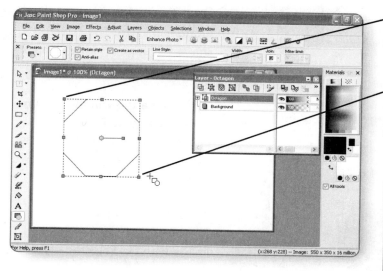

5. Position the **mouse** at the point you want the rectangle to begin.

6. Click and **drag** the **mouse** diagonally on the image. An outline of the rectangle will appear as you draw.

TIP

Hold down the Shift key to constrain your drawing to a perfect circle, square, or other shape.

7. Release the **mouse button**. The rectangle will appear on the image with handles surrounding it, indicating that the object is selected.

Drawing Shapes with Style

If, when choosing a preset shape, you leave the Retain style box checked, Paint Shop Pro draws the shape with the color and fill as displayed in the Tool Options palette sample box. You can, however, choose your own stroke and fill for a preset shape.

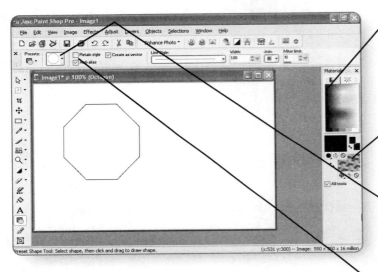

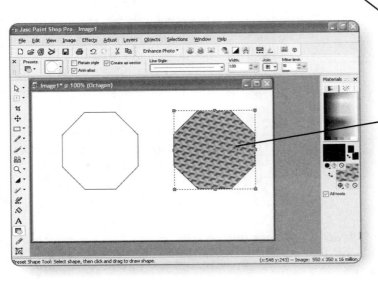

1. **Select** a **stroke color**, **gradient**, or **pattern**. Remember that stroke style is the outline of the object, not the interior.

2. **Select** a **fill color**, **gradient**, or **pattern**. The fill style is the interior of an object.

3. **Select** a **shape** from the Tool Options palette. The selected shape will appear in the sample box.

4. **Remove** the √ in the **Retain style check box**. Removing the √ tells Paint Shop Pro to use the colors and styles you selected in steps 1 and 2.

5. **Draw** the **object** as usual. The object will appear on the image with the selected styles.

Adding Vector Lines

In Chapter 3, "Discovering Drawing Tools," you learned how to use the Pen tool to draw various types of lines; however, editing the lines after drawing them is difficult when they are raster lines. When lines are drawn as vector objects, you can easily move and edit them without affecting the rest of the image objects.

Drawing Vector Lines

You draw vector lines just like you draw raster lines. However, after you complete a vector line, handles remain at the ends of the lines awaiting your next movement. You can create continuous lines or single lines. As with raster lines, you need to click the New button when you want to create a new series of lines.

1. Click on the **Pen tool**. The mouse pointer will display a black arrowhead with a cross below it.

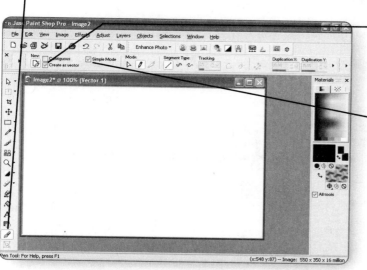

2. Click on **Create as vector** if it's not already checked. A √ will appear in the box when the option is selected.

3. Click on **Simple Mode**. The option will be selected.

TIP

If you like to draw freehand, you might want to check into using an electronic pressure-sensitive drawing tablet, which lets you draw with better precision. Paint Shop Pro supports most tablets on the market today.

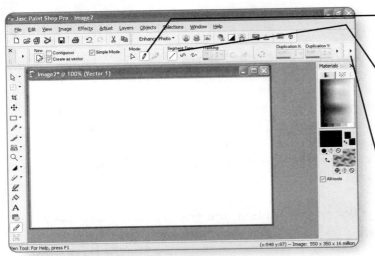

4. Click on **Drawing Mode**. The option will be selected.

5. Click on a **Segment Type**. You can draw single line segments, point-to-point lines, or freehand lines.

6. Click on the **Tool Options arrow**. More Tool Options choices will appear.

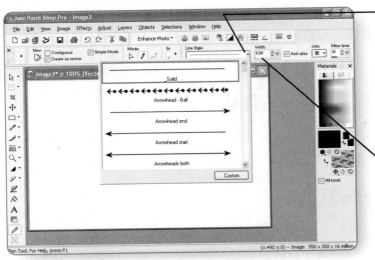

7. Click on the **Line Style drop-down box**. A selection of line styles will appear.

8. Click on a **line style**. The selected line style will appear in the Line Style box.

9. Enter a **line thickness value** in the **Width box**. The higher the value, the heavier the line.

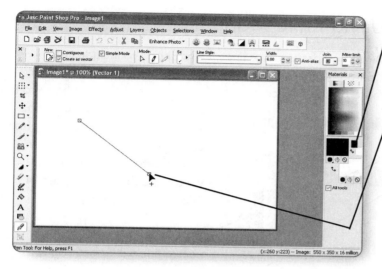

10. **Select** a **foreground stroke color**. The selected color will appear in the first color box.

11. **Click** and **drag** the **mouse** along the path you want the line to take. Paint Shop Pro will draw an outline to show the width of the line.

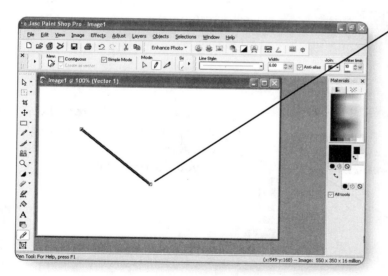

12. **Release** the **mouse button**. Paint Shop Pro will draw the line based on the selected options. Selection handles will appear at each end of the line.

Using Knife Mode

When you draw vector lines, Paint Shop Pro includes a Contour Knife tool that allows you to slice a line into two or more pieces. The contour knife tool is new to Paint Shop Pro 8.

Using the Contour Knife is one way to modify a vector line after you've drawn it. You will learn lots of different ways to edit vector graphics in Chapter 14, "Editing Vector Graphics."

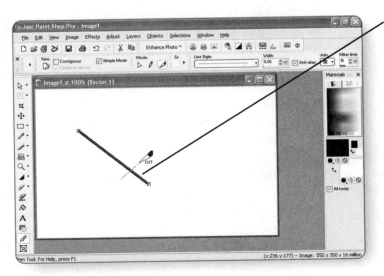

1. **Draw** a **vector line**. The vector line will appear on the canvas.

2. **Click** on **Knife mode**. The mouse pointer will appear as a knife blade.

3. **Click** and **drag across** the **line** where you want to make a cut. A temporary line will appear as you make the cut.

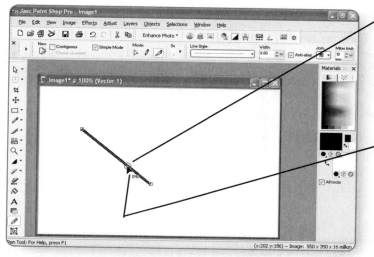

4. Release the **mouse button**. The temporary line will disappear and a circle marker will appear on the image. The circle marker marks the end of the lines.

5. Position the **mouse pointer** over the circle marker. The mouse pointer will appear with a black arrowhead and the word *END*.

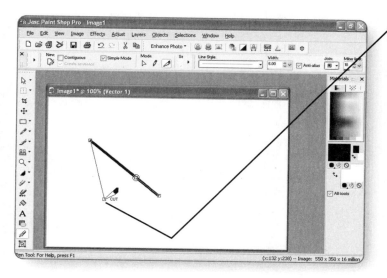

6. Click and **drag** from the **circle marker** to a different location on the canvas. A thin black line will appear representing a split segment of the original line.

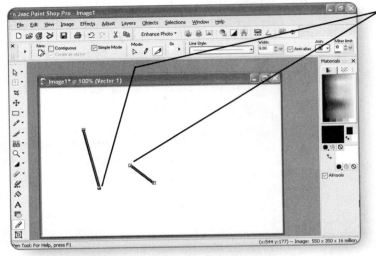

7. Release the **mouse button**. The line will split into two segments, and one of the lines will rotate and resize to the new position.

14

Editing Vector Graphics

Paint Shop Pro files can have many vector layers, and each layer can have many objects. Because vector objects are independent elements, you can modify, move, reshape, or delete any of them without affecting the rest of the image objects. In this chapter, you'll learn how to

- Select vector objects
- Move, resize, rotate, and flip vector objects
- Delete vector objects
- Edit vector nodes
- Arrange, align, and distribute space between objects
- Convert vector objects to raster images

Selecting Vector Objects

Before you can modify a vector object, the object(s) must be selected. Only objects on the active layer can be selected at any one time. You cannot select objects that exist on different layers at the same time.

Selecting with the Vector Selector

Paint Shop Pro provides a tool called the Object Selector for working with vector objects. The Object Selector is available only when the current active layer is a vector layer.

Selecting Individual Objects

Use the Object Selector to choose which objects you want selected.

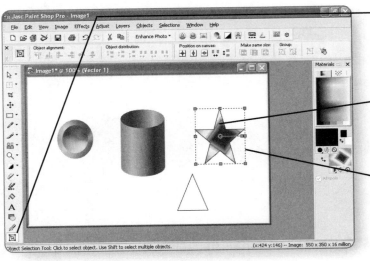

1. Click on the **Object Selector**. The mouse pointer will turn into a white cross with a boxed arrowhead beside it.

2. Click on the **object**. Selection handles and a box will appear around the object.

If the object is filled in the center, you can click anywhere on the object to select it; however, if the object has no fill, you have to smile, hold your mouth just right, and click on the outline of the image.

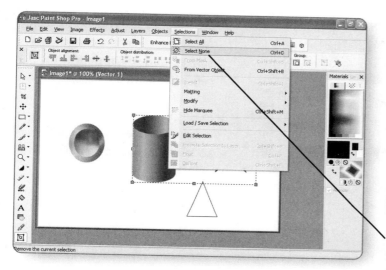

TIP

Hold down the Shift key and click to select additional objects (the mouse pointer will display a plus sign), or hold down the Ctrl key and click to deselect objects (the mouse pointer will display a minus sign).

To deselect all objects, choose Selections, Select None or press Ctrl+D.

Drawing Around Objects

Another method of selecting objects with the Object Selector tool is to draw a boundary box around the objects you want to select. Paint Shop Pro selects all objects that are *completely* surrounded by the boundary box.

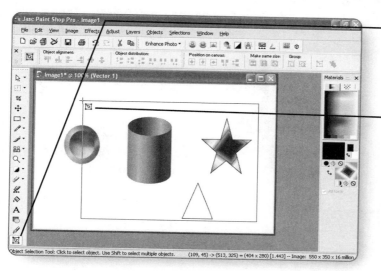

1. Click on the **Object Selector**. The mouse pointer will turn into a white cross with a boxed arrowhead beside it.

2. Click and **drag** the **mouse** to surround the objects you want to select. A black border will surround the perimeter of the objects.

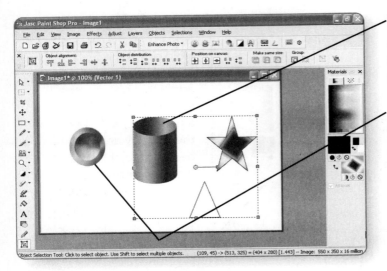

3. Release the **mouse button**. All objects that are completely surrounded will appear with selection handles.

In this example, the button wasn't completely surrounded, so it isn't included in the selection.

Selecting in the Layer Palette

An optional method to select objects is from the Layer palette.

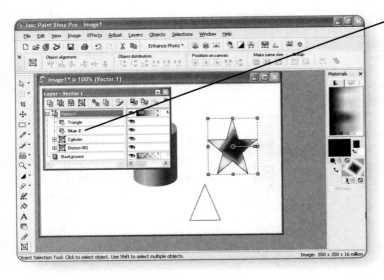

1. Click on the **object name** on the Layer palette. The object will become selected. Selected items will appear on the Layer palette in a bold font.

TIP

If you can't see the objects, click on the plus sign next to the layer name. The layer will expand to display all objects.

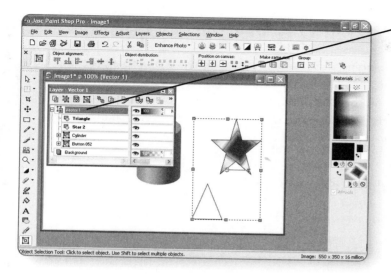

2. If desired, **hold** down the **Shift key** and **click** on additional **layer objects**.

To deselect objects, choose Selections, Select None.

Deleting a Vector Object

You can easily delete unwanted objects from your image.

1. Select the **object** you want to delete. The object will appear with selection handles.

2. Press the **Delete key**. The object will disappear.

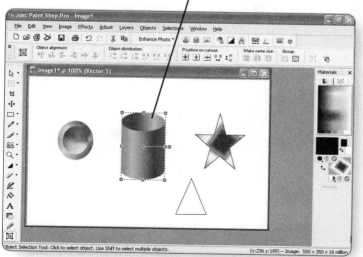

TIP

Don't forget that if you make a mistake and delete the wrong object, you can click the Undo button.

Resizing a Vector Object

Changing the size of a vector object is a simple process. You can change the object size from a selected side, in an equal conformed amount, or you can skew or distort the object. Additionally, if you created several objects, you can make them equal in size.

Manually Resizing

You use your mouse to change the size of a vector object.

1. Select the **object** you want to resize. The object will appear with selection handles.

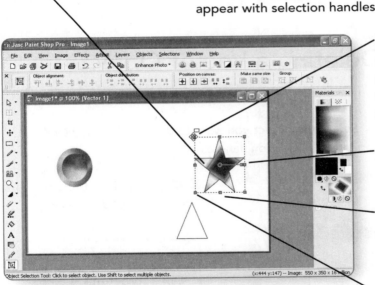

2. Place the **mouse pointer** over one of the **handles**. The mouse pointer will turn into a white two- or four-headed arrow.

- Use the handle on either side of the object to resize the width of the object.

- Use the handle at the top or bottom of the object to resize the height of the object.

- Use any corner handle to resize both width and height at the same time.

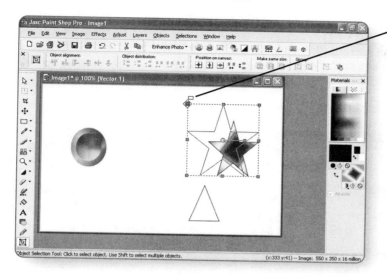

3. **Click** and **drag** a **handle**. An outline of the object will indicate the new size.

TIP

Use the right mouse button with a corner handle to maintain height to width proportions.

---

4. **Release** the **mouse button**. The object will retain the new size.

Deforming a Vector Object

When you deform an image, you distort its original shape. Technically, resizing an image is a form of deforming an image, but other types of deformation include Skew, Distort Change Perspective, and Shear. You can use any of these types of deformation with vector shapes, lines, and vector text objects.

1. **Select** the **object** you want to resize. The object will appear with selection handles.

2. **Position** the **mouse** over an image handle. Whether you select a corner handle or a side or top handle depends on how you want to deform the object.

Deforming an object is similar to resizing it, but you need to hold down one or more additional keys before dragging a selection handle.

- To change the image perspective, hold down the Ctrl key and drag a corner handle.

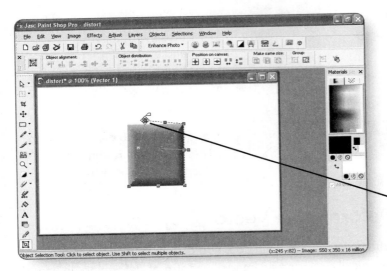

- To skew the image, hold down the Shift key and drag a corner handle.

- To distort the image, hold down the Ctrl and Shift keys and drag a corner handle.

- To shear the image, hold down the Shift key and drag a side or top handle.

3. Hold the appropriate **key** and **drag** the selection **handle** until the selected object outline displays the shape you want.

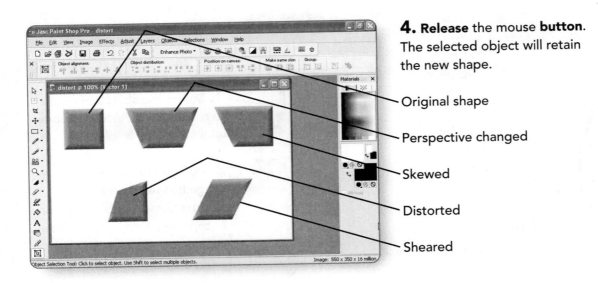

4. Release the mouse **button**. The selected object will retain the new shape.

Original shape

Perspective changed

Skewed

Distorted

Sheared

Making Objects the Same Size

If you have multiple objects and want them to be the same size, Paint Shop Pro includes a tool to quickly resize them. You can make the objects the same height, the same width, or both the same height and width.

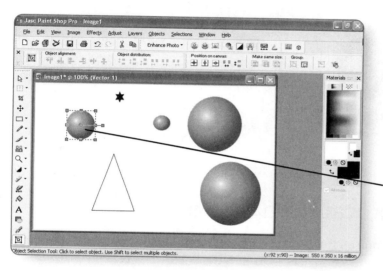

The secret to working with most multiple object features is the order of selection. The object you select *first* is considered the "base" object—the one the others will adjust to. This applies to alignment, spacing, and resizing features.

1. Select the **object** you want the objects to imitate in size. The object will be selected.

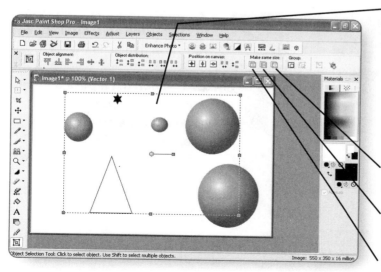

2. Hold down the **Shift key** and **click** on the **objects** you want to resize. A selection box will surround the selected objects.

3. Click on a **resize button** from Make same size buttons on the Tools Options palette.

Make the selected objects the same width and height.

Make the selected objects the same height.

Make the selected objects the same width.

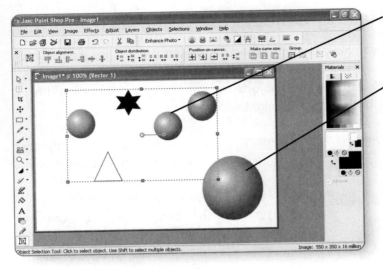

The selected objects will be uniform in size to the first selected object.

This sphere did not resize because it was not included in the selection.

Rotating a Vector Object

You can freely rotate any vector object to any angle by using the rotation handle to turn the vector object.

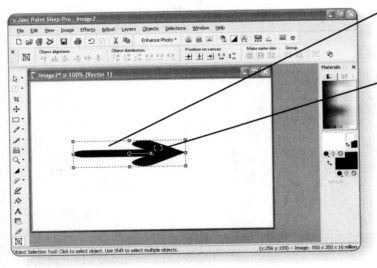

1. Select the **object** you want to rotate. The object will appear with selection handles.

2. Position the **mouse pointer** over the **rotation handle** (a small square box) in the selected object. The mouse pointer will turn into two curved arrows.

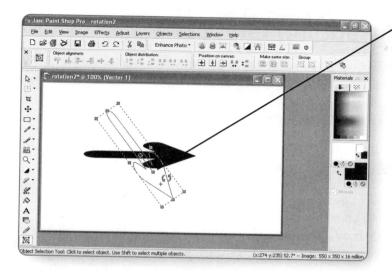

3. Click and **drag** the **rotation handle**. An outline of the image rotation will appear.

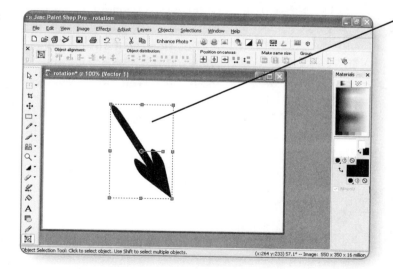

4. Release the **mouse button**. The image will move to the new rotation.

Arranging Objects

Paint Shop Pro includes several handy features for working with positioning objects. You'll find features to line up object edges, to create equal spaces between objects, to make objects equal in size, and even to combine multiple objects into one.

Moving a Vector Object

If an object is not in the position you require, move it easily by using your mouse. Moving vector objects is a little different from moving raster objects. With raster objects, you use the mover tool, but with vector objects, you don't use the mover tool; instead you simply use your mouse.

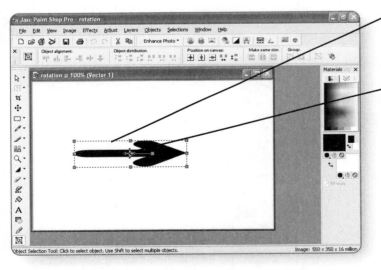

1. **Select** the **object** you want to move. The object will appear with selection handles.

2. **Position** the mouse in the center of the object, over the move circle. The mouse pointer will turn into a black four-headed arrow.

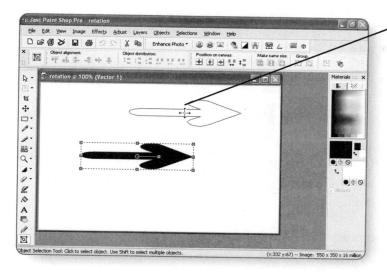

3. Click and **drag** the **object** to the new position. An outline of the object will indicate the move location.

4. Release the **mouse button**. The object will move to the new position.

Reordering Objects

When a vector layer has multiple objects, the elements are stacked according to their order in the Layer palette. The element at the top of the list is at the top of the other elements as well, making it visible in front of all other objects on that layer. The object at the bottom of the layer is at the bottom of the stack and might appear to be behind the other objects.

1. Select the **object** you want to reorder. Selection handles will appear around the object.

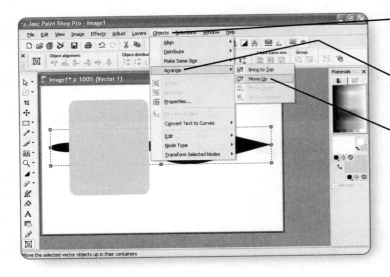

2. Click on **Objects**. The Objects menu will appear.

3. Click on **Arrange**. The Arrange submenu will appear.

4. Click an arrangement **option**. The selected object will move to the new order in the stack of objects.

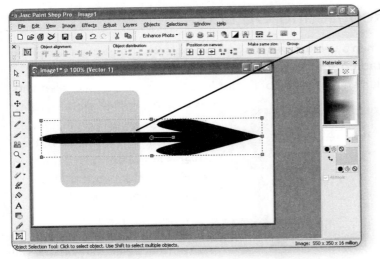

In this example, the black arrow moved on top of the red box.

Aligning Objects Together

Suppose that you have two or more objects and you want them to be at the same vertical position on the image, or you want one (or more) of the objects to be centered in another. Well, you could use your mouse to move the objects, but sometimes it can be difficult to visually align them. Instead, let the alignment feature do the guesswork for you.

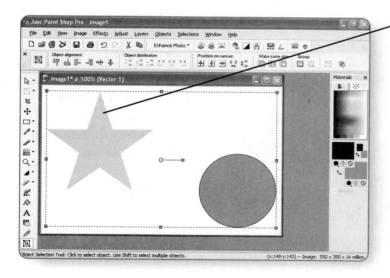

Remember: The secret is in the order in which you select the objects. The first selected object is the one that the other selected objects will match up to.

1. Select the **object** you want the others to line up to. Selection handles will appear around the selected object.

2. Hold down the **Shift key** and **select** the remaining **objects** you want to line up to the first object. A selection box will appear around the selected objects.

In this example, to line up the star even with the circle, select the circle first and then select the star.

3. Select an **alignment option** from the Tools Options palette. The following list explains each option:

- **Align Top.** All selected objects will match up to the top edge of the first selected object.

- **Align Bottom.** All selected objects will match up to the bottom edge of the first selected object.

- **Align Left.** All selected objects will match up to the left edge of the first selected object.

- **Align Right.** All selected objects will match up to the right edge of the first selected object.

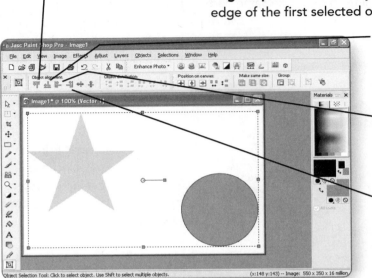

- **Align Vertical Center.** All selected objects will match up vertically to the center of the first selected object.

- **Align Horizontal Center.** All selected objects will match up horizontally to the center of the first selected object.

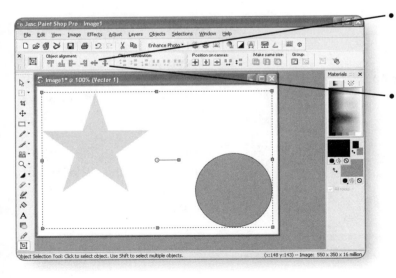

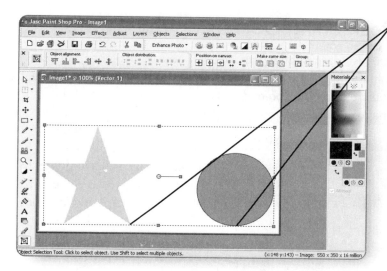

The Objects will align together. In this example, the bottom edges of the star and circle align.

TIP

You can also make alignment selections through the Objects menu.

Some alignment choices might take two steps. In this example, to get the star in the center of the circle, the alignment is accomplished in two steps. First they were aligned Vertical Center, and then they were aligned Horizontal Center.

Positioning Objects on the Canvas

You just learned how you can align objects together, but you can also align one or more object to the canvas. For example, you created a button and you need it in the middle of the image. You could turn on the ruler and the grid and visually move the button until it looks like it is in the center of the canvas, but by using the Align to canvas feature, you only need to make a mouse click and let Paint Shop Pro do the work for you.

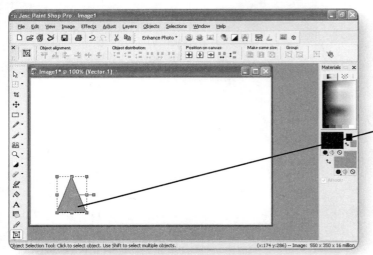

1. Select the **object(s)** you want to line up. Selection handles will appear around the selected objects.

2. Click on an **option** from the Position on canvas buttons:

- **Center on Canvas.** Moves all selected objects to the exact center of the canvas.

- **Horizontal Center in Canvas.** Moves all selected objects horizontally in the center of the canvas, but not vertically center.

- **Vertical Center in Canvas.** Moves all selected objects vertically to the center of the canvas but not horizontally center.

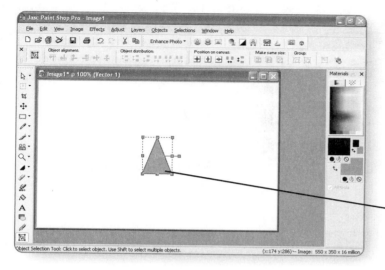

- **Space Evenly Horizontal.** Places all selected objects so that there is equal horizontal space between the canvas.

- **Space Evenly Vertical.** Places all selected objects so that there is equal vertical space between the top and bottom of the canvas.

The triangle is centered on the canvas.

Distributing Space Between Objects

Any time you have multiple objects, Paint Shop Pro can distribute the space between the objects evenly, either horizontally or vertically.

At least three objects should be selected to distribute space evenly. If you choose to distribute evenly three or more objects horizontally, the objects that are closest to the left and right boundaries of the group become the two target objects. When you distribute evenly three or more objects vertically, the objects that are closest to the top and bottom of the group boundaries become the target objects. The distance between these target objects determines the spacing of the objects between them.

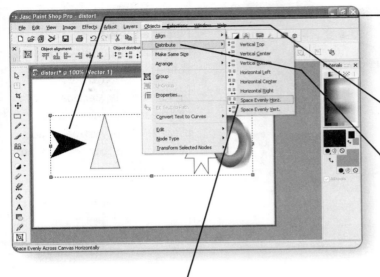

1. Select the **objects** you want to distribute. The objects will appear in a group surrounded by selection handles.

2. Click on **Objects**. The Objects menu will appear.

3. Click on **Distribute**. The Distribute submenu menu will appear.

4. Click on an **alignment option**. There are a number of ways to distribute space evenly:

- **Distribute Vertical Top.** Spaces objects evenly between the top edges of the top and bottom targets.

- **Distribute Vertical Center.** Spaces objects evenly between the centers of the top and bottom targets.

- **Distribute Vertical Bottom.** Spaces objects evenly between the bottom edges of the top and bottom targets.

- **Distribute Horizontal Left.** Spaces objects evenly between the left edges of the left and right targets.

- **Distribute Horizontal Center.** Spaces objects evenly between the centers of the left and right targets.

- **Distribute Horizontal Right.** Spaces objects evenly between the right edges of the left and right targets.

- **Space Evenly Horizontal.** Divides horizontal space on the canvas equally between all selected objects.

- **Space Evenly Vertical.** Divides vertical space on the canvas equally between all selected objects.

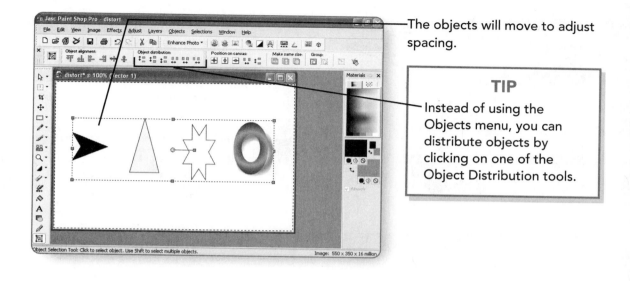

The objects will move to adjust spacing.

TIP

Instead of using the Objects menu, you can distribute objects by clicking on one of the Object Distribution tools.

Grouping Multiple Objects

Grouping multiple objects is like linking the objects for easier manipulation. Grouped objects can be ungrouped at any time. When you select multiple objects, Paint Shop Pro treats them as a temporary group but ungroups the objects when you deselect the object. Using the grouping feature, however, keeps them grouped together unless you ungroup them.

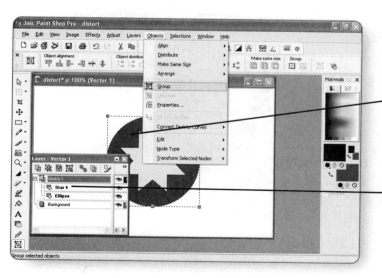

1. Select the **objects** you want to group together. Selection handles appear around the objects.

The objects are listed independently in the Layer palette.

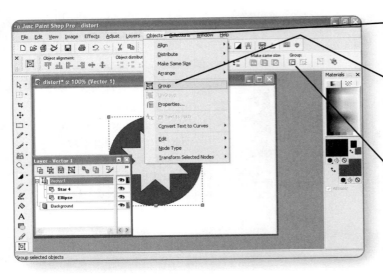

2. Click on **Objects**. The Objects menu will appear.

3. Click on **Group**. The multiple objects are melded into a single selected object.

TIP

Optionally, click on the Group button.

Only a single object appears in the Layer palette.

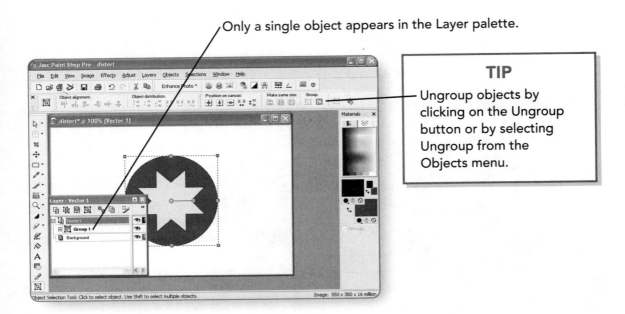

TIP

Ungroup objects by clicking on the Ungroup button or by selecting Ungroup from the Objects menu.

Altering Vector Properties

Even after you create a vector object, you can easily change its line style, color, style, thickness, and other properties.

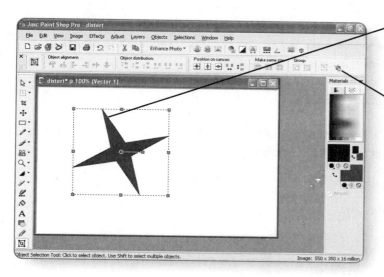

1. Select the **object** you want to modify. The object will appear with selection handles.

2. Click on the **Properties button**. The Vector Properties dialog box will open.

TIP

Optionally, right-click on the object and from the shortcut menu, selected Properties.

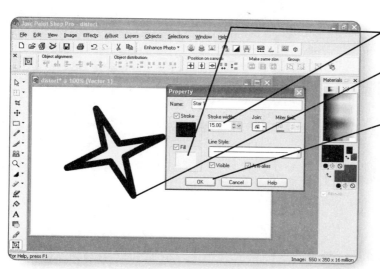

3. Modify any desired **options**.

The changes reflect on the object as you make them.

4. Click on **OK**. The Vector Properties dialog box will close.

NOTE

If you have multiple objects selected, all objects take on the property change.

Naming a Vector Object

As you place your objects on a layer, you might find it helpful to give the individual object a name to help you easily identify each object. When you create the object, Paint Shop Pro assigns a name that corresponds to the shape, such as ellipse, rectangle, or star, but you can easily rename the object to something more to your liking.

Default names as displayed on the Layer palette.

1. Select the **object** you want to rename. Selection handles will appear around the selected object.

2. Click on the **Properties button**. The Property dialog box will open.

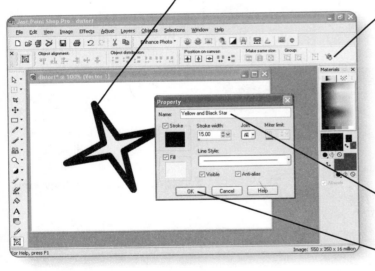

> ### NOTE
> You can only rename one object at a time.

3. Type a new **name** for the object in the **Name box**.

4. Click on **OK**. The Property dialog box will close.

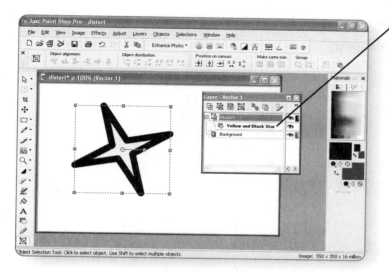

The Layer palette will reflect the object's new name.

Editing Nodes

A handy feature when you're working with vector graphics is the ability to create new shapes from an existing vector object. Each vector graphic has a form of control point called a *node* stored along the outline or path of the object. By adjusting the nodes, you change the shape of the vector graphic. Control the overall shape of an object by using Paint Shop Pro's Node Editing feature available from the Pen tool.

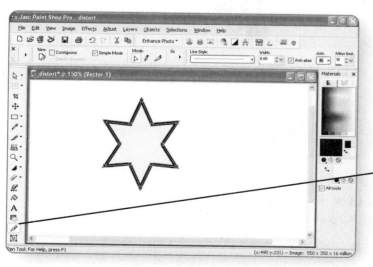

1. Select the **object** you want to edit. Selection handles will appear around the object.

2. Click on the **Pen tool**.

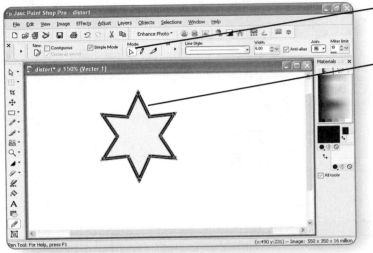

Paint Shop Pro automatically selects the Edit Mode button.

Nodes boxes surround the image at and between each corner of the object.

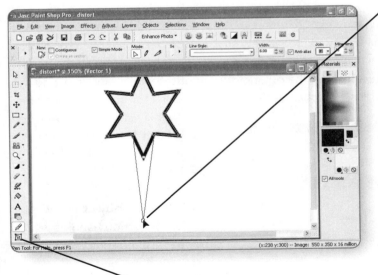

3. Click and **drag** a **node** to a different area. The node stretches as you drag the mouse, thereby reshaping the image.

4. Click the **Object Selection tool** to close Edit mode and return to vector object selection.

Converting Vector Objects to Raster

The main drawback to vector objects is that you cannot apply effects and filters to vector images. Don't give up hope, though! Paint Shop Pro includes a feature to convert vector layers with all its objects to raster objects on a raster layer. From there, you can apply effects.

Another reason to convert a vector image to raster is file size. A raster file might be smaller than a vector file if the image has several vectors and many areas of uniform color.

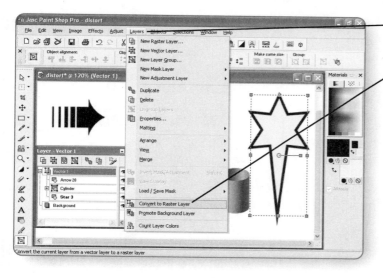

1. **Click** on **Layers**. The Layers menu will appear.

2. **Click** on **Convert to Raster Layer**. The vector layer and all its vector objects will become a raster layer with raster objects.

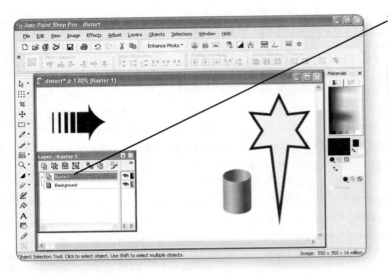

The Layer Palette reflects the change to a raster layer.

NOTE

If you save the image as a .gif, a .jpeg, or any format other than .psp, Paint Shop Pro automatically converts the image to a raster image.

15

Generating Text

We've been told that a picture is worth a thousand words, and Paint Shop Pro has certainly proved that statement to be true over and over. However, sometimes you just *have* to spell it out. You can create text with Paint Shop Pro's text feature. In this chapter, you'll learn how to

- Create text objects
- Work with the Text Entry dialog box
- Edit text
- Change the appearance of text
- Move or resize a text object

Entering Text

You use the Text tool to create text in Paint Shop Pro. As with the other tools you've used so far, when you select the Text tool, you will have additional options in which you determine items such as font, size, style, alignment, kerning, and leading as well as deciding what method you want Paint Shop Pro to use when placing the text on your image.

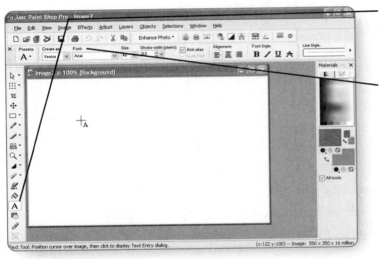

1. Click on the **Text tool**. The mouse pointer will resemble a cross with the letter A beside it.

The Tools Options palette will display options for working with text.

Selecting a Text Type

Paint Shop Pro provides three types of text: vector, floating, or selection. The type you choose determines what kind of editing you can do. The text object type cannot be changed after the text object appears on the image. Paint Shop Pro places vector text on a vector layer and selection text on a background or raster layer. Floating text is placed on a floating layer above a background or raster layer.

1. Click the **Create as arrow**. A list of text types will appear.

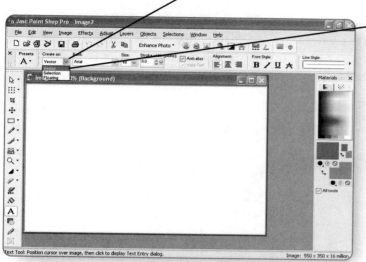

2. Click a text **type**. The option you select will appear in the Create as box.

- **Vector.** Creates the text as a vector object and adds a new vector layer, if necessary. Remember that vector objects are easily moved or edited, but effects cannot be added.

- **Floating.** Creates the text as a selection that floats above the current layer. The text is moveable and you can apply effects, but you can't modify either the text or the style. After effects are applied, you can "defloat" the text, which places it on the next lowest raster layer. After you place the text on the raster layer, you cannot move it easily.

- **Selection.** Creates the text as an empty selection on the current layer. You cannot move or edit the text without leaving behind the background color, although you can apply a few effects to the text.

TIP

You will probably find it most practical to create the text as vector text, until you are absolutely sure you are finished with the placement and appearance of the object. You can then convert the vector layer to a raster layer and apply desired effects.

Choosing Basic Text Options

Later in the chapter, in the section titled "Editing Text," you will see where you can change text options after you create the text object, but you will find it much easier to select the options prior to creating the actual text.

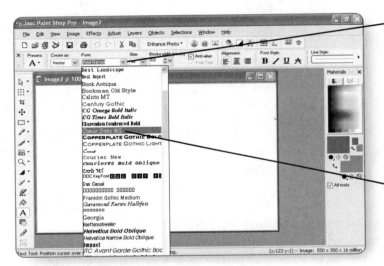

1. **Click** on the **Font list box**. A list of available fonts will appear.

NOTE

Your fonts might vary from the ones shown here.

2. **Click** on a **font**. You can use any font that is installed on your computer.

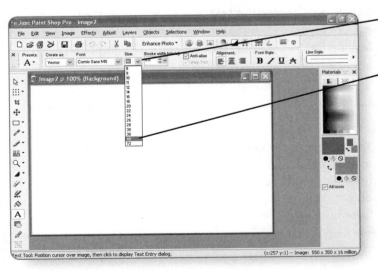

3. **Click** on the **Size list box**. A list of font sizes will appear.

4. **Click** on a font **size**. As a rule of measurement, when printing, a 72-point font is 1-inch tall, but when viewing text on a computer screen, the sizes vary depending on the screen resolution.

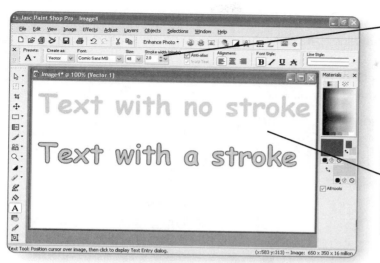

5. Optionally, **select** a **stroke width**. When you have a stroke width of 1 or greater, your text will take the stroke color and form a line around the text characters.

TIP

In this example, you see text with a stroke and text without a stroke.

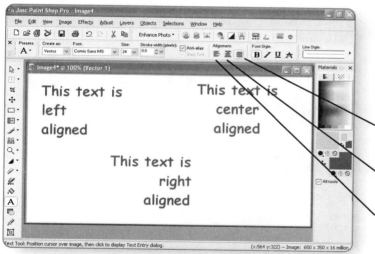

6. Click an **Alignment button**. Alignment determines how multiple lines of text line up with each other. Alignment choices include the following:

- **Right.** The right edges of each text line align together.

- **Center.** Each line centers to the one above it.

- **Left.** The left edges of each text line align together.

Paint Shop Pro provides text enhancements such as bolding, underlining, italic, or strikethrough on any portion of your text.

7. Click on one or more of the four available text **enhancements**. Enhancements include the following:

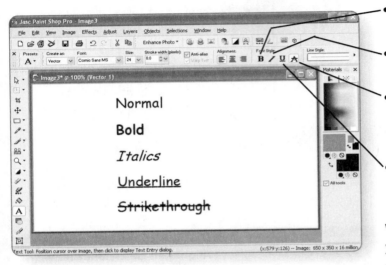

- **Bold**. Makes the text characters darker and thicker.

- *Italic*. Makes the text characters slightly slanted.

- ~~Strikethrough~~. Provides a line through the middle of each character and space.

- <u>Underline</u>. Provides a line under each character and space.

When you're working with text, you have the same materials options available as with other Paint Shop Pro objects. The stroke style is the color of the edge around the letters, whereas the fill style is the center or body of the letters.

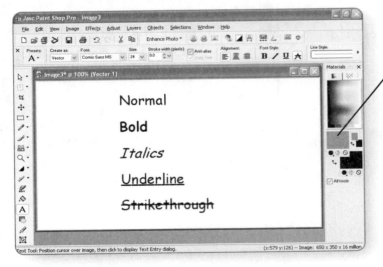

8. Select a **color**, **gradient**, or **pattern** for the stroke and fill of your text. The current selections will appear on the Materials swatches.

TIP

You cannot choose Null for both the stroke and fill. Choosing Null for the fill creates outlined text.

Setting Kerning and Leading Options

Two additional features that are available when you're working with text are kerning and leading. *Kerning* refers to the spacing between letters and *leading* (pronounced like *sledding* without the *s*) refers to the space between lines of text. Positive kerning or leading values increase the amount of space between adjacent characters (kerning) or lines (leading), whereas negative values decrease the amount of spacing.

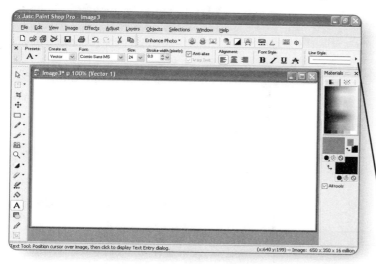

1. Click the Text Style **Options arrow**. Kerning and leading text options will appear.

In most cases, you can let Paint Shop Pro make the kerning decision by leaving Auto kern checked.

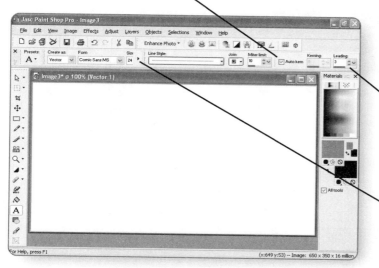

However, if you have multiple lines of text, you might want to adjust the leading.

2. Click on a **leading arrow**. Click on the up arrow (▲) to increase the space between the text lines or the down arrow (▼) to decrease the spacing.

3. Click the Text Format **Options arrow**. The Text Format Options Tool palette will reappear.

Typing Text

Now that you have set your options, you are ready to create the text. Paint Shop Pro provides a dialog box in which to type your text. However, unlike your use of a word processor, the text does not automatically wrap around to the next line. You need to tell Paint Shop Pro when you want the text to begin on a new line.

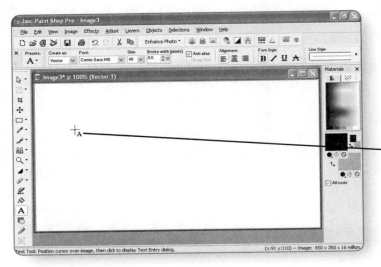

1. With the Text tool selected, **click** on the **canvas** where you want the text to appear. The Text Entry dialog box will open.

2. Type the **text** you want. The text will appear in the Enter text here box.

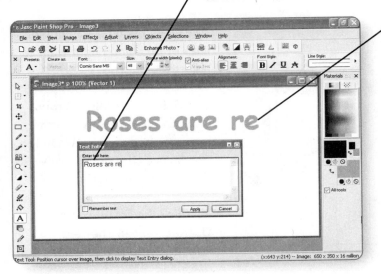

The formatted text will appear on the canvas as you type it.

3. Press Enter if you have more text to add under the first line. The insertion point will drop to the next line.

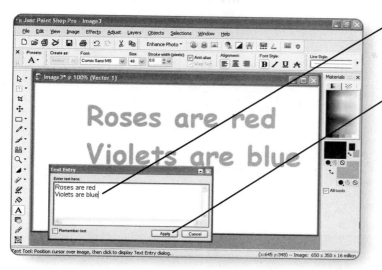

4. Type the **additional text.**
Add as many lines of text as you would like.

5. Click on **Apply**. The Text Entry box will close.

Editing Text

Suppose that after you created your text, you see a problem. Perhaps you misspelled a word, or you want a different font or style. Depending on the text type that you created, you might be able to edit the object.

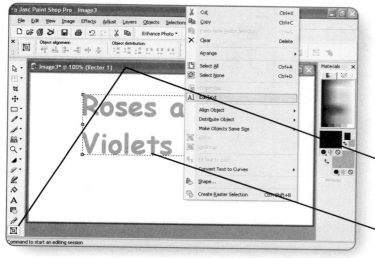

Modifying Vector Text

You can only modify the text on vector text type objects, not selection or floating text types.

1. Click on the **Vector Selection tool.** The tool will become selected.

2. Click on the **text object.** The text vector object will become selected.

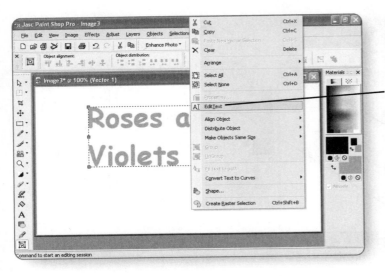

3. **Click** the **right mouse button** while over the selected text. A menu will appear.

4. **Click** on **Edit Text**. The Text Entry dialog box will open.

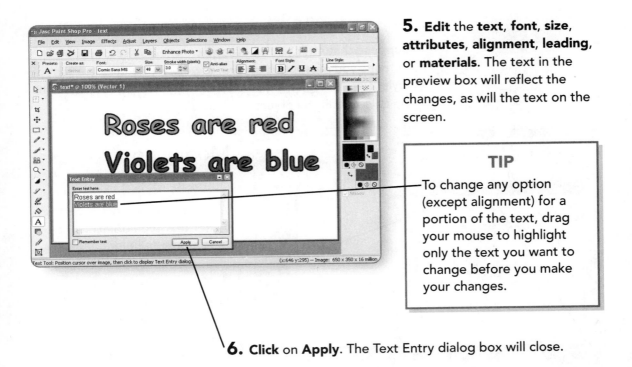

5. **Edit** the **text**, **font**, **size**, **attributes**, **alignment**, **leading**, or **materials**. The text in the preview box will reflect the changes, as will the text on the screen.

TIP

To change any option (except alignment) for a portion of the text, drag your mouse to highlight only the text you want to change before you make your changes.

6. **Click** on **Apply**. The Text Entry dialog box will close.

Resizing a Text Object

You can only resize vector type text. Resize vector text in the same manner that you resize any vector object.

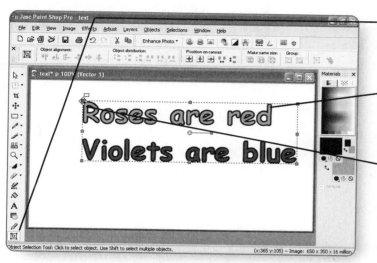

1. Click on the **Vector Selection tool**. The tool will become selected.

2. Click on the **text object**. The object will become selected.

3. Position the **mouse** over a resize handle. The mouse pointer will turn into a white four-headed arrow.

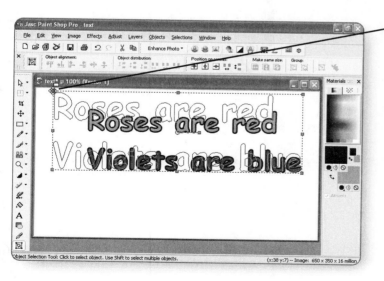

4. Click and **drag** any of the selection **handles**. An outline of the text will appear as you drag the handle.

5. Release the **mouse button**. The text object will remain at the new size.

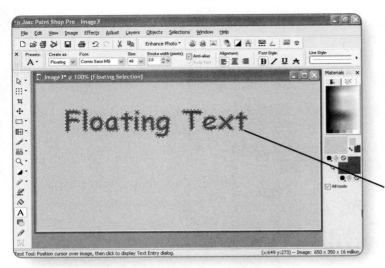

Floating Text

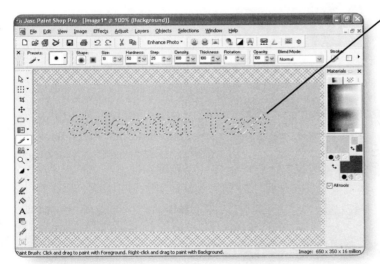

Selection Text

Changing Floating and Selection Styles

Although you cannot easily edit the font size or the actual text on floating or selection type text, you can edit the style with the Paint Brush tool.

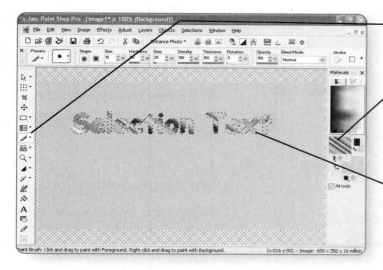

1. Click on the **Paint Brush tool**. The tool will become selected.

2. Select a foreground **color**, **gradient**, or **pattern**. The selection will appear in the Materials foreground swatch.

3. Paint over the **text**. Because the text is selected, the paint will not go over the boundaries of the selection. (See—you really *can* color within the lines!)

Moving Text

You can move all three text types—but with totally different results.

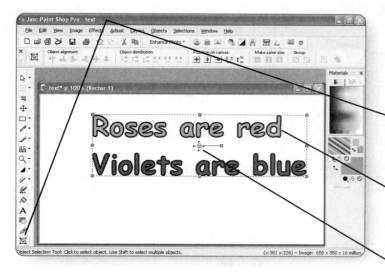

Moving Vector Text

Move vector text in the same manner as moving any vector object.

1. Click on the **Vector Selection tool**. The tool will become selected.

2. Click on the **vector text object**. The object will become selected.

3. Position the **mouse** over the center move box. The mouse pointer will turn into a four-headed arrow.

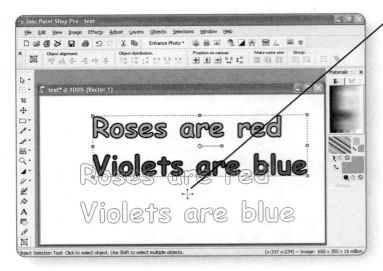

4. Click and **drag** the **text** to a new position. An outline of the text will appear.

5. Release the **mouse button**. The text will move to the new position.

Moving Floating Text

Floating text is raster-style text, but you can move it anywhere on the image as long as the text is still floating and is on a raster layer, not a background layer.

1. Click on the **Move tool**. The mouse pointer will resemble a four-headed arrow.

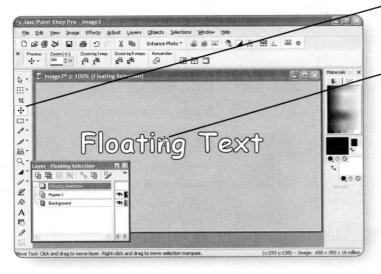

2. Position the **mouse** anywhere over the floating text object until the mouse pointer turns into a four-headed arrow.

3. Click and **drag** the **text** to a new position. The text will move as you drag the mouse.

4. Release the **mouse button**. The text will remain in the new position and will remain selected.

NOTE

If the floating text is on a background layer, Paint Shop Pro prompts you to promote it to a full raster layer.

Moving Selection Text

Moving selection text is quite different from moving the other two types of text. When you move selection text, the fill color remains underneath the moved selection. In fact, moving selection text just a tiny bit can give the effect of 3D text.

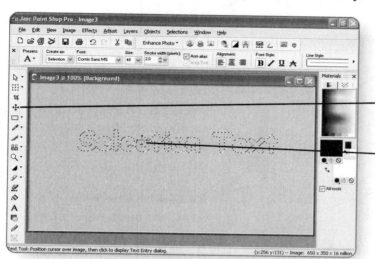

1. **Click** on the **Move tool**. The tool will become selected.

2. **Position** the **mouse pointer** over the text, making sure the mouse pointer is a four-headed arrow.

3. **Click** and **drag** the **text**. The area that is outlined by the marquee will move to the new location.

Notice that the selection fill color remains.

4. **Release** the **mouse button**. The selection will remain in the new position.

TIP

To deselect the selection text, choose Selections, Select None or press Ctrl+D.

Defloating Text

After you've placed the floating text where you want it, you'll need to defloat it to the next lowest raster layer.

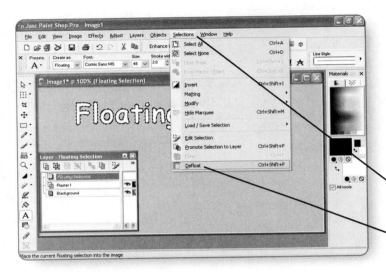

If you want special effects applied to the text only, apply the effect before you defloat it. After you defloat the text, unless you reselect the text, you cannot apply effects only to the text; the effects apply to the entire layer.

1. Click on **Selections**. The Selections menu will appear.

2. Click on **Defloat**. The text will no longer float above the layers; it will merge with a raster layer. The text will still be selected and surrounded by a marquee.

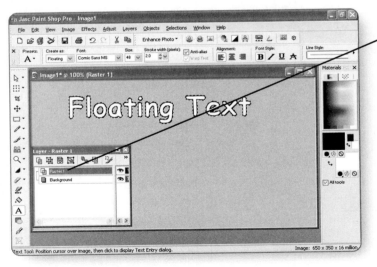

Notice that the Layer palette no longer displays *Floating Selection*.

TIP

To deselect the text, choose Selections, Select None or press Ctrl+D.

Deleting Text Objects

The method to delete text objects depends on the type of object.

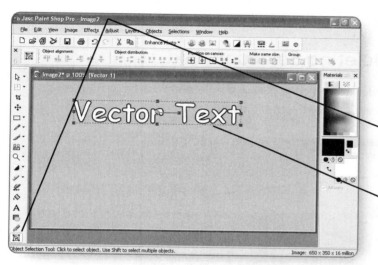

Deleting Vector Text

Delete vector text in the same manner that you would delete any vector object.

1. Click on the **Vector Selection tool**. The tool will become selected.

2. Click on the **text object**. The object will become selected.

3. Press the **Delete key**. Paint Shop Pro will delete the text object.

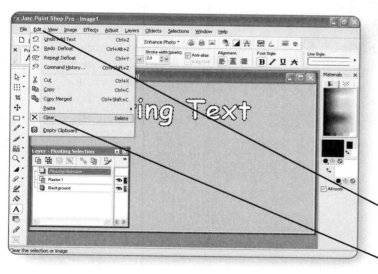

Deleting Floating Text

As long as the floating text is still floating, you can delete it easily. If the floating text is defloated, you'll need to paint over the area with a desired background color.

1. Click on **Edit**. The Edit menu will appear.

2. Click on **Clear**. The floating text will disappear.

TIP

If the floating text doesn't delete, make sure you're on the Floating Selection layer.

Deleting Selection Text

Deleting selection text is a little different because it isn't really a text object; it's a selection.

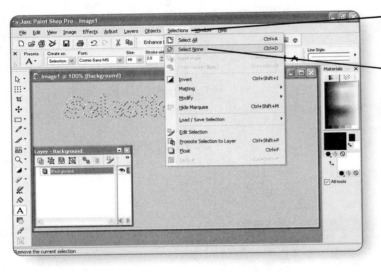

1. Click on **Selections**. The Selections menu will appear.

2. Click on **Select None**. The area that is outlined with the marquee will disappear.

This method works only if the selection text has not been painted or moved.

TIP

If the selection text has been painted or moved, deselect the text and then paint over the entire image with your desired background color.

16
Creating Text Effects

This chapter is a little different from the chapters you've seen so far. By following this book, you've learned how to work with objects, tubes, effects, and text. This chapter shows you how you can combine some of those Paint Shop Pro features along with specific options to create some spectacular text effects. Adding special effects to text objects is a lot of fun—you're limited only by your imagination! In this chapter, you'll learn how to

- Add special effects to text
- Color individual letters
- Use picture tubes to fill text
- Combine special effects
- Create text around shapes

Adding Bevels and Shadows

Give your gradient text a three-dimensional stenciled effect with a combination of the Inner Bevel effect and a Drop Shadow effect.

1. Click on the **Text tool**. The Text tool will become selected.

2. Select the text type as **Floating**.

3. Select a **font**.

4. Select a **font size**.

5. Click the **Background and Fill Materials swatch**. The Materials dialog box will open.

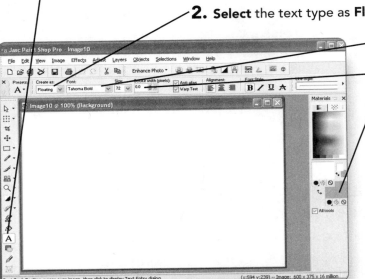

6. Click the **Gradient tab**. The Gradient tab will come to the front.

7. Click the **Gradient arrow**. A list of gradients will appear.

8. Select a **gradient**. In this example, a Metallic Silver gradient will be used.

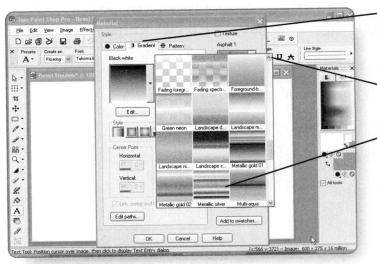

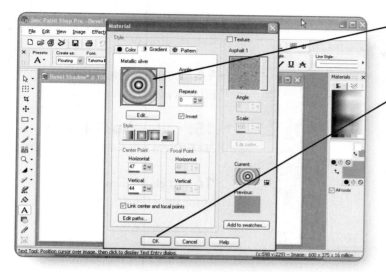

9. Select any desired **style** or **angle**. In this example, a Sunburst style will be used.

10. Click on **OK**. The Material dialog box will close.

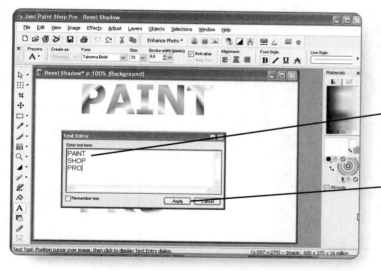

11. With the Text tool selected, **click** on the **canvas**. The Text Entry dialog box will open.

12. Type your text. The formatted text will appear on the canvas.

13. Click on **Apply**. The Text Entry dialog box will close.

Now it's time to add a few special effects.

14. **Click** on **Effects**. The Effects menu will appear.

15. **Click** on **3D Effects**. The 3D Effects submenu will appear.

16. **Click** on **Inner Bevel**. The Inner Bevel dialog box will open.

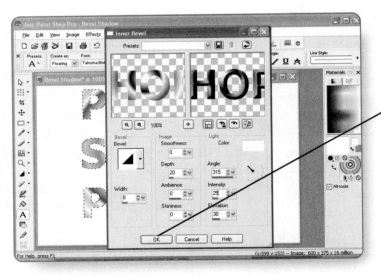

17. **Make** any desired **changes** to the settings. In this example, the Intensity was decreased to 25.

18. **Click** on **OK**. The Inner Bevel dialog box will close.

19. **Click** on **Effects**. The Effects menu will appear.

20. **Click** on **3D Effects**. The 3D Effects submenu will appear.

21. **Click** on **Drop Shadow**. The Drop Shadow dialog box will open.

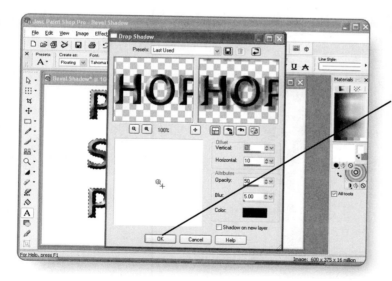

22. **Make** any desired **changes** to the settings. In this example, no changes are needed.

23. **Click** on **OK**. The Drop Shadow dialog box will close.

24. **Click** on **Selections**. The Selections menu will appear.

25. **Click** on **Select None**. The marquee will disappear and the text will be defloated.

The finished text with the special effects applied

Filling Text with Tubes

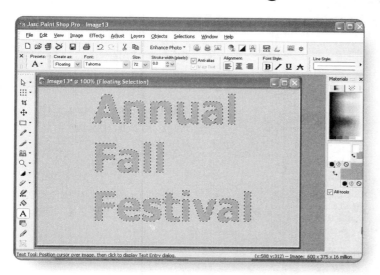

Create text and fill it with any picture tube image. This works best with smaller picture tubes.

1. Using the Text tool, **create** some **floating text** with a large heavy font. The text will appear on the canvas.

2. Click on the **Picture Tube tool**. The tool will become selected.

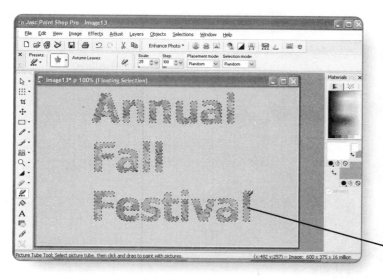

3. From the Tool Options palette, **select** a **picture tube**, preferably a small one. In the example shown, it's a collection of autumn leaves.

TIP

If the image you want to use is larger than you need, decrease the scale.

---

4. Using the Picture Tube tool, **paint over** the **text letters**. Because the text is selected, the tube images do not extend beyond the letters of text.

5. Optionally, **apply** an **effect**. Select your effects from the Effects browser or the Effects menu. In this example, a 3D drop shadow was added.

6. Click on **Selections**. The Selections menu will appear.

7. Click on **Select None**. The marquee will disappear.

The finished text with the special effects applied

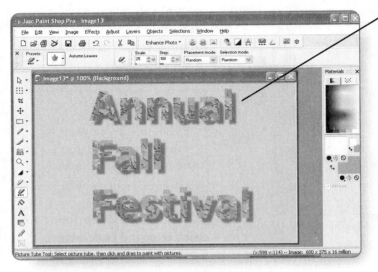

Coloring Individual Letters

A colorful way to present your text is to individually color each letter of the text. This example works best if you select a solid color when creating the text. You can add patterns, textures, or gradients to the individual letters when you select them later in this example.

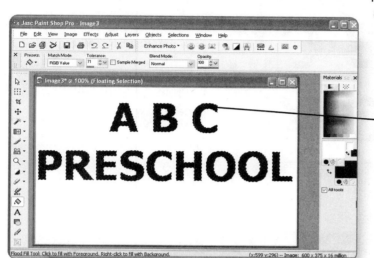

1. Using the Text tool, **create** some **floating text**. The text will appear on the canvas.

2. Press Ctrl+D to deselect the text. The text will become deselected.

Next, you need to select each letter individually and apply a style to it.

3. Click on the **Magic Wand tool**. Use the Magic Wand to select the individual letters.

TIP

You might want to increase the feather and tolerance amounts to make sure that all edges of the letter are included.

4. Click on the **first letter** you want to modify. The letter will become selected.

TIP

If you want to select additional letters, hold down the Shift key and click on the additional letters with the Magic Wand tool.

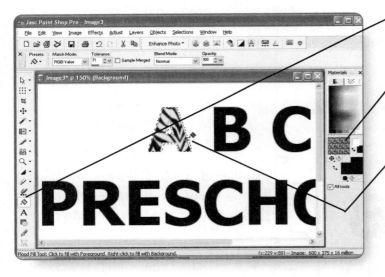

5. Select the **Flood Fill tool**. The Flood Fill tool will become selected.

6. Select a **color**, **pattern**, or **gradient** for the foreground Materials swatch.

7. Click on the **selection** to flood fill the selected letter. The letter will appear in the new material.

8. Press Ctrl+D. The letter will be deselected.

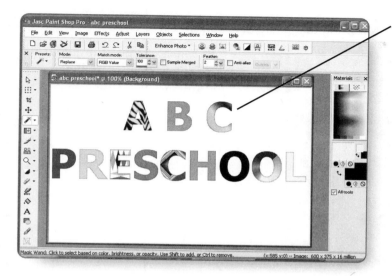

9. Repeat steps 3 through **8** for each letter of your text.

Creating Reflection Magic

This is one of my favorites. You just have to try it to see the effect! Again, this looks best against a dark background.

1. Using the Text tool, **create** some **text** with the following guidelines.

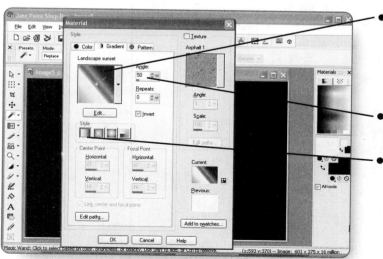

- Set the background fill pattern to a gradient type. This is especially pretty with the gradient called Landscape Sunset.

- Set the gradient angle at 50 degrees.

- Set the gradient style to Linear.

● Make the text a "floating" type.

● Select a large script type font, such as Monotype Corsiva.

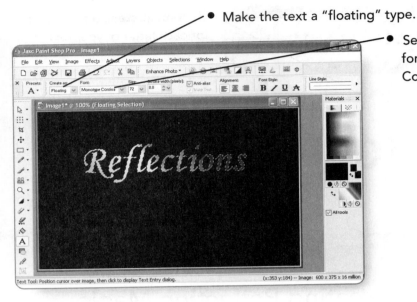

2. While the text is still floating and selected, **click** on **Edit**. The Edit menu will appear.

3. Click on **Copy**. The text will copy to the Windows Clipboard.

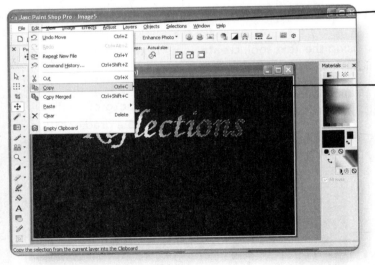

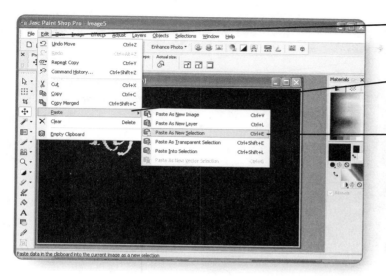

4. Click on **Edit**. The Edit menu will appear.

5. Click on **Paste**. The Paste submenu menu will appear.

6. Click on **Paste As New Selection**. You now have two identical copies of the text. The new copy of the text will be "stuck" to your mouse.

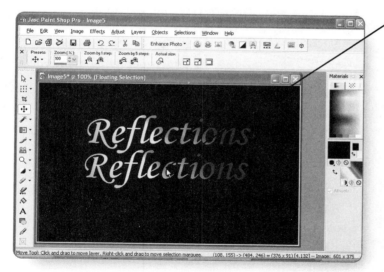

7. Move the **mouse** under the original text and **click**. The new text will be laid down and selected.

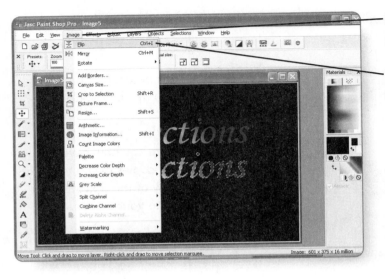

8. **Click** on **Image**. The Image menu will appear.

9. **Click** on **Flip**. The selected text will flip upside down.

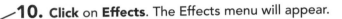

10. **Click** on **Effects**. The Effects menu will appear.

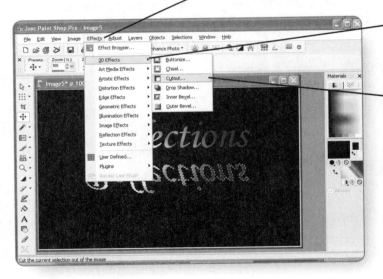

11. **Click** on **3D Effects**. The 3D Effects submenu menu will appear.

12. **Click** on **Cutout**. The Cutout dialog box will open.

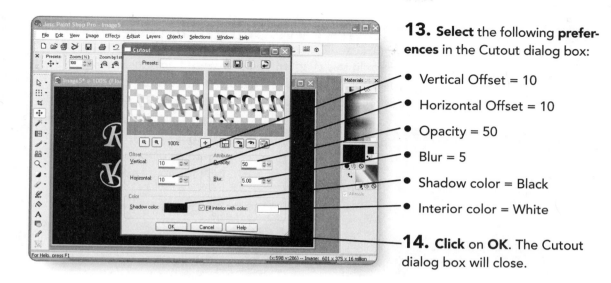

13. Select the following **preferences** in the Cutout dialog box:

- Vertical Offset = 10
- Horizontal Offset = 10
- Opacity = 50
- Blur = 5
- Shadow color = Black
- Interior color = White

14. Click on **OK**. The Cutout dialog box will close.

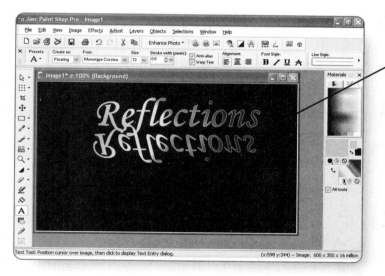

TIP

If necessary, move the selected text closer to the original text.

15. Press Ctrl+D to deselect the text.

The image takes on the appearance of a reflection.

Making Woodburned Text

Earlier in this chapter, you discovered how to generate a 3D effect for your text. You used two effects to achieve the desired look: the cutout and drop shadow effects. In this section, you'll see how you can use those same two effects to create a completely different look for your text.

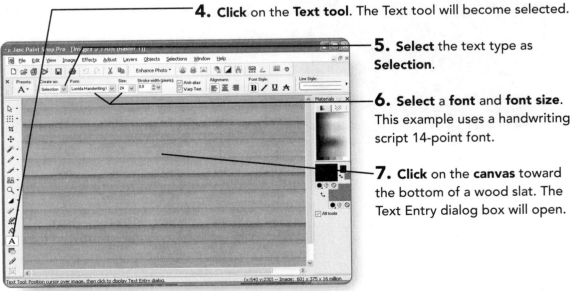

1. Create a new **image** with the Woodgrain 02 pattern background.

2. Set the **foreground materials swatch** to **Black**.

3. Set the **background materials swatch** to a **medium brown**.

4. Click on the **Text tool**. The Text tool will become selected.

5. Select the text type as **Selection**.

6. Select a **font** and **font size**. This example uses a handwriting script 14-point font.

7. Click on the **canvas** toward the bottom of a wood slat. The Text Entry dialog box will open.

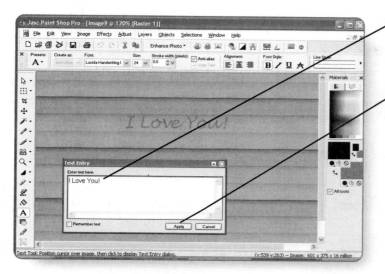

8. Type your **text**. The text will appear on a board slat of your background canvas.

9. Click on **Apply**. The Text Entry dialog box will close.

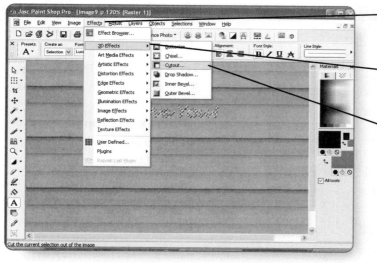

10. Click on **Effects**. The Effects menu will appear.

11. Click on **3D Effects**. The 3D Effects submenu will appear.

12. Click on **Cutout**. The Cutout dialog box will open.

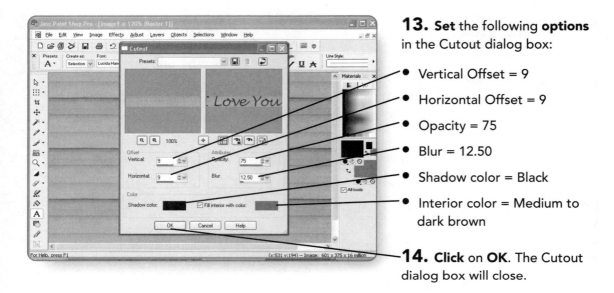

13. **Set** the following **options** in the Cutout dialog box:

- Vertical Offset = 9

- Horizontal Offset = 9

- Opacity = 75

- Blur = 12.50

- Shadow color = Black

- Interior color = Medium to dark brown

14. **Click** on **OK**. The Cutout dialog box will close.

15. **Click** on **Effects**. The Effects menu will appear.

16. **Click** on **3D Effects**. The 3D Effects submenu will appear.

17. **Click** on **Drop Shadow**. The Drop Shadow dialog box will open.

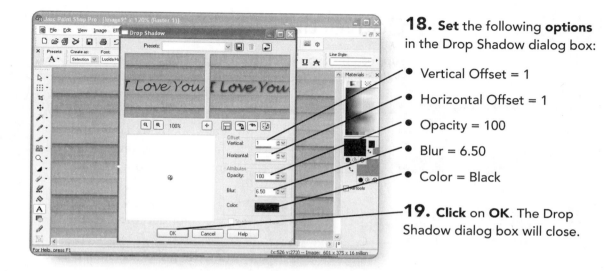

18. **Set** the following **options** in the Drop Shadow dialog box:

- Vertical Offset = 1
- Horizontal Offset = 1
- Opacity = 100
- Blur = 6.50
- Color = Black

19. **Click** on **OK**. The Drop Shadow dialog box will close.

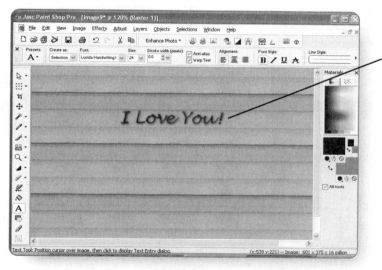

20. **Press Ctrl+D**.

The text is deselected and you can see the woodburned appearance on your text.

Converting Text to Curves

Suppose that you want to place your text in a sort of helter-skelter pattern. You could create one letter at a time, place it, and then move on to the next one, but there's an easier way. Paint Shop Pro has a Convert Text to Curves feature that does most of the work for you!

1. Create a new **image** with any color background you want.

2. Using the Text tool, **create** some **vector text**. Using vector text enables you to break the text into individual characters.

3. Click on **Objects**. The Objects menu will appear.

4. Click on **Convert Text to Curves**. The Convert Text to Curves submenu menu will appear.

5. Click on **As Character Shapes**. Paint Shop Pro will convert each letter of the text into separate vector objects.

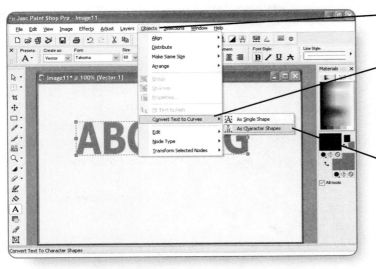

It doesn't look like anything happened because all objects are selected together as a group.

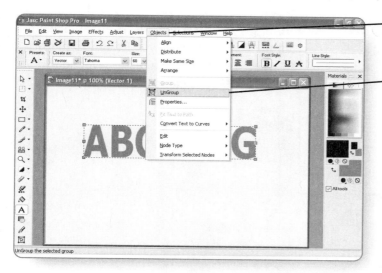

6. Click on **Objects**. The Objects menu will appear.

7. Click on **Ungroup**. The items will become internally ungrouped from each other.

8. Press Ctrl+D (or click on Selections, Select None). The letters will become deselected.

9. Click on the **Vector Selection tool**. The tool will become selected.

10. Click on the **first letter** of your text. The individual letter will appear with selection handles.

11. Position the **mouse** over the rotation handle. The mouse pointer has two curved arrows.

12. Rotate or **move** the **letter** to a new position.

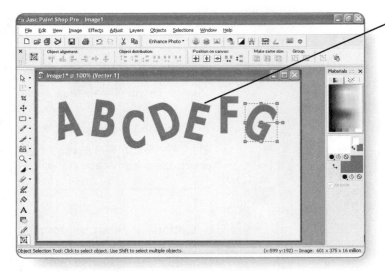

13. **Repeat steps 8** through **10** for each letter of the text.

After the letters are sufficiently jumbled, you'll need to place them on a raster layer so that you can apply an effect.

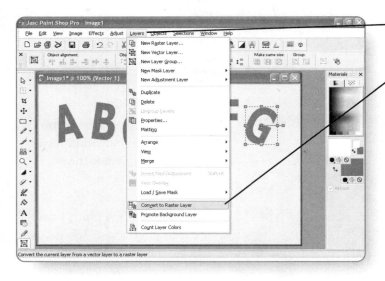

14. **Click** on **Layers**. The Layers menu will appear.

15. **Click** on **Convert to Raster Layer**. The text will convert to raster text. You can now apply any desired special effect.

Before applying special effects, you might want to merge all the layers into one.

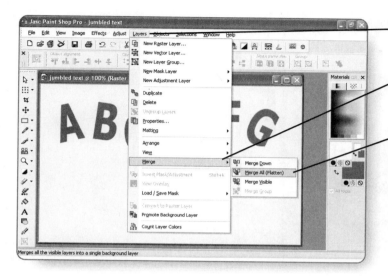

16. **Click** on **Layers**. The Layers menu will appear.

17. **Click** on **Merge**. The Merge submenu will appear.

18. **Click** on **Merge All (Flatten)**. All layers will be combined into a single background layer.

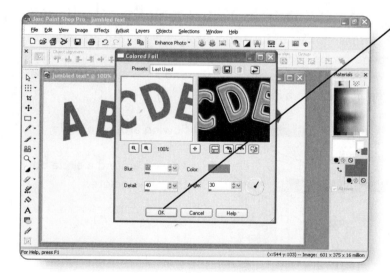

19. **Apply** any desired special **effects**. This figure shows settings for the Artistic, Colored Foil effect.

The final result

Wrapping Text Around Shapes

Text doesn't have to flow on a straight path. You can wrap it around circles, make it wave along a line, or generally have it take on any shape you want. Paint Shop Pro calls this feature Creating Text on a Path.

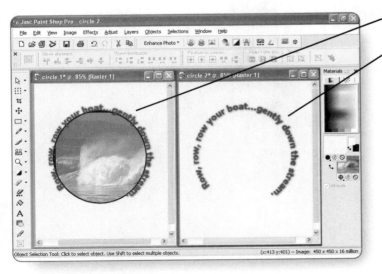

Text flowing around a circle

Text flowing around a circle but with the circle deleted

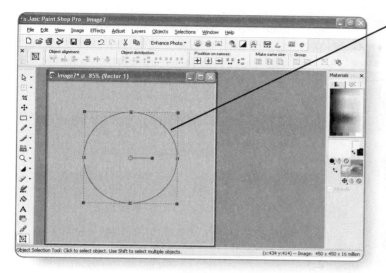

The first thing you'll need is a path or shape for the text to follow. The path can be a line, a circle, a star, or almost any vector object.

NOTE

The 3D vector shapes, such as the 3D arrows, buttons, or traffic signs, are actually made up of multiple objects. Therefore, you cannot use them to create text on a path unless you ungroup the object first.

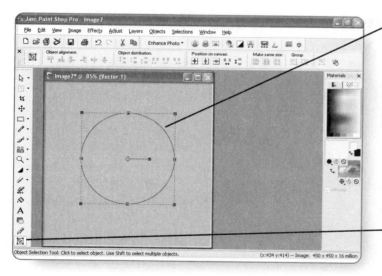

1. Draw a vector **shape**. Use either the preset shapes or the line tools to draw the shape.

NOTE

You can use any background fill you want or you can create the shape on a transparent layer.

2. If it's not already selected, use the Vector Selection tool to **select** the vector **object**. Selection handles will appear around the object.

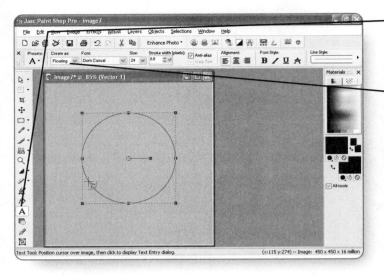

3. Click on the **Text tool**. The mouse pointer will resemble a cross with the letter A under it.

4. Set the text type to **Floating**. You can create shaped text with vector text, but it works best with Floating.

NOTE

Remember that you can apply special effects only to the floating raster text; however, you can rotate and move vector text easily. If you create floating text, you can later delete the vector image and the text will remain shaped. If you delete the vector shape with vector text, the text will lose the shape and return to a straight line.

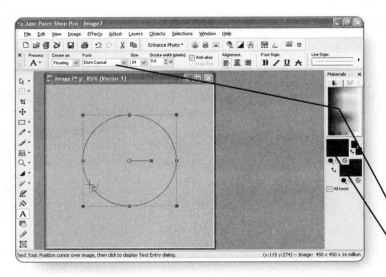

5. Select a **font** and **font size**.

6. Select a background **color**.

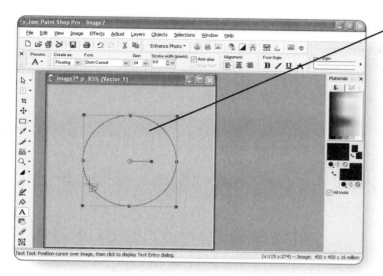

7. Position the **mouse** over the vector shape until the mouse pointer has a half circle under the pointer. This indicates that the text you create should wrap around the vector object.

TIP

The text will begin where you click your mouse.

8. Click the **mouse**. The Text Entry dialog box will open.

9. Enter some **text**. The text will appear around the vector object.

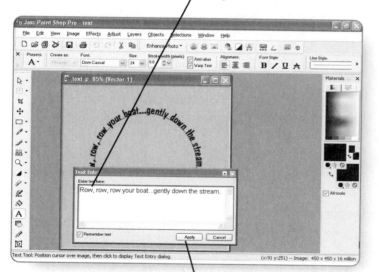

TIP

Depending on the font and size you've selected as well as the shape you're wrapping around, you might have to experiment with the kerning. Make sure you can see the object and text and adjust the kerning until the letters flow the smoothest. Keeping the shape and font simple creates better text flow.

10. Click on **Apply**. The Text Entry dialog box will close and the text will appear wrapped around the image with a selection marquee.

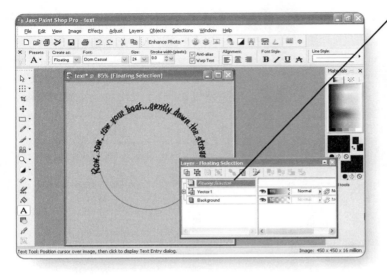

The text is placed on a new layer called Floating Selection.

11. **Press Ctrl+D** to deselect your text.

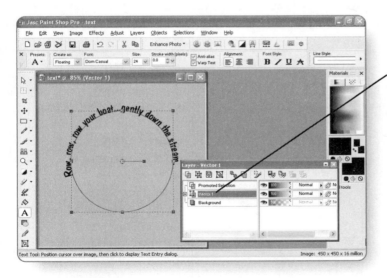

The text is placed on a new layer called Promoted Selection.

If you don't want the vector shape to be included with the text, click on the vector layer and delete it.

17

Designing Web Page Components

Today's Web pages must not only look good, but also convey your message accurately. The competition for "hits" on a Web site is fierce. Paint Shop Pro can help you create backgrounds and patterns that are designed to catch the eye of the surfer. Pages that contain similar topics should have a similar look and feel.

Although you can create your backgrounds and graphics in Paint Shop Pro, in most situations, Paint Shop Pro doesn't do the HTML code for you. You'll need to either create the HTML text yourself or use one of the many Web page creation applications such as FrontPage or Dreamweaver. In this chapter, you'll learn how to

- Create a Web page background
- Resize an image
- Preview in a Web browser
- Save in Web graphics formats

Creating a Simple Web Background

Use Paint Shop Pro to create exciting backgrounds for use on your Web pages. Although there are a number of different ways to create Web page backgrounds, here's one of the easier methods.

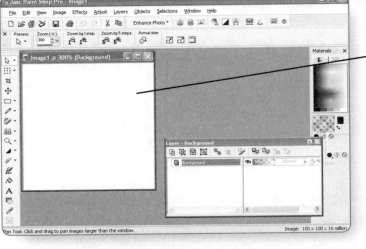

1. Create a new **image** that is approximately 100 pixels wide by about 100 pixels high. The blank image will appear in the Paint Shop Pro Window.

TIP

Don't make the background image too big or it will take too long to load in the Web page. When the background is small, the Web browser automatically repeats (tiles) the image to cover the entire page.

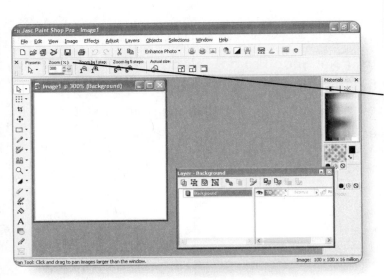

2. If desired, **click** on the **Zoom tool** and then **click** on the **image** to enlarge the view.

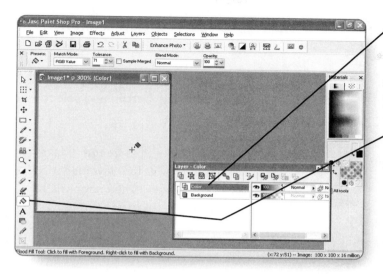

3. Add a new **raster layer**, naming the layer **Color**. To review the addition of raster layers, see Chapter 9, "Developing Layers."

4. Click on the **Flood Fill tool**. The mouse pointer will take the shape of a paint bucket.

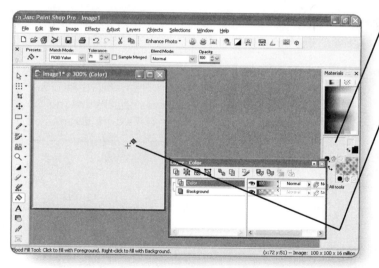

5. Click on the **Foreground Materials box** and **select** a **color** or **style** for your Web page background.

6. Click in the **image**. (Make sure the Color layer is the active layer.) The image will fill with the selected color.

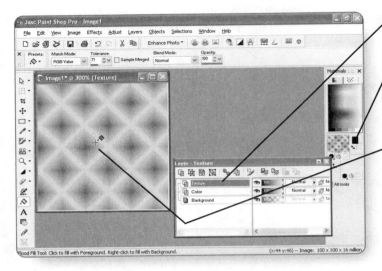

7. **Add** another new **raster layer**, naming the layer **Texture**.

8. **Click** on the **Foreground Materials button** and **select** a **texture**.

9. **Click** in the **image**. (Make sure the Texture layer is the active layer.) The image will fill with the selected texture.

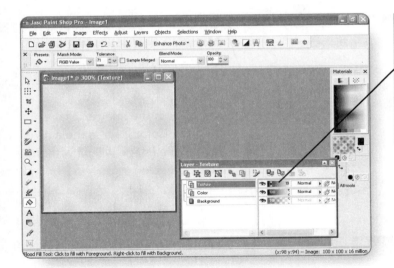

TIP

If you don't see the texture or it's too dark, you might need to reduce the layer opacity for the Color or Texture layers.

Creating Seamless Background Tiles

Web browsers take the background images and automatically replicate them in a tiled pattern so that they fill an entire page. If your Web page background is a single color that has no texture or pattern, you won't be able to see where your tile starts and begins. With patterns and textures, however, sometimes you can see where one square ends and the next one starts. Paint Shop Pro includes a feature to assist in creating a seamless tile effect.

You need to merge all layers in the background tile before you can achieve good results with the Seamless Tiling effect.

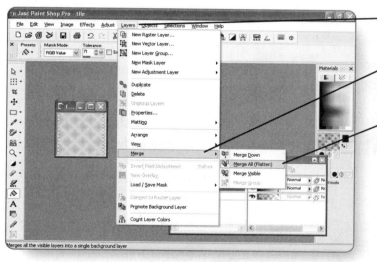

1. Click on **Layers**. The Layers menu will appear.

2. Click on **Merge**. The Merge submenu will appear.

3. Click on **Merge All (Flatten)**. The layers will merge into a single background layer.

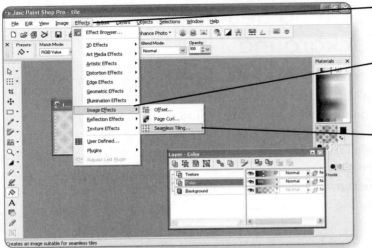

4. Click on **Effects**. The Effects menu will appear.

5. Click on **Image Effects**. The Image Effects submenu will appear.

6. Click on **Seamless Tiling**. The Seamless Tiling dialog box will open.

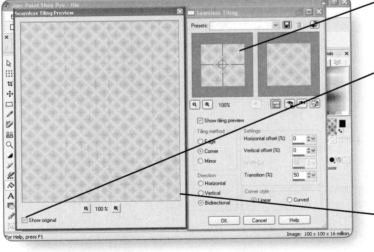

7. Click on **Show tiling preview** if it's not already selected. A preview window will open.

8. Click on **Show original** if it's not already selected. The Preview window will show you how tiled your original image looks.

TIP

To get a larger representative view of your image, drag a border of the preview window to resize it.

Notice the striping effect from the original textured tile.

9. **Remove** the ✔ from Show original. You can now use the preview window to see the changes you make in the Seamless Tiling dialog box.

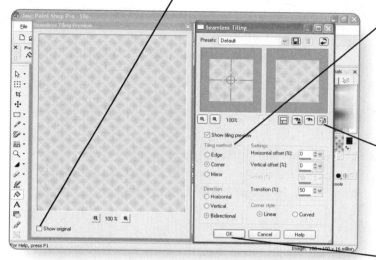

10a. Manually **change** the **settings** until the preview window displays the look you want for your background.

OR

10b. **Click repeatedly** on the **Randomize button** until the preview window displays the look you want for your background.

11. **Click** on **OK**. The Seamless Tiling dialog box will close.

Understanding Web Graphics Formats

Up to this point, you've been saving all your images in the standard Paint Shop Pro format, which applies a .psp extension to files. Unfortunately, the Web doesn't support the PSP format. The two most widely used graphics formats supported by today's Web browsers are Graphics Interchange Format (GIF) and Joint Photographic Experts Group (JPEG).

NOTE

The new kid on the Internet graphics block is Portable Network Graphics (PNG) format. Paint Shop Pro can save images as PNG formats, but, unfortunately, many older Web browsers don't support that format.

Always save your image in the standard Paint Shop Pro format before you begin saving it as other formats. If you've saved the only copy of your new background or logo as a GIF image and then decide you want to save it as a JPEG (or vice versa), you'll lose quite a bit of valuable graphics data should you ever need to edit the image.

Saving Images in Paint Shop Pro Format

Saving an image in Paint Shop Pro format retains support for layers, selections, and other features that the other formats don't support. Image compression does not occur when you're saving an image in Paint Shop Pro format.

1. Click on **File**. The File menu will appear.

2. Click on **Save As**. The Save As dialog box will open.

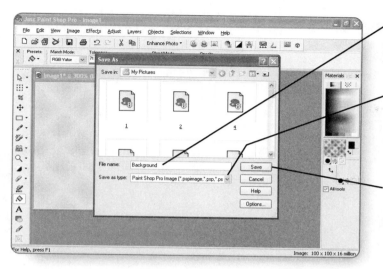

3. Type a **name** for the image. The filename will appear in the File name text box.

4. Click on the **Save as type arrow** and **select Paint Shop Pro Image**. The file type will appear in the Save as type box.

5. Click on **Save**. The image will be saved as a Paint Shop Pro image.

Saving Images as Compressed JPEG

You can compress JPEG images into smaller file sizes, which translates to faster loading time for the Web surfer. Although JPEG images can support high file colors and frequently produce better quality in an image such as a photograph, JPEGs do not support transparent areas and are not the best format to use for line art, cartoons, or other high-contrast images.

NOTE
Although you can just save your file as a JPEG without using optimization, an uncompressed file size might be too large to work well on a Web page.

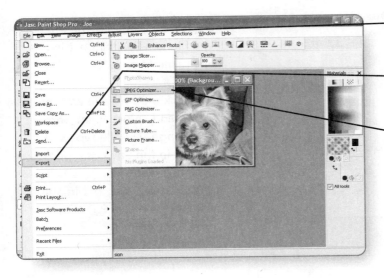

1. Click on **File**. The File menu will appear.

2. Click on **Export**. The Export submenu will appear.

3. Click on **JPEG Optimizer**. The JPEG Optimizer dialog box will open.

JPEG Compression

When you're saving images as JPEG, you must determine a compression factor between 1 and 99. The larger the factor, the more compression, which results in smaller file size but lower quality.

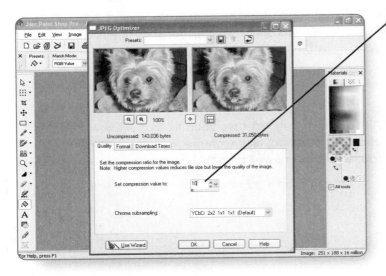

1. Click on the **Set compression value to up/down arrows** ($\updownarrow$). The compression value will display in the text box.

View the before and after compression images along with uncompressed and compressed file sizes.

JPEG Format

Next, you need to select a format option for use when displaying the image.

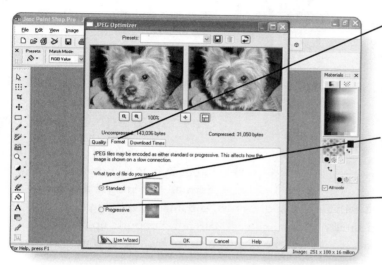

1. Click on the **Format tab**. The Format tab will come to the front.

2. Click on a **format option**. Two options are available:

- **Standard.** The image downloads one line a time, starting from the top.

- **Progressive.** The image is displayed in several passes with greater detail added each time. (This option works better for larger images.)

JPEG Download Times

View the approximate download times for your image by using your current settings and various modem speeds.

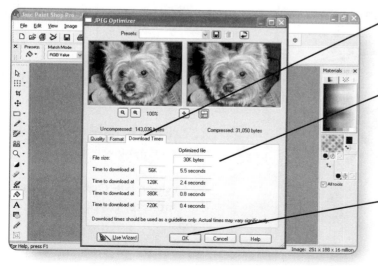

1. Click on the **Download Times tab**. The Download Times tab will come to the front.

2. View the **download times** for various modem speeds. The values will change with the compression factor you've selected.

3. Click on **OK**. The Save As dialog box will open.

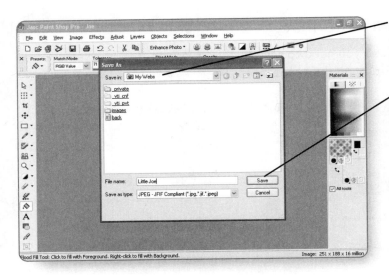

4. Type a **name** for the image. The filename will appear in the File name text box.

5. Click on **Save**. Paint Shop Pro will save the image in a JPEG format.

Saving Images as Transparent GIF

Save any image with transparent areas in it as an optimized GIF format. GIF images also work well with cartoons, drawings, and images with high contrast and similar colors; however, GIF only supports up to 256 colors, so it's not the best choice for high-color photographs.

> ## NOTE
> Although you can save your file as a GIF without optimization, an uncompressed file size might be too large to work well on a Web page.

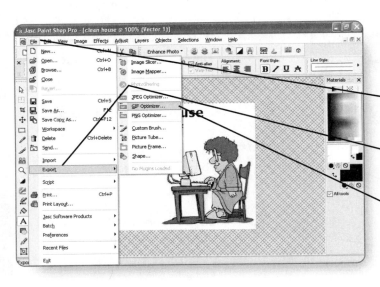

1. Click on **File**. The File menu will appear.

2. Click on **Export**. The Export submenu menu will appear.

3. Click on **GIF Optimizer**. The GIF Optimizer dialog box will open.

GIF Transparency

The first screen of the GIF Optimizer dialog box relates to how you want Paint Shop Pro to handle transparency.

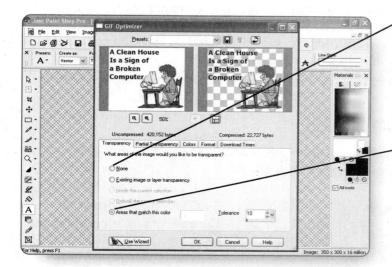

1a. Click on **None** if you have no transparent areas in the image. Paint Shop Pro won't block any area of the image.

OR

1b. Click on **Areas that match this color** if you need a particular color on the image blocked out. Areas that match the color box will appear transparent.

TIP

Click on the color box to select a color to block. In the example shown, Paint Shop Pro blocks out all white areas in the image.

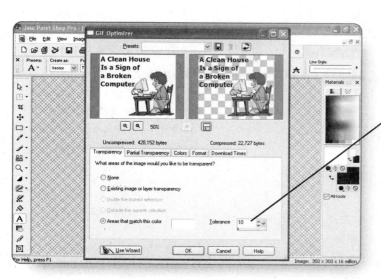

2. Optionally, **adjust** the **Tolerance scale** from 1–200. The tolerance factor indicates how closely colors must match the color in the box before they are selected.

> **NOTE**
>
> The higher the tolerance, the wider the range of color matching. For example, at a low tolerance of the color red, images that contain light red might not be included, however, if the tolerance were increased to say, 150, not only would light red be included, but perhaps pink or magenta as well.

GIF Format

Next, you need to select a format option for use when displaying the image.

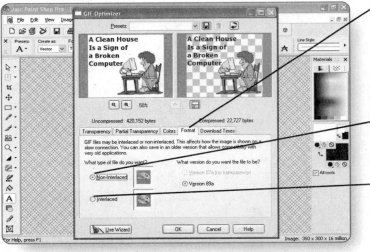

1. Click on the **Format tab**. The Format tab will come to the front.

2. Click on a **format option**. Two options are available:

- **Non-Interlaced.** The image downloads one line a time, starting from the top.

- **Interlaced.** The image is displayed in several passes with greater detail added each time. (This option works better for larger images.)

GIF Download Times

View the approximate download times for your image by using your current settings and various modem speeds.

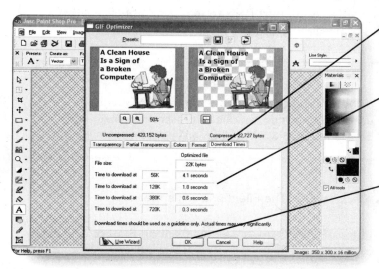

1. **Click** on the **Download Times tab**. The Download Times tab will come to the front.

2. **View** the **download times** for various modem speeds. The values will change with the options you previously selected.

3. **Click** on **OK**. The Save As dialog box will open.

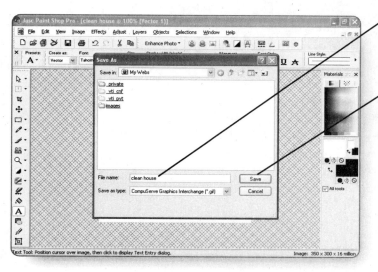

4. **Type** a **name** for the image. The filename will appear in the File name text box.

5. **Click** on **Save**. Paint Shop Pro will save the image in a GIF format.

Saving Images as PNG

The newer PNG format is the best of both GIF and JPEG worlds, but remember that most Web browsers in use today don't yet fully support PNG format. Additionally, PNG files tend to be slightly larger than JPEG or GIF files.

NOTE

Although you can save your file as a PNG without using optimization, an uncompressed file size might be too large to work well on a Web page.

---

1. **Click** on **File**. The File menu will appear.

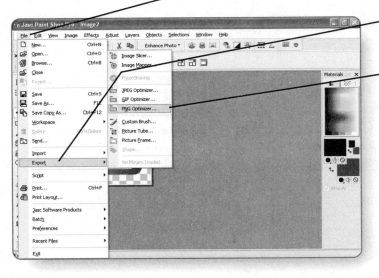

2. **Click** on **Export**. The Export submenu will appear.

3. **Click** on **PNG Optimizer**. The PNG Optimizer dialog box will open.

PNG Colors

The PNG format works similarly to a combination GIF and JPEG. The PNG format supports higher-color image types plus transparency.

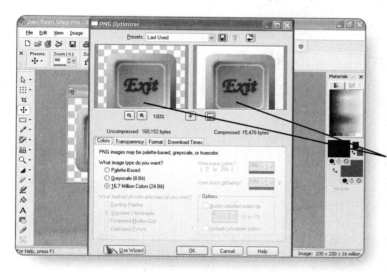

1. Select an **image type**. The option will appear selected.

If you select Palette-Based, you'll need to specify a maximum number of colors.

View the before and after images along with uncompressed and compressed file sizes.

PNG Transparency

The transparency screen of the PNG Optimizer dialog box relates to how you want Paint Shop Pro to handle transparency.

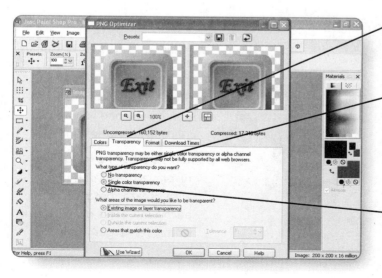

1. Click on the **Transparency tab**. The Transparency tab will come to the front.

2a. Click on **No transparency** if you have no transparent areas in the image. Paint Shop Pro won't block any area of the image.

OR

2b. Click on **Single color transparency** if you need a particular color on the image blocked out.

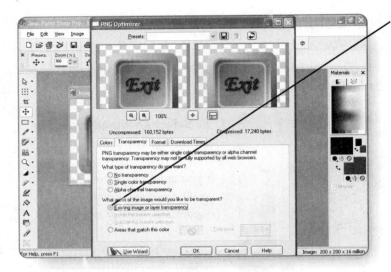

3. Click on **Existing Image or layer transparency**. The option will become selected.

PNG Format

Next, you need to select a format option for use when displaying the image. PNG format options are identical to GIF options.

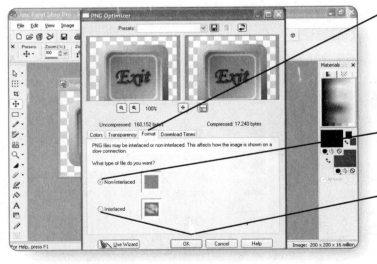

1. Click on the **Format tab**. The Format tab will come to the front.

2. Click on a **format option**. Two options are available:

- **Non-Interlaced.** The image downloads one line a time, starting from the top.

- **Interlaced.** The image is displayed in several passes with greater detail added each time. (This option works better for larger images.)

PNG Download Times

View the approximate download times for your image by using your current settings and various modem speeds.

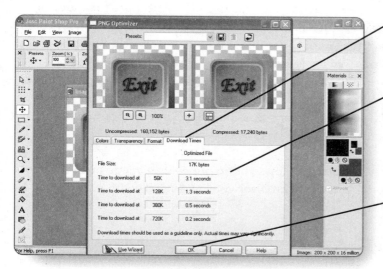

1. Click on the **Download Times tab**. The Download Times tab will come to the front.

2. View the **download times** for various modem speeds. The values will change with the compression factor you've selected.

3. Click on **OK**. The Save As dialog box will open.

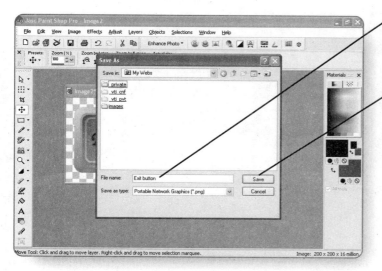

4. Type a **name** for the image. The filename will appear in the File name text box.

5. Click on **Save**. Paint Shop Pro will save the image in a PNG format.

Previewing Images in a Web Browser

Internet Explorer and Netscape Navigator are two popular browsers; however, a number of different Web browsers are on the market today including a relatively new browser, called Opera, which is quickly gaining popularity. When you're working with Web graphics, you should view the graphic in a variety of different browsers because each one supports different features. If possible, view your images in different versions of different browsers as well.

Paint Shop Pro allows you to preview an image in a variety of formats on each browser you have installed on your computer.

1. **Click** on **View**. The View menu will appear.

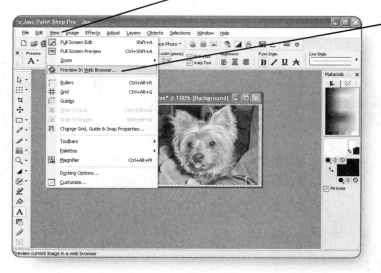

2. **Click** on **Preview in Web Browser**. The Preview in Web Browser dialog box will open.

Paint Shop Pro lists the Web browsers that are installed on your computer.

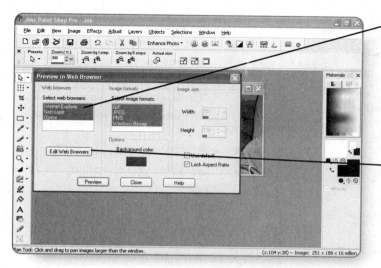

3. Click on the **Web browser** in which you want to view your image. For comparison purposes, try to view the image in all available Web browsers.

Paint Shop Pro supports four types of Web graphics: GIF, JPEG, PNG, and BMP.

4. Click on the **formats** in which you would like to preview your image. Again, I suggest you view the image in a variety of formats. The more the better!

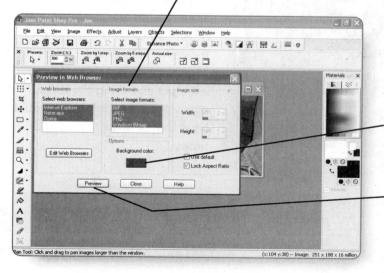

5. Click on the **Background color box** and **select** a **background color** for the Web page.

6. Click on **Preview**. If you selected the GIF, JPEG, or PNG formats, the Optimizer window for the appropriate graphics type will appear.

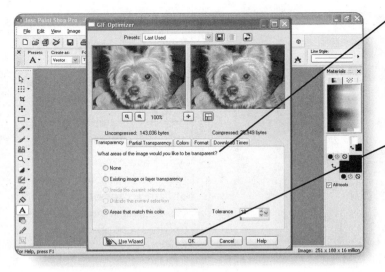

7. Enter compression, transparency, and other **options** for the selected graphics types. Refer to "Understanding Web Graphics Formats" earlier in this chapter.

8. Click on **OK**. The Web browsers you specified will open.

The Web browser previews your image in each format you selected along with display size and approximate loading time.

The following table illustrates approximate file sizes and download times at 56.6 Kbps for various file types. Using a 4" × 3" photograph as an example and using the default compression options, you would have the following download times:

GIF	JPEG	PNG	BMP
31.14 Kb	78.47 Kb	112.52 Kb	175.56 Kb
5.50 seconds	13.86 seconds	19.88 seconds	31.02 seconds

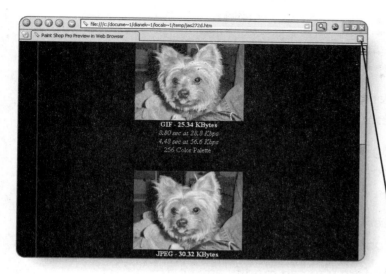

TIP

If you preview a file type that your browser does not support, a white box appears indicating that the browser cannot display the image.

9. Click the **Close box**. The Web browser window will close.

Part III Review Questions

1. Can vector and raster objects be mixed on the same layer? *See "Creating a Vector Layer" in Chapter 13.*

2. When you're drawing preset shapes, what does leaving the Retain style box checked do to the shape? *See "Drawing Shapes with Style" in Chapter 13.*

3. What tool can you use to slice a line into multiple pieces? *See "Using Knife Mode" in Chapter 13.*

4. What must you do before you can modify any vector object? *See "Selecting Vector Objects" in Chapter 14.*

5. When you're aligning multiple selected objects, which object does Paint Shop Pro use as the base that the other objects will align to? *See "Making Objects the Same Size" in Chapter 14.*

6. Can grouped objects be ungrouped? *See "Grouping Multiple Objects" in Chapter 14.*

7. When you're typing text in the Text Entry dialog box, will the text automatically wrap around to the next line? *See "Typing Text" in Chapter 15.*

8. After you defloat text, can you apply effects to only the text? *See "Defloating Text" in Chapter 15.*

9. Can text be filled with pictures? *See "Filling Text with Tubes" in Chapter 16.*

10. What does Paint Shop Pro call the feature to make text wrap around circles or other shapes? *See "Creating Text on a Path" in Chapter 16.*

PART IV

Special Photo Projects

18

Removing Photo Red-Eye

Often when you see a photo of a person or an animal, their eyes seem to glare at you and appear red or blank, giving an effect called red-eye. Red-eye is caused by flash, and it frequently occurs in photographs of humans and animals. You can also use this feature to enhance or change a person's or animal's eye color. In this chapter, you'll learn how to

- Select a red-eye removal method
- Make red-eye automatic adjustments
- Adjust red-eye options
- Adjust red-eye manually

Opening the Red-Eye Removal Dialog Box

The Red-eye Removal option does not work on an image that contains a selection. Before you access the Red-eye Removal dialog box, deselect any selections by pressing Ctrl+D to make the Red-eye Removal option available.

> ## NOTE
>
> If your image is not 24-bit color, the Red-eye Removal option is unavailable. You'll need to convert your image by clicking on Colors, Increase Color Depth, 16 million colors.

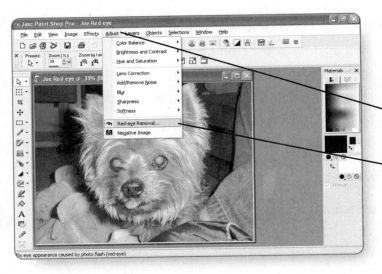

1. Open an **image** with red-eye. Red-eye doesn't have to be red; it can also be white or another color.

2. Click on **Adjust**. The Adjust menu will appear.

3. Click on **Red-eye Removal**. The Red-eye Removal dialog box will open.

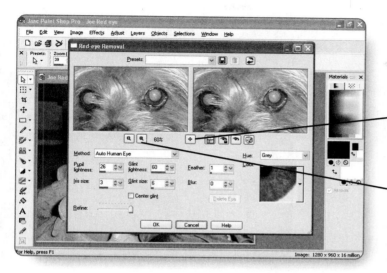

4. The "before" preview displays on the left, and the "after" preview displays on the right.

5. If necessary, **click** on the **placement box** to relocate the preview area to the eyes.

6. If necessary, **click** on the **Zoom in button** to get a good view of the eye. The preview boxes will display the enlarged images.

Selecting a Red-Eye Removal Method

Paint Shop Pro provides several methods for making red-eye corrections:

- **Auto Human Eye.** Automatically selects the correction area and makes the appropriate corrections to a human eye.

- **Auto Animal Eye.** Automatically selects the correction area and makes the appropriate corrections to an animal eye.

- **Freehand Pupil Outline.** Lets you manually select the correction area by using a Freehand selection tool. Use this method for difficult situations, such as a partially obscured-eye.

- **Point-to-Point Pupil Outline.** Lets you manually select the correction area by using a Point-to-Point selection tool. Use this method for difficult situations, such as a partially obscured eye.

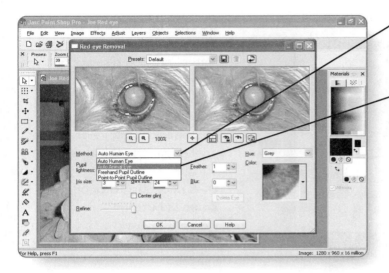

1. **Click** on the **Method down arrow** (⌄). A list of methods will appear.

2. **Click** on a **method**. The fastest and easiest methods are the automatic selections.

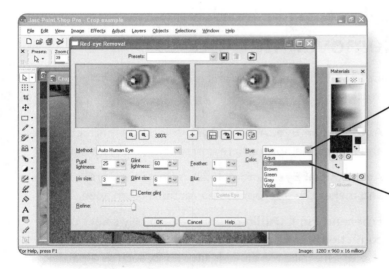

Next, you'll need to decide on an eye hue and color. Eye hue is not available when you're working with an animal eye.

3. If you are working on a human eye, **click** the **Hue down arrow** (⌄). A list of Hue colors will appear.

4. **Click** on a **hue**. The selection will appear in the Hue box.

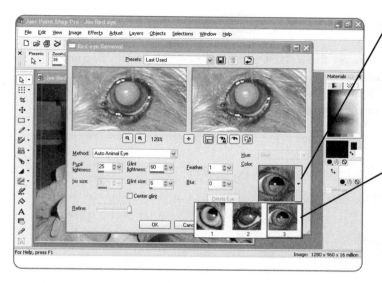

5. **Click** on the **Color down arrow** (-). A selection of eye colors and types will appear. When you're working with animal eyes, selection #1 is for a cat, whereas selections #2 and #3 are for dogs.

6. **Click** on an **eye type/color**. The selection will appear in the Color box.

Now you're ready to define the eye area.

Using Automatic Selections

By using the automatic selections, you select the eye area and let Paint Shop Pro do the rest of the work.

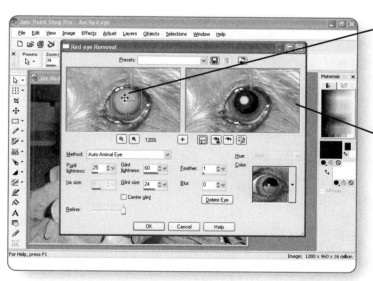

1. In the left preview box, **click** anywhere **inside** the red-eye area of one of the **eyes**. A selection control box will appear around the eye.

The correction will appear in the "after" preview box on the right.

NOTE

Because the default settings can automatically correct a wide range of red-eye effects, you might only need to click the eye. However, in the next section, you'll see how to customize the selection area and red-eye options.

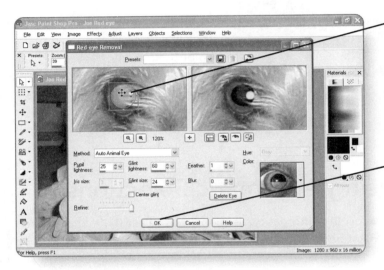

2. In the left preview box, **click** anywhere **inside** the red-eye area of the **other eye**. A selection control box will appear around the eye and the right preview box will display the change.

3. Click on **OK**. The Red-eye Removal dialog box will close.

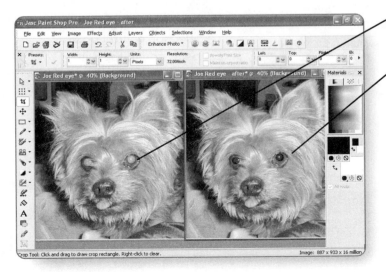

Image before red-eye corrections

Image after red-eye corrections

Adjusting Red-Eye Options

Even though the Red-eye Removal feature can automatically correct a wide range of red-eye effects, sometimes you'll need to adjust the settings yourself.

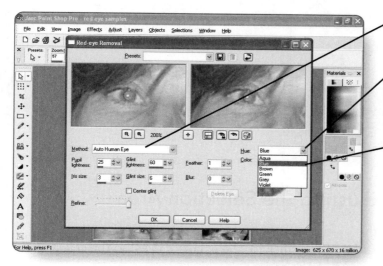

1. Click on a **method**. This image needs Auto Human Eye.

2. Click on the **Hue down arrow** (⌄). A list of eye color selections will appear.

3. Click on a **hue**. The option will become selected.

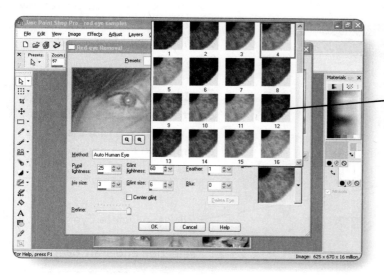

4. Click on the **Color down arrow** (⌄). Thumbnails of the color variations will appear.

5. Click on a **color**. The selection will appear in the Color box.

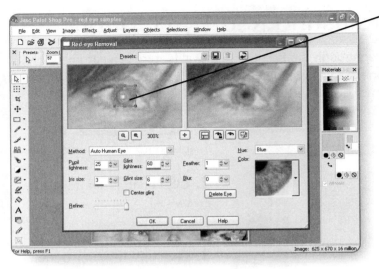

6. In the left preview box, **click** anywhere **inside** the **"red" area** of one of the **eyes**. A selection control box will appear around the eye and the current settings will apply to the eye.

Adjusting the Selection Area

In this example, the automatic selection process selected an area that is too small for the woman's eyes, so the selection area needs to be resized.

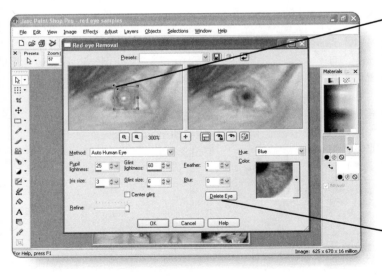

1. Position the **mouse** over any control handle. The mouse will turn into a double-headed arrow.

2. Click and **drag** any of the **control handles**. The selection area will resize and the settings will apply to the new size.

TIP
Click the Delete Eye button to remove a selection and start over.

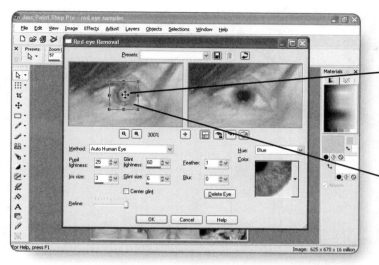

Move the selection box if it is not exactly in the correct position.

3. Position the **mouse** over the selection box, but not over a control handle. The mouse pointer will resemble a four-headed arrow.

4. Drag the **selection box** to the new **location**, and then **release** the **mouse button**. The selection area will move and the settings will apply to the new location.

TIP

Because the default settings can automatically correct a wide range of red-eye effects, you might only need to click the eye. However, in the next section, you'll see how to customize the selection area and red-eye options.

Adjusting Settings

There are settings for the iris area around the pupil, the pupil lightness and glint, feathering the selection, and blurring the area.

Modifying Iris Size

When you're correcting the eye, look at the corrected eye in the right preview box and determine whether you need to modify the iris area around the pupil.

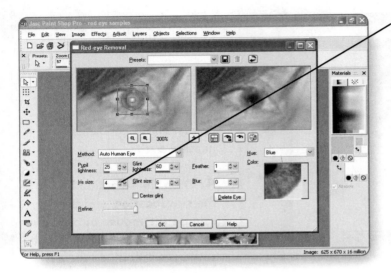

1. **Click** the **up/down arrows** (‡) on the Iris size box. A larger number increases the size of the iris and decreases the pupil size.

Adjusting the Pupil

Determine whether the pupil should be lighter or darker, and, if necessary, adjust the settings.

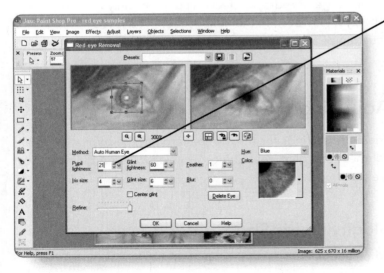

1. **Click** the **up/down arrows** (‡) on the Pupil lightness box. A lower value darkens the pupil, whereas a higher value lightens it.

Modifying Glint

A glint in the eye adds a natural, lively look to the eye, whereas absence of a glint makes the eye dull.

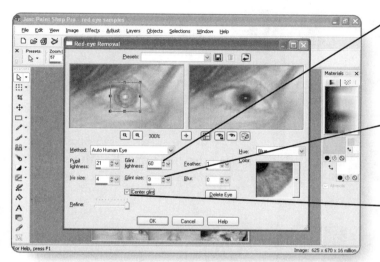

1. Click the **up/down arrows** (‡) on the Glint lightness box. A larger number lightens the glint, whereas a lower value darkens the glint.

2. Click the **up/down arrows** (‡) on the Glint size box. A larger number increases the size of the glint.

3. Optionally, **click** on the **Center glint check box** to move the glint to the center of the pupil.

Refining the Eye Settings

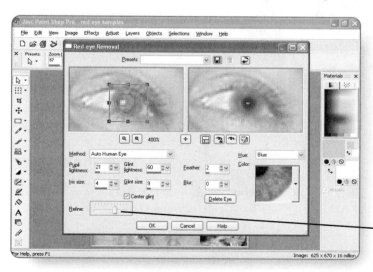

Look at the eye in the left preview box. If part of the eye is obscured in the original image, adjust the corrected eye to look the same. For example, if the eyelid is covering part of the eye in the original, you should make it look that way in the corrected eye. Use the Refine, Blur, and Feather settings to make refinements.

1. Click and **drag** the **Refine slider** to the left one notch at a time until the visible area of the corrected eye looks similar to the eye in the original image.

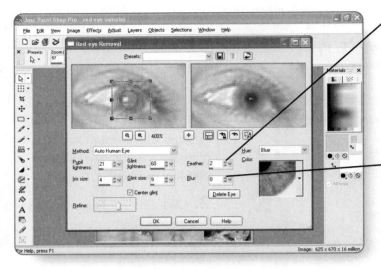

2. Optionally, **click** the **up/down arrows** (⬍) on the Feather box. Smaller values make the edges more pronounced, whereas larger values make them less pronounced.

3. Click the up/down arrows (⬍) on the Blur box. A larger number increases the blending of the surrounding pixels. Use this function when the photo has a grainy appearance.

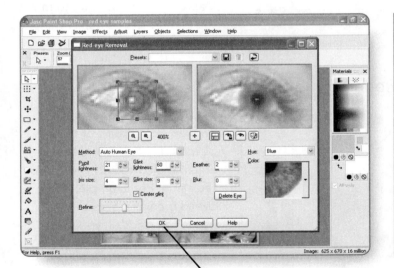

TIP

As you correct the next eye, the controls retain their settings from the first correction, making it much easier to correct the second eye. When you select the next eye, the previously corrected eye still has a circle around it. You can click this circle to go back and make further corrections to the eye.

4. Click on OK. The Red-eye Removal dialog box will close.

Getting Rid of Red-Eye Manually

If, after trying the red-eye reduction feature, you are still unhappy with the image, you can try adjusting the eye, pixel by pixel. It's tedious, but sometimes you need to use this method. You can use the Paint Brush tool to do the editing.

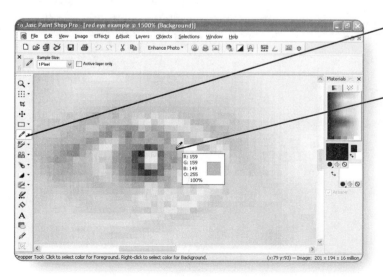

1. Click on the **Zoom tool**. The Zoom tool will become selected.

2. Click to **zoom in** on the **eye area** of the image until you can see the individual pixels.

You need to determine the surrounding color choices to get a good match.

3. Click on the **Dropper tool**. The mouse pointer will turn into an eyedropper shape.

4. Position the **mouse pointer** over a pixel color you want to duplicate. The color settings will appear under the mouse pointer.

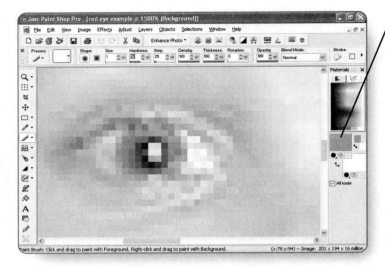

5. Click the **mouse pointer**. The foreground color box will pick up the color you clicked.

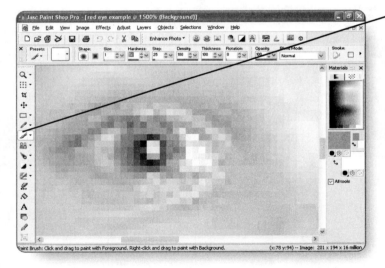

6. Click on the **Paint Brush tool**. The Paint Brush tool will become selected.

7. From the Tool Options palette, **set** the **brush Size** to 1. This allows you to change the image one pixel at a time.

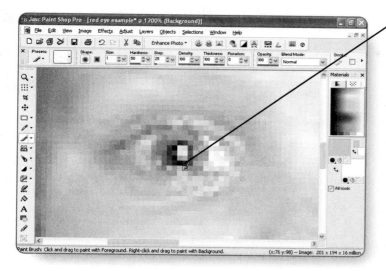

8. Click on an eye **pixel**. The pixel will change to the new color.

9. Repeat steps 3 through **8** for each color variation and pixel of the eye area.

TIP

Use different color shade variations. Using all brown or all blue, for example, leaves the eye looking hardened and unrealistic.

---

10. Click on **View**. The View menu will appear.

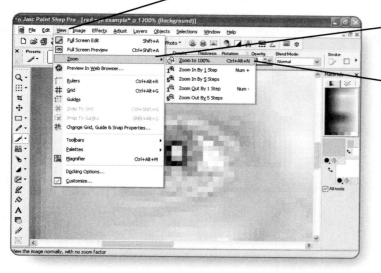

11. Click on **Zoom**. The Zoom submenu will appear.

12. Click on **Zoom to 100%**. The image will resize to normal.

19

Restoring a Photo

Even the most professional photographers sometimes need to edit and fix a few features on their images. Paint Shop Pro includes a number of tools to assist you in cleaning up your less than perfect shots, including many that are designed for nonprofessionals. In this chapter you'll learn how to

- Use the One Step Photo Fix feature
- Remove scratches from a photo
- Modify image contrast
- Adjust color saturation
- Age a photo

Using One Step Photo Fix

Paint Shop Pro has long included numerous features to enhance photographs. The problem was, you needed to know what you needed to change, and most of us amateurs didn't have a clue how to fix what was wrong with the image. New, however, to Paint Shop Pro 8 is a One Step Photo Fix that, with a single click of a mouse, does a magnificent job of enhancing your photographs. You don't need to be a photographic expert to use this feature; Paint Shop Pro calculates all the needed requirements.

1. Open the **image** you want to enhance. The image will appear on the screen.

In this example, the child's face is dark and overpowered by the white snow in the background.

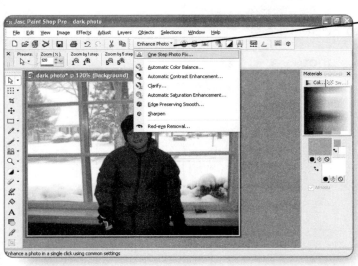

2. From the Photo toolbar, **click** the **Enhance Photo button**. A menu of options will appear.

TIP

If you don't have the Photo toolbar displayed, click on the View menu, and choose Photo from the Toolbars submenu.

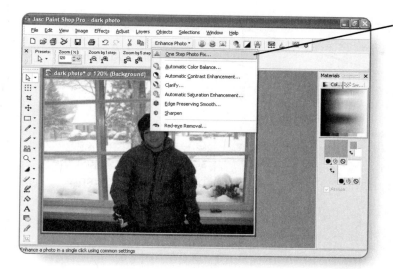

3. Click on **One Step Photo Fix**. Paint Shop Pro will begin the photo enhancement process.

During the process, Paint Shop Pro will adjust the color balance, contrast, clarity, saturation, edge preservation, and sharpness.

Original photograph

Enhanced photograph

TIP

You might want to run the One Step Photo Fix a second time to adjust the photograph even more.

Removing Photo Scratches

Sometimes older photographs, due to aging and handling, acquire scratches or cracks that can deter from the photo image. Paint Shop Pro includes a scratch remover tool that can help you in getting rid of photo scratches.

NOTE

Paint Shop Pro also includes an Automatic Scratch Removal feature (Under the Adjust, Add/Remove Noise menus) that looks at the entire image for what it considers scratches and adjusts them. Unfortunately, this tool sometimes causes more distortion in the image than it fixes. If the scratches are highly visible, you are better off using the scratch remover tool than the Automatic Scratch Removal feature.

1. **Open** the **image** you want to work with. The image will appear on the screen.

In this example, notice the three large scratches in the upper-right quadrant of the photograph.

2. **Click** on the **Scratch Remover tool**. The Scratch Remover tool is located by the Clone brush.

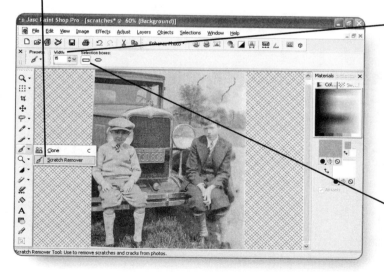

3. From the Tool Options palette, **set** a tool **width**. The tool uses pixels from outside the selection box to correct the scratch, so you need your tool width to be wider than the scratch width. The area can be 4 to 500 pixels wide, although the default is set to 20.

4. **Select** a tool **shape**. Click either the flat-end or pointed-end option to set the shape of the ends of the enclosure box. Wider scratches typically work best with the flat-end option.

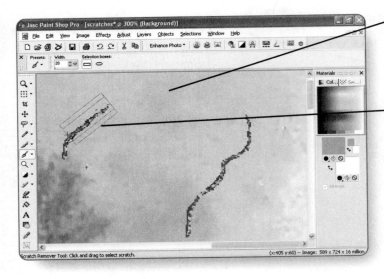

5. **Zoom** in on the **area** you want to work with. You need to be able to easily see the scratch area.

6. **Drag** the **mouse pointer** along the area where you want to start removing the scratch. A box will display around the selected area.

> **TIP**
>
> It's generally better to work with a small portion of the scratch at a time, especially if the scratch has curves and turns in it. You can maintain better control of the scratch area by working with smaller areas.

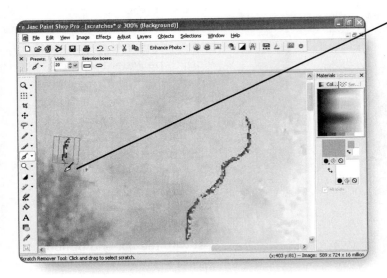

7. **Release** the **mouse button**. The tool will use pixels from outside the selection box to correct the scratch. It will also apply some feathering to reduce the amount of correction applied to the scratch, which then causes the pixels to blend from the scratch area back into the image.

8. **Repeat steps 6** and **7** until the scratched or cracked areas are removed.

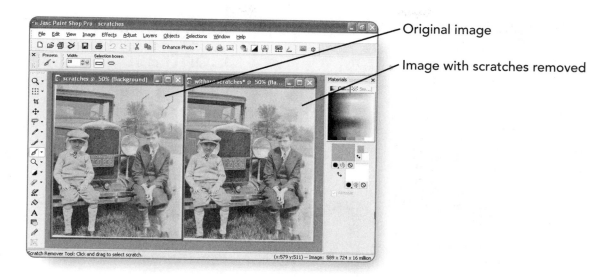

Original image

Image with scratches removed

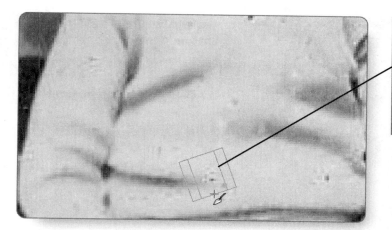

TIP

Also use the Scratch Removal tool to rid a photograph of unwanted artifacts and blemishes.

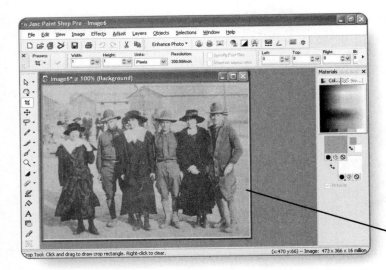

Modifying Contrast

If a photograph is faded and washed out, adjusting the contrast can bring it back to a more natural look. You can use the contrast adjustments on color or black-and-white photographs.

1. Open the **image** you want to work with. The image will appear on the screen.

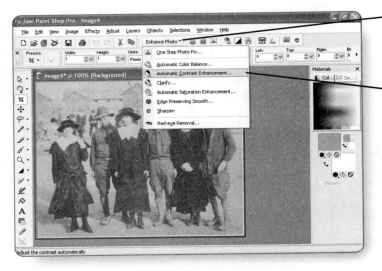

2. Click on the **Enhance Photo button**. A menu of options will appear.

3. Click on **Automatic Contrast**

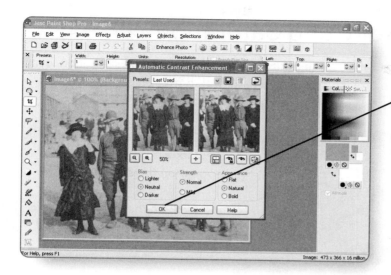

4. Adjust any desired **settings** until the right preview window displays the effect you want.

5. Click on **OK**. The Automatic Contrast Enhancement dialog box will close.

The original image

The contrast-adjusted image

Adjusting Saturation

Saturation is the purity of color. Increasing the saturation level can provide a brighter image with better color and color depth. Lowering saturation adds more grey to the colors.

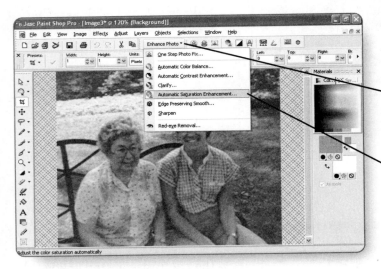

1. Open the **image** you want to work with. The image will appear on the screen.

2. Click on the **Enhance Photo button**. A menu of options will appear.

3. Click on **Automatic Saturation Enhancement**. The Automatic Saturation Enhancement dialog box will open.

4. Adjust any desired **settings** until the right preview window displays the effect you want.

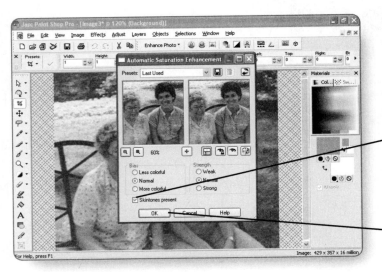

TIP

Setting the saturation level too high can make the image look unnatural.

5. If your image includes people, **click** on the **Skintones Present** box. The option will be selected.

6. Click on **OK**. The Automatic Saturation Enhancement dialog box will close.

The original image

The saturation-adjusted image

Aging a Photo

So far in this chapter, you've learned how to modify the color and sharpness in old photographs to restore them to a newer look. Sometime you might want to make a current photograph look older and more aged.

1. Open the **image** you want to work with. The image will appear on the screen.

Because colors in aged photos tend to be less saturated, you'll probably want to dull the image saturation.

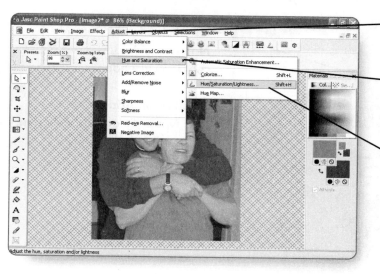

2. Click on **Adjust**. The Adjust menu will appear.

3. Click on **Hue and Saturation**. The Hue and Saturation submenu will appear.

4. Click on **Hue/Saturation/Lightness**. The Hue/Saturation/Lightness dialog box will open.

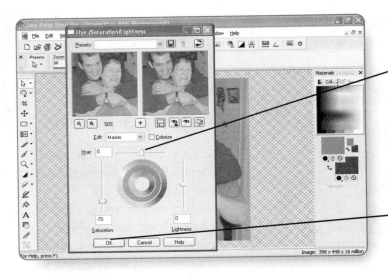

You want to remove a lot of the color, but not all of it.

5. **Set** the Saturation value to a high negative number (which reduces the color), such as somewhere between –40 and –80. Keep an eye on the preview window for the tone you are looking for.

6. **Click** on **OK**.

Most older photographs, due to older technology, weren't as clear as the images taken today. That less clear look is called noise.

7. **Click** on **Adjust**. The Adjust menu will appear.

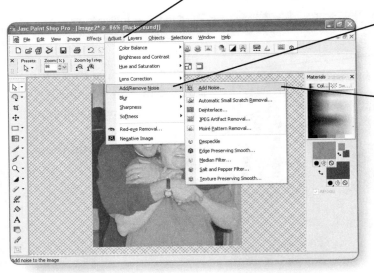

8. **Click** on **Add/Remove Noise**. The Add/Remove Noise submenu will appear.

9. **Click** on **Add Noise**. The Add Noise dialog box will open.

Rather than have the noise "dots" randomly placed, they should be in a more even pattern.

10. **Click** on **Uniform**. The option will be selected.

By default, the noise dots are in color, but for an aging photograph, you want them in a solid gray scale pattern.

11. **Click** on **Monochrome**. The option will be selected.

Next, you need to determine the amount of noise.

12. **Set** the **Noise value**. The amount will vary depending on the age effect you want, but an average amount is 15.

13. **Click** on **OK**. The Add Noise dialog box will close.

Finally, for a great additional aging effect, add one of Paint Shop Pro's effects called Aged Newspaper.

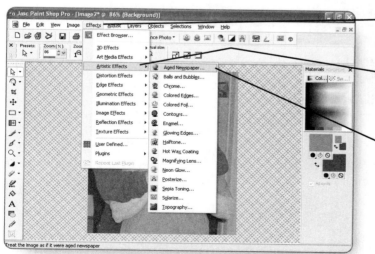

14. **Click** on **Effects**. The Effects menu will appear.

15. **Click** on **Artistic Effects**. The Artistic Effects submenu will appear.

16. **Click** on **Aged Newspaper**. The Aged Newspaper dialog box will open.

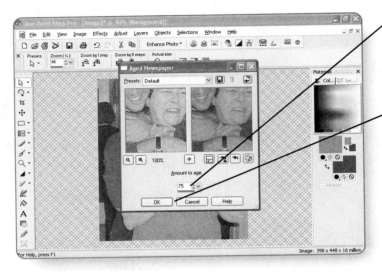

17. Select an aging **number**. The higher the number, the older the photograph will appear.

18. Click on **OK**. The Aged Newspaper dialog box will close.

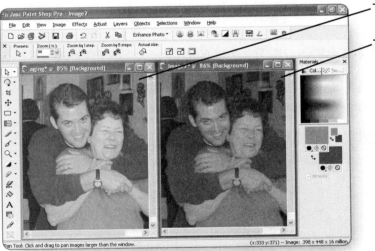

The original image

The aged image

20

Working with Picture Frames

Paint Shop Pro contains a variety of picture frames ranging from wood to metal, stone, and other decorative surfaces. Additional frames are available through the Internet. In this chapter, you'll learn how to

- Work with the Picture Frame dialog box
- Position the frame on an image
- Add additional picture frames

Applying a Picture Frame

Paint Shop Pro includes a Picture Frame dialog box that takes all the work out of adding a frame to your image.

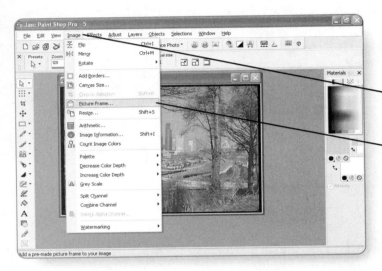

1. Open an **image** for which you want to add a picture frame.

2. Click on **Image**. The Image menu will appear.

3. Click on **Picture Frame**. The Picture Frame dialog box will open.

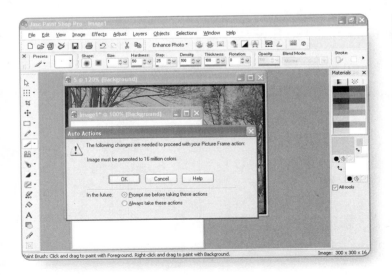

NOTE

If your image is not 32-bit color or grey scale, then when you access the Picture Frame, a dialog box will appear prompting you to increase your color depth.

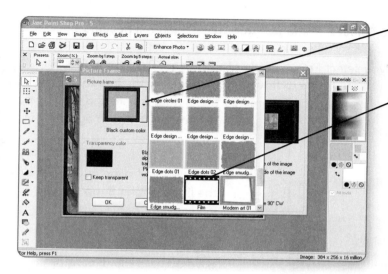

4. Click on the **frame list down arrow** (▾). A list of available picture frames will appear.

5. Click on a **picture frame**. A sample will appear in the preview window.

NOTE

Don't pay much attention to whether the frame is tall or wide. The Picture Frame Wizard will fit the frame to your image.

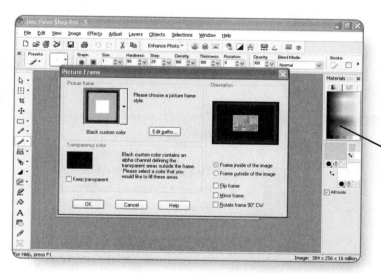

Depending on the shape of the frame you selected, you might need to select a color to fill the transparent areas outside of the frame. Odd-shaped frames usually have a transparent area.

6. If available, **select** a **color** from the color box. The color you select will replace any transparent area outside the frame.

7. Select a **frame position**. The option will become selected.

If you select Frame inside of the image, Paint Shop Pro will resize the frame to fit within the edges of the image. Part of the image will be covered by the picture frame, and the dimensions of the image will not be altered.

If you select Frame outside of the image, Paint Shop Pro will increase the canvas size to accommodate the frame. The original image will not be covered, and the dimensions of the image will be increased by the size of the frame.

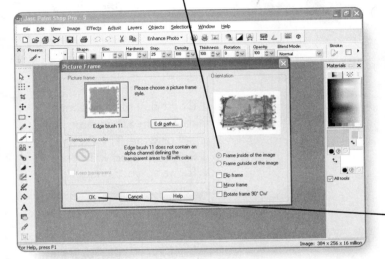

8. Click on **OK**. Paint Shop Pro will apply the frame with your specifications to the image.

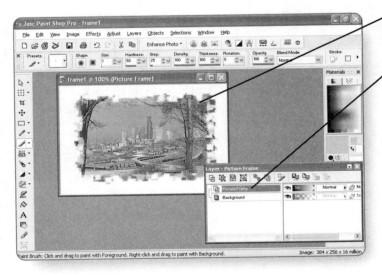

The picture frame will surround the image.

The picture frame will appear on its own layer entitled Picture Frame.

The same image without a picture frame and with three different styles of picture frames

Saving Images as Picture Frames

Whether you've downloaded an image from the Internet to use as a frame or whether you've created it yourself, you need to tell Paint Shop Pro that you plan to use the image as a frame.

The image must meet two criteria for a frame:

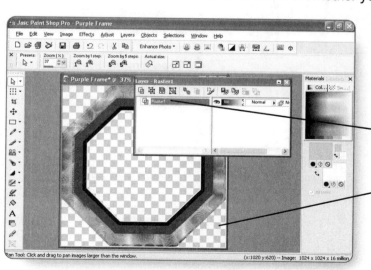

- The image must have only one layer and the layer must be a raster layer.

- All areas of the image canvas other than the frame must be transparent.

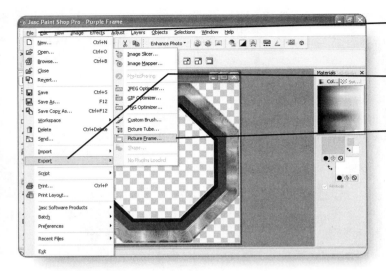

1. Click on **File**. The File menu will appear.

2. Click on **Export**. The Export submenu will appear.

3. Click on **Picture Frame**. The Export Picture Frame dialog box will appear.

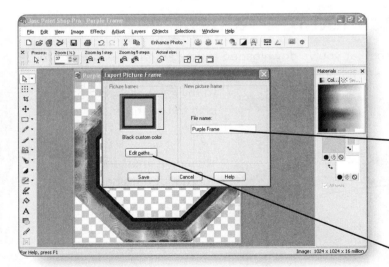

By default, Paint Shop Pro stores picture frames you create in the folder C:\Documents and Settings*your name*\My Documents\My PSP8 Files\Picture Frames.

4. Type a **name** for the picture frame. The picture frame name will appear in the File name box.

TIP

Click on Edit paths if you want to store your frames in a different folder location.

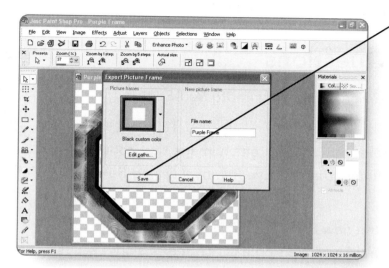

5. Click on **Save**. The image will be saved as a Paint Shop Pro frame.

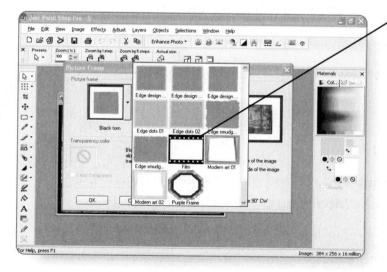

The saved frame will appear in the Picture Frame dialog box.

Part IV Review Questions

1. What causes red-eye? *See "Removing Photo Red-Eye" in Chapter 18.*

2. Will the red-eye removal option work on an image that contains a selection? *See "Opening the Red-Eye Removal Dialog Box" in Chapter 18.*

3. What is the name of the new Paint Shop Pro feature that can enhance your photographs with a single click? *See "Using One-Step Photo Fix" in Chapter 19.*

4. What tool can you use to remove scratches from old photographs? *See "Removing Photo Scratches" in Chapter 19.*

5. What is saturation? *See "Adjusting Saturation" in Chapter 19.*

6. Does increasing saturation or decreasing saturation add more gray to an image? *See "Adjusting Saturation" in Chapter 19.*

7. Name one effect you can use to age a photograph. *See "Aging a Photo" in Chapter 19.*

8. If a photograph is faded and washed out, how can you give it a more natural look? *See "Modifying Contrast" in Chapter 19.*

9. What color depth must your image be to use the Picture Frame feature? *See "Applying a Picture Frame" in Chapter 20.*

10. What two criteria must an image have to save it as a picture frame? *See "Saving Images as Picture Frames" in Chapter 20.*

PART V

Appendixes

A
Keyboard Shortcuts

Like most Windows applications, there's usually more than one way to accomplish a single task or access a particular feature. Included with Paint Shop Pro are a number of shortcut keystrokes that you can use to access tools or menu options without having to reach for your mouse.

Tool Shortcuts

Shortcut	Function
A	Arrow/Pan tool
B	Paint Brush tool
C	Clone tool
D	Deform tool
E	Dropper tool
F	Flood Fill tool
I	Picture Tube tool
J	Dodge tool
L	Lighten/Darken tool
M	Move tool

Shortcut	Function
O	Vector Object Selection tool
P	Preset Shapes tool
R	Crop tool
S	Selection tool
T	Text tool
V	Pen tool
X	Eraser tool
Z	Zoom tool
Shift+Alt+F6	Swap materials
Ctrl+Shift+F6	Reset materials palette

Menu Shortcuts

Most commonly accessed menu functions include a shortcut key combination that you can use instead of clicking the top-level menu and selecting options under that menu. These shortcuts are organized by the different top-level menu items.

File Menu Shortcuts

Shortcut	Function
F12	File, Save as
Ctrl+B	File, Browse
Ctrl+N	File, New
Ctrl+O	File, Open
Ctrl+P	File, Print
Ctrl+S	File, Save
Ctrl+F12	File, Save copy as
Ctrl+Delete	File, Delete
Shift+C	File, Import, Screen capture, Start
Shift+Alt+D	File, Workspace, Delete
Shift+Alt+L	File, Workspace, Load
Shift+Alt+S	File, Workspace, Save

Edit Menu Shortcuts

Shortcut	Function
Delete	Edit, Clear
Ctrl+C	Edit, Copy
Ctrl+E	Edit, Paste as new selection
Ctrl+G	Edit, Paste as new vector selection
Ctrl+L	Edit, Paste as new layer
Ctrl+V	Edit, Paste as new image
Ctrl+X	Edit, Cut
Ctrl+Y	Edit, Repeat
Ctrl+Z	Edit, Undo
Ctrl+Shift+C	Edit, Copy merged
Ctrl+Shift+E	Edit, Paste as transparent selection
Ctrl+Shift+L	Edit, Paste into selection
Ctrl+Shift+Z	Edit, Command history
Ctrl+Alt+Z	Edit, Redo

Selections Menu Shortcuts

Shortcut	Function
Ctrl+A	Selections, Select all
Ctrl+D	Selections, Select none
Ctrl+F	Selections, Float
Ctrl+H	Selections, Modify feather
Ctrl+Shift+B	Selections, Select from vector object
Ctrl+Shift+F	Selections, Defloat
Ctrl+Shift+I	Selections, Invert
Ctrl+Shift+M	Selections, Hide marquee
Ctrl+Shift+P	Selections, Promote selection to layer
Ctrl+Shift+S	Selections, Select from mask

View Menu Shortcuts

Shortcut	Function
Num+	View, Zoom in by 1 step
Num-	View, Zoom out by 1 step
F2	Hide palettes
F3	View, Palettes, Script output
F4	View, Palettes, Tool options
F6	View, Palettes, Materials
F7	View, Palettes, Histogram
F8	View, Palettes, Layers
F9	View, Palettes, Overview
F10	View, Palettes, Learning center
F11	View, Palettes, Brush variance
Ctrl+Shift+A	View, Full screen preview
Ctrl+Shift+G	View, Snap to grid
Ctrl+Shift+T	Show hidden toolbars
Ctrl+Alt+G	View, Grid
Ctrl+Alt+N	View, Zoom to 100%
Ctrl+Alt+R	View, Ruler
Ctrl+Alt+M	View, Magnifier
Shift+A	View, Full screen edit
Shift+Alt+G	View, Snap to guides

Window Menu Shortcuts

Shortcut	Function
Ctrl+W	Window, Fit to image
Shift+D	Window, Duplicate
Shift+W	Window, New window

Help Menu Shortcuts

Shortcut	Function
Shift+F1	Help, Context help

Layers Menu Shortcuts

Shortcut	Function
Shift+K	Layers, Invert Mask/Adjustment
Shift+Y	Layers, New Mask Layer, Hide all

Image Menu Shortcuts

Shortcut	Function
Ctrl+I	Image, Flip
Ctrl+M	Image, Mirror
Ctrl+R	Image, Rotate, Free rotate
Shift+I	Image, Image information
Shift+O	Image, Palette, Load palette
Shift+P	Image, Palette, Edit palette
Shift+R	Image, Crop to selection
Shift+S	Image, Resize
Shift+V	Image, Palette, View palette transparency
Ctrl+Shift+1	Image, Decrease color depth, 2 colors
Ctrl+Shift+2	Image, Decrease color depth, 16 colors
Ctrl+Shift+3	Image, Decrease color depth, 256 colors
Ctrl+Shift+4	Image, Decrease color depth, 32K colors
Ctrl+Shift+5	Image, Decrease color depth, 64K colors
Ctrl+Shift+6	Image, Decrease color depth, x colors
Ctrl+Shift+8	Image, Increase color depth, 16 colors
Ctrl+Shift+9	Image, Increase color depth, 256 colors
Ctrl+Shift+0	Image, Increase color depth, 16 million colors
Ctrl+Shift+V	Image, Palette, Set palette transparency

Adjust Menu Shortcuts

Shortcut	Function
Shift+B	Adjust, Brightness & Contrast, Brightness & contrast
Shift+G	Adjust, Brightness & Contrast, Gamma correction
Shift+E	Adjust, Brightness & Contrast, Histogram equalize
Shift+L	Adjust, Hue & Saturation, Colorize
Shift+M	Adjust, Brightness & Contrast, Highlight, Midtone/shadow
Shift+T	Adjust, Brightness & Contrast, Histogram stretch
Shift+U	Adjust, Color Balance, Red/Green/Blue
Ctrl+Shift+H	Adjust, Brightness & Contrast, Histogram adjustment

B

Exploring Useful Web Sites

The World Wide Web has hundreds, maybe thousands, of sites that are dedicated to using Paint Shop Pro. If you have Internet access, take the time to check out some of the links listed in this appendix. Some are general Paint Shop Pro help information whereas others are step-by-step tutorials on special tasks that you can accomplish with Paint Shop Pro. Still others are links to free, or mostly free, things you can download to use with Paint Shop Pro—things like picture tubes, masks, filters, and frames.

Many of these sites refer to prior versions of Paint Shop Pro, but you'll find that you can use most of the information they offer with Paint Shop Pro 8 as well. Some of these sites offer help that is specifically designed for new users, others have tutorials to guide you step by step through various Paint Shop Pro processes, and still others are freebies (along with a few non-freebies) such as tubes, masks, frames, and other various goodies.

I apologize in advance if any listed site closes or modifies its content. Although these links were active and accurate at the time of publication, Web sites change frequently. Also, make sure that your anti-virus software is up to date before you download anything from the Internet. You cannot be too safe!

http://www.psptoybox.com

http://moonsdesigns.com

http://www.campratty.com

http://loriweb.pair.com

http://www.jasc.com

http://www.lvsonline.com

http://www.alienskin.com

http://autumnweb.com/Roxys

http://www.brovik.com

http://www.comm-unique.com.au

http://www.compusmart.ab.ca/lastwords

http://www.cutups.org

http://www.designsbydonna.com

http://www.digitalartresources.com/PSP/
ArtResources.htm

http://www.dizteq.com

http://www.extenuation.net/psp

http://www.flamingpear.com/blade.html

http://www.flashpowdergraphics.com

http://www.fortunecity.com/westwood/alaia/354

http://www.fortunecity.com/westwood/idea/909/
index.html

http://www.frontiernet.net/~willshak/index.html

http://www.geocities.com/haylers

http://www.geocities.com/Heartland/Cabin/6995/
RaindropImages.htm

http://www.geocities.com/Heartland/Plains/6524/
frames.html

http://www.geocities.com/Heartland/Plains/9316/
masktut.html

http://www.geocities.com/mcjd83/Tutorials.htm

http://www.graphicallusions.com

http://hem.passagen.se/grafoman/plugtool/plugs.html

http://home.freeuk.net/brooksbank/frames.html

http://htmlhelp.rootsweb.com/imagehelp

http://mardiweb.com/web

http://members.madasafish.com/~blue_daffodil/
tutorials/tutorials.htm

http://millerfg.home.mindspring.com/wpf2.htm

http://www.nanettes-place.com

http://net-buddies.org/TL/index.htm

http://www.netins.net/showcase/wolf359/plugins.htm

http://www.nobledesktop.com/guide.html

http://www.onstagegraphics.com

http://www.plugin-filters.com

http://pspimaginarium.com

http://www.pspiz.com

http://www.psplinks.com

http://www.psppower.com

http://psptips.com

http://www.putertutor.net

http://ronstoons.com

http://www.rorony.net

http://www.serialpurrs.org

http://www.state-of-entropy.com

http://suzshook.topcities.com/tutorials/8custtoolbars

http://www.thekoala.com

http://www.the-taskbar.com/tbdesignspsp8.htm

http://westwood.fortunecity.com/vivienne/150/
stationery_from_hrlyville.htm

http://www.v-d-l.com

http://www.visionsnet.com/web/index.html

One final note: If you like to read newsgroups, here are a few of them. You can post Paint Shop Pro questions and receive answers from other Paint Shop Pro users or even the Jasc programmers.

comp.graphics.apps.paint-shop-pro (If you don't have a newsreader program, you can access this newsgroup from http://www.google.com.)

alt.binaries.paint-shop-pro

http://www.egroups.com/group/PSP7Newbies

C

Sample Effects

As you've already discovered, Paint Shop Pro has many powerful effects available to enhance your images, whether the image is a photograph or a drawing.

Here are just a few of the applied effects. Remember that effects can be combined for even more effects!

Original Image

Reflection—Kaleidoscope

Artistic—Magnifying Lens

Artistic—Balls and Bubbles

Original Image

Edge—Dilate

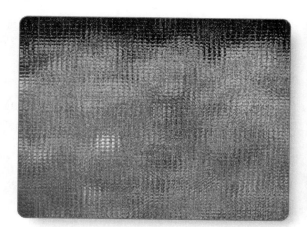

Texture—Mosaic Glass

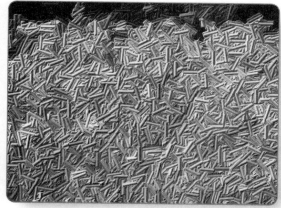

Texture—Straw Wall

Original Image

Geometric—Circle

Art Media—Colored Pencil

Illumination—Sunburst

Original Image

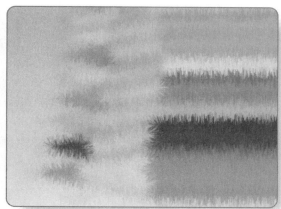

Texture—Fur

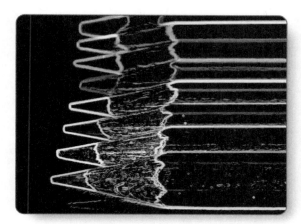

Artistic—Glowing Edges

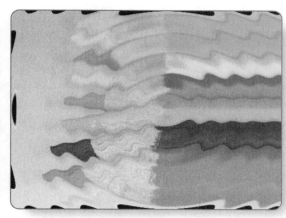

Distortion—Ripple

Original Image

Illumination—Lights

Image—Page Curl

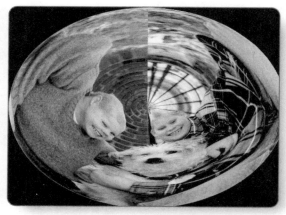

Distortion—Polar Coordinates

Original Image

3D—Buttonize

Reflection—Feedback

Art Media—Black Pencil

Glossary

1-bit image. An image that contains a maximum of 2 colors.

4-bit image. An image that contains a maximum of 16 colors.

8-bit image. An image that contains a maximum of 256 colors.

15-bit image. An image that contains a maximum of 32,768 colors.

16-bit image. An image that contains a maximum of 65,536 colors.

24-bit image. An image that contains a maximum of 16,777,216 colors.

Adjustment layer. A layer that is used to apply color adjustments to the layers below it.

Animation. A series of sequential images with an optional transition effect to create the illusion of movement.

Animation Shop. An application that is included with Paint Shop Pro to create animations.

Animation Wizard. A tool that is supplied by Animation Shop to assist you in creating animations.

Anti-alias. The smoothing and blending of pixel edges to eliminate jagged edges on curved and slanted lines.

Aspect ratio. The ratio of width to height.

Attribute. Items that determine the appearance of text, such as bolding, underlining, italics, font, or size.

Automatic rollups. Floating objects that open automatically as you hover your mouse in their area but then close up again when you move your mouse out of their vicinity.

AutoSave. A feature that periodically saves a temporary version of your document.

AVI. Abbreviation for Audio Video Interlaced. A Windows multimedia file format used for video and audio.

Background. The canvas on which graphics display.

Background color. The canvas color on which graphics display.

Background layer. The bottom layer in many images.

Banner Wizard. An Animation Shop feature that assists you in creating animated text banners.

Bevel. A three-dimensional edge on an object.

Bit. The smallest unit of digital information that a computer handles.

Bit depth. *See* color depth.

Bitmapped image. An image that is composed of small squares, called pixels, that are arranged in columns and rows. Each pixel has a specific color and location.

Blend. To combine two layers or areas of an image.

Blur. An effect that reduces areas of high contrast and softens the appearance of an image.

BMP. File format abbreviation for a bitmapped image.

Brightness. The amount of light or white color in an image.

Browse. A feature of Paint Shop Pro and Animation Shop that allows you to see multiple thumbnail images.

Browser toolbar. Displays useful tools when you're browsing images.

Canvas. The area on which an image is displayed.

Canvas size. The size of the area within an image window.

Clone. To duplicate a portion of an image.

CMYK. Abbreviation for Cyan/Magenta/Yellow/Black, which are the four standard ink colors used in printing.

Color depth. The number of bits of color information that is available for each pixel.

Color palette. Contains a selection of available colors, styles, and textures and displays the current foreground and background colors and styles.

Color wheel. The circular color area from which you can create a custom color.

Colorize. An effect that converts an image or selection to a uniform hue and saturation while retaining its lightness.

Compression. A process that is applied to saved images to reduce file size.

Contract command. Shrinks a selection by a specific number of pixels.

Contrast. The difference between the light and dark areas of an image.

Crop. To remove part of an image outside a selection.

Defloat. To merge a floating selection into a layer.

Deformation. To change an image appearance by moving data from one area to another.

Defringe. To clean the edges of a selection by removing pixels of the background color.

Digital. Information that a computer reads and processes.

Digital camera. A camera that takes pictures and stores them in its memory or on a disk.

Dithering. When a computer monitor substitutes a color it cannot display with a similar color.

DPI. Abbreviation for Dots Per Inch. A unit of measurement that measures the number of dots that fit horizontally and vertically into a one-inch measure.

Effect. A graphics function that creates a modification to an image.

Emboss. An effect that causes the foreground of an image to appear raised from the background.

Expand a selection. Increases the size of a selection by a specified number of pixels.

Export. The process of saving a file into a different format.

Feather. The process of fading an area on all edges of a selection. Measured in pixels.

File associations. A method of determining which files your computer opens automatically using Paint Shop Pro.

File format. The structure of a file that defines the way it is stored.

Filter. A tool that applies special effects to an image.

Flip command. The command that reverses an image vertically.

Float command. The command that temporarily separates a selection from an image or layer.

Floating objects. Screen elements appearing in the middle of the Paint Shop Pro window that can be moved to other areas of the window. Floating objects have automatic rollup.

Foreground color. The primary color for the painting and drawing tools.

Format. The shape and size of an image or text. Also, the method that a browser uses to display an image.

FPS. Abbreviation of Frames Per Second. The rate at which animations are displayed.

Frame. A single complete image in a series of images, usually animations, that indicates a step in the image movement.

GIF. File format abbreviation for a Graphic Interchange Format image. GIF images support transparency but only 8-bit (256) color. Commonly used with Web graphics.

Gradient Fill. A fill that is created by the gradual blending of colors.

Grey scale image. An image that uses up to 256 shades of grey.

Grid. An equally spaced series of vertical and horizontal lines to help align objects.

Grow command. Adds color pixels that are adjacent to an active selection.

Handles. Control points on vector objects that are used to edit the object.

Highlight. The lightest part of an image.

Histogram. A graphics representation showing the distribution of color and light in an image.

HSL. Abbreviation for Hue/Saturation/Lightness. A method of defining colors in an image.

HTML. Abbreviation for Hypertext Markup Language. A programming language that is used to create Web pages.

Hue. A color.

Image window. The area in which you work on your image.

Internet. A global network of computers used to transfer information.

JPEG. Abbreviation for Joint Photographic Experts Group. Same as JPG file format.

JPG file format. A file format that supports 24-bit (16,777,216) color but not transparency. Commonly used with Web graphics.

Kerning. The distance between characters of text.

Layer. A level of an image that can be edited independently from the rest of the image.

Layer palette. Lists each layer in the current image.

Leading. The distance between lines of text.

Line art. An image that is composed of one color.

Logo. A name or symbol that many businesses use for easy recognition.

Luminance. A physical measurement of the brightness information in an image.

Magic Wand. A selection tool that works by selecting content rather than defining edges.

Marquee. A selection area that is represented by "marching ants."

Mask. A feature that allows some portion of an image to be hidden.

Mirror. An exact copy of an image that is placed in reverse of the copied image.

Negative image. A photographic image in reversed form where the light areas become dark and the dark areas become light.

Node. A control point on a vector object.

Noise. The grainy appearance in some images.

Object. A single element in an image.

Opacity. The density of a color or layer.

Overview window. Displays entire image when zooming in to a small area.

Path. The guiding line for a vector object.

Picture tubes. Fun little pictures that you paint with your brush.

Pixel. The smallest element in an image.

PNG. Abbreviation for Portable Network Graphics. A file format designed for Web graphics that supports both transparency and 24-bit (16,777,216) color.

Posterize. Effect that replaces areas of continuous color tone with single colors.

Preferences. The area in which each user maintains customized settings for Paint Shop Pro.

Print Preview. The feature that allows you to view an image prior to printing it on paper.

Raster image. A bitmapped image made up of pixels.

Rasterize. To convert a vector image to raster.

Red-eye. A photographic effect that frequently occurs in photographs of humans and animals, giving a shiny or red appearance to eyes.

Replace Color command. The Paint Shop Pro feature that allows you to pick a specific color and replace it with any other color.

Resize. The ability to make an image or object larger or smaller.

Resolution. The measurement of the detail in an image.

RGB (Red/Green/Blue). The three primary colors that compose most images.

Rotate. To turn an image or object.

Saturation. The measure of strength of an image's color.

Scanner. A hardware device used to translate pictures and text into digital language that a computer can interpret.

Selection. The outline that appears around an area to be modified.

Shadow. The darkest area of an image. Sometimes applied as an effect.

Sharpen. An effect that increases the contrast in an image.

Skew. A deformation that tilts an image along its horizontal or vertical axis.

Solarize. An effect that inverts all colors above a selected value.

Status bar. The line at the bottom of an application window that displays help and image details.

Stroke. An outline of text.

Text banner. Animations often seen on Web pages—usually at the top—that have text moving around.

Thumbnail. A miniature version of an image.

TIFF. Abbreviation for Tagged Image File Format. A format that scanners commonly use.

Title bar. The bar at the top of the application that displays the Paint Shop Pro Control icon, the application name, and the name of the active image and its format, as well as the standard Windows buttons.

Toggle. To switch an item back and forth from one state to another. Frequently used to turn the display of layers on and off.

Tool palette. Contains the image-editing tools.

Toolbar. Displays tools to manage files and commonly used menu functions.

Tools Option palette. Displays options for the currently selected tool.

Transparency. An area that lacks color.

TWAIN. A common computer interface among scanners, digital cameras, and computers.

Undo. The ability to reverse actions.

VCR controls. An Animation Shop toolbar that controls viewing an animation.

Vector graphic. An object that uses mathematics to create images. Vector graphics can be edited, moved, and resized easily.

Watermark. Embedded information in an image that is used to mark an image with copyright and author information.

Web browser. A software program that is designed specifically to view Web pages on the Internet.

Workspace. The portion of the Paint Shop Pro window where you work on your image.

Zoom. The process of viewing an image in a larger or smaller magnification.

Index